Who Fired The First Shot?

And Other Untold Stories of the Civil War

HAWTHORN BOOKS INC. • PUBLISHERS • NEW YORK

WHO FIRED THE FIRST SHOT?

and other
untold stories
of the Civil War

By ASHLEY HALSEY, JR.

FIRST EDITION

April, 1963

Contents

List of Illustrations   6

Preface   7

Foreword   11

1—Was the War Inevitable?   17

2—Who Fired the First Shot?   27

3—The Forts Come Tumbling Down   37

4—What They Fought With   48

5—Inventions for Better Killing   65

6—The Indians in Blue and Gray   82

7—Duels and Plain Murder   92

8—The Stealthy Snipers   111

9—What Is a Massacre?   128

10—Whose Prison Camps Were Worse?   143

11—The Deadly Medical Practices   169

12—How Wives Influenced Generals   181

13—Brother Against Brother   190

14—The Infidel's Sword   205

15—Why One Hero Never Reached the Front   210

Index   219

The Author and His Book   224

List of Illustrations

	BETWEEN PAGES
FAMOUS CIVIL WAR CANNON	9-11
WHO FIRED THE FIRST SHOT?—CLAIMANTS TO THE HONOR	27-28
INVENTIONS FOR BETTER KILLING	69-70
AERIAL NAVIGATION; THE BATTLE OF PEA RIDGE	81-82
THE INDIANS IN BLUE AND GRAY; COL. RHETT; LT.-GEN. HAMPTON	91-92
JEFFERSON DAVIS; STONEWALL JACKSON; GEN. NELSON; ADMIRAL SEMMES	107-108
TECHNIQUE OF LOADING A HEAVY SIEGE GUN	141-142
BEATTY'S BRIGADE AT BATTLE OF STONE'S RIVER	169-170
GENERALS AND WIVES; BROTHER AGAINST BROTHER	189-190
THE BURNING OF THE "CONGRESS"	203-205

Preface

A book such as this represents the end result of researching, analyzing, assimilating, of comparing facts and eliminating palpable fallacies. This is at best an imperfect process. Events are what their recorders make them. No two eyewitnesses today see a street corner accident identically. No two generals a century ago shared absolutely the same viewpoint of a battle. Even if they happened to be riding the same horse, only one was in the saddle. And no two professional historians agree on anything, apparently, unless one has copied blindly from the other. Therefore common sense and intuition must temper conclusions drawn from history.

Civil War history is not an exact science. Too many of its writers lack such prime qualifications as a military education, mind, or experience; years of skeptical newspaper reporting; months behind a department-store complaint window, quietly doubting people; and a polite ability to disbelieve their own grandmothers. The author does not recall any such paragon and does not set himself up as one.

As nearly as possible in this book, blatant fictions in history have been either appropriately labeled or consciously avoided. Yet some statements undoubtedly are open to question if not exception. The author, in his own good time, will discuss questions with anyone seeking tranquil discussion. To anyone taking violent exception, the author can only express regret—regret that dueling is forbidden. He would gladly demonstrate his antique but operable dueling pistols in any suitably isolated place to convince the boorishly irate that violence should be avoided.

Chapters 2, 6, 13, 14 and 15 first appeared in *The Saturday Evening Post* in substantially their present form as part of the *Post* centennial series, which the author conceived and edited. Other chapters written especially for this particular book bear no relationship to any magazine in content, viewpoint, or any other way. Several reflect the sentiments of the author, a Southerner, rather than non-Southern or anti-Southern views. This must be stated because the preponderance of Civil War literature is Northern. The author does not, for example, share in the cultish idolization of Mr. Lincoln. He respects Mr. Lincoln for many great deeds—as he respects Franklin D. Roosevelt, for whom he often voted, for his achievements—but he feels that both of these wartime Presidents, in being consummate politicians, detracted from their stature as great statesmen. He does not "blame" Mr. Lincoln for the Civil War any more than he blames F.D.R. for Pearl Harbor. He simply wonders whether dedicated statesmanship, devoid of political considerations, might have averted those wars.

As with any human effort, the author owes a debt to his fellow humans. He is especially obliged for research assistance and inspiration to a lady whose name speaks volumes in a Southern tone, Miss Georgia Pepper, of Atlanta; for an encyclopedic knowledge of "the" war and for much kindly help to Erd Brandt, long a senior editor of *The Saturday Evening Post*; to Ben Hibbs, under whose editorship the *Post* centennial series was published; and for generous assistance in the form of information, permissions and so on to the following:

F. R. Paxton, New York City, a V.M.I. alumnus and true Civil War buff; Col. George M. Chinn, Frankfort, Ky.; Robert E. Hickman, Esq., Benton, Ill.; W. B. Edwards, Skokie, Ill.; Claude Crowley, Nashville, Tenn.; W. G. Conrad, III, and Victor Marine, Ship Bottom, N. J.; and Walter Easterbrook, Brant Beach, N. J.

Mrs. Waveland S. FitzSimons, of ½ Tradd St., Charleston, S.C.; Miss Virginia Rugheimer and her associates of the Charleston Library Society; James Gray, Hudson, N.Y.; Norman Mason, Sedro Woolley, Wash.; Emerson Wilson, Wilmington, Del.; J. B. Blackford, Richmond, Va.; R. Baker Harris, Masonic librarian and biographer of Albert Pike, Washington, D.C.; Richard Gibbon, Charlotte, N.C.; Mrs. Jennie Engle Staudt, Union City, Indiana; The Confederate Museum, Richmond; The Marine Corps Museum, Quantico; The West Point Museum, U.S.M.A., West Point, N.Y.; The Buffalo (N.Y.) Museum; The Pennsylvania Historical Society; Col. W. A. Lee, USMC (Ret.) and Lt. Col. J. A. Magruder, USMCR, Quantico; Gerald C. Stowe, curator, The West Point Museum; Lt. Col. Willard L. Jones, Silver Spring, Md.; Lt. Col. E. H. Hoffman, USA (Ret.), Woodstock, Va.; Jac Weller, Princeton, N.J.; W. A. Albaugh, III, Falls Church, Va.; Mrs. Vivian C. Ward and Miss Barbara McKnight, of Philadelphia, and many others.

The author also acknowledges his appreciation not only of such well-worked standbys as *Battles and Leaders of the Civil War*, Miller's *Photographic History of the Civil War* and the *Official Records of the War of the Rebellion* but of three latter-day publications which he humbly regards as outstanding in the overgrown field of Civil War literature: The State University of Iowa's quarterly *Civil War History*, edited by James I. Robertson, Jr.; the Premier Civil War Classics, edited with keen comprehension of the period by Philip Van Doren Stern; and *The Civil War Times*, published at Gettysburg, appropriately, by Maj. Gen. E. J. Stackpole under the editorship of Robert H. Fowler.

In conclusion, let it be said emphatically that this book is *not* a history of the Civil War. It simply attempts to highlight some little-known aspects of what Robert Penn Warren termed "the greatest single event in our history."

A. H.

FAMOUS CIVIL WAR CANNON

This cannon is prominently displayed in the front entrance of the State House on Smith Street, Providence, Rhode Island. It is presumed to be a bronze Napoleon 12-pounder and saw service at the battle of Gettysburg with a Rhode Island unit. Engraved on the top of the barrel is this legend: *U.S. Battery B, Rhode Island Light Artillery. This Gun was disabled during the cannonade at Gettysburg July 3, 1863: At the point where Pickett's Division made the charge upon the Union lines. William Jones and Alfred G. Gardiner were killed by a rebel shell while placing the shot now in its muzzle.* The explosion of the Confederate shell, which killed the two men, caused the shell to become fused while it was being loaded into the cannon.

Foreword

The Civil War is the longest cold war in our nation's history. It began in 1775 over an exalted ideal and it has not yet ended. Possibly it will never end, because the ideal remains still unfulfilled.

This cold Civil War started in a three-story brick house on the southwest corner of Seventh and Walnut Streets in Philadelphia, now the site of a hot-dog stand. There Thomas Jefferson, drafting the Declaration of Independence, penned the momentous words that all men are entitled to "liberty" and the debatable phrase that they are "created equal."

Ever since then, there has been conflict hot and cold over what the idealistic gentleman from Virginia actually meant. Perhaps he was so radically far ahead of his times and our times that the nation has not yet caught up with him. Conceivably the United States has misinterpreted and muddled its colonial recipe for freedom. It becomes a matter of definition. What is freedom? What is equality?

If Mr. Jefferson had meant his brave words literally, he should have freed his hundred or more slaves before sundown. In the present-day socialistic interpretation of "equality," he should have divided his worldly goods, which they helped to earn, equally with them. He did nothing of the kind, of course. Although Mr. Jefferson, while our third President, opposed the westward spread of slavery, he owned Negroes virtually all his life. In stressing equality, he apparently thought, as a scholar of the classics, in terms of the Athenian republic with its citizens and slaves. To Mr. Jefferson, it might seem, equality meant equal rights for citizens. And it meant equality before the law rather than a personal parity in dollars and opportunity. Today progressive Mr. Jefferson might be condemned in some parts of the nation and world as a pawn of capitalism and an insincere, lily-white liberal. At any rate, his words have gone marching on and it is for anyone to say whether or not they have lost their sense of direction.

In Massachusetts, Mr. Jefferson's dictum on liberty was soon clasped to the bosom of a quick-minded slave woman.

11

She asked a kindly lawyer whether those words didn't set her free. The lawyer thought they did. In a test case against her owner, Colonel John Ashley, the Massachusetts courts in 1781 agreed.[1] Slavery was forevermore ended in Massachusetts as a result of slave-owner Jefferson's words. But not in the United States.

In 1788, by which time Massachusetts and five other Northern states had formally abolished slavery, the Constitution of the United States was adopted. It recognized slavery in no fewer than three places although it avoided the ugly expression. For political and financial reasons, the free states accepted this.

Article I, Section 2, provided that Congressional representation and direct taxes should be apportioned among the states according to their populations, "which shall be determined by adding to the whole number of free persons, including those bound to service for a term of years, and excluding Indians not taxed, *three-fifths of all other persons.*" The "all other persons" obviously meant Negro slaves. Adding them to the proposed tax base, even at 60 per cent of their numerical total, meant more taxes from the South. This apparently helped to influence the North to go along with the proposal.

Article I, Section 9, read: "The Migration or Importation of such Persons as any of the States now existing shall think proper to admit, shall not be prohibited by the Congress prior to the Year 1808, but a Tax or duty may be imposed on such Importation, not exceeding ten dollars for each Person." The "Persons," even though the "P" was dignified by a capital, meant Negro slaves, of course, and again there was a sort of national profit motive evident in the provision for a ten-dollar head tax.

Article IV, Section 2, contained the famous Fugitive Slave clause which caused vast altercation before the Civil War. It read: "No Person held to Service or Labour in one State, under the Laws thereof, escaping into another, shall, in Consequence of any Law or Regulation therein, be discharged from such Service or Labour, but shall be delivered up upon Claim of the Party to whom such Service or Labour may be due."

---

[1] No kin to the author, one of whose Massachusetts ancestors was run out of the colony more than a century earlier for the high misdemeanor of being a Baptist.

Here then, in the very Constitution of the United States, arose the foundations of a nation "half slave and half free" such as Abraham Lincoln said could not exist. It had existed that way for some 90 uneasy years before he stated his conclusion.

(Almost half a century later, another President, an eminent historian, gave a somewhat different interpretation of the role of slavery in bringing on the Civil War. Woodrow Wilson, Southern-born son of a pro-Confederate Ohioan and an English mother, with uncles who served the Union, said in his *The Proper Perspective of American History*, that the great issue was not the existence of slavery but whether slavery should expand into the Western territories: "Kansas showed us what the problem was, not South Carolina.")

Although totally absent from the Constitution, another issue arose like a spectre to haunt the peace of the new nation after the Constitutional Convention of 1787. This was an ominous thing called secession. It was based somewhat upon the theory that the Union was a marriage of sovereign states and that a state could divorce itself from this Union at any time. Almost mysteriously, the Constitution nowhere suggested that secession was possible—or impossible.

An answer to this mysterious omission was advanced years later by an eminent lawyer, a protégé of Benjamin Franklin, who had sat as a spectator at the sessions of the Constitutional Convention in Philadelphia. Lawyer William Rawle, a Philadelphia Quaker and abolitionist or anti-slavery leader, brought out in 1825 probably the first learned legal analysis of the Constitution.[2] Entitled "A View of the Constitution of the United States of America," it soon ran through several editions.

One assertion in this sedate tome proved sensational and eventually nation-shaking. Rawle stated that the Constitution failed to spell out the right of secession only because that right, while "not expressed, was mutually understood."

Certainly, events bore him out on this. There were secession movements in 1798, 1801, 1811, 1814, 1832, 1845 and 1856

---

[2] William Rawle's law firm is still in active practice in Philadelphia under the name of Rawle and Henderson. One of the partners, the late Joseph Henderson, Esq., was President of the American Bar Association in 1943–44. The firm library contains a second edition of Rawle on the Constitution.

—and five of the seven were generated in disgruntled Northern states, the last only four years before South Carolina actually withdrew from the Union. The 1856 secession movement arose that year after Democrat James Buchanan was elected President over Republican John C. Fremont. The extreme abolitionists, who had publicly damned the Constitution years before because of its slavery clauses, announced that any country which kept on electing Democrats to the Presidency was hopeless. They called a national secession convention to meet in Cleveland, Ohio, in 1857. The financial panic of that year thwarted them. Most of the delegates went so broke that they lacked train fare and the convention fizzled.

All these outbursts of discontent with the Union indicated only one thing. To many early Americans, the right to "liberty" included the privilege of seceding from any national government that they disliked. Rawle's book found its way onto the shelves at West Point and served as a civics or political text for a number of future Confederate generals, among them possibly Joseph E. Johnston, P. G. T. Beauregard, Braxton Bragg, A. P. Hill and Stephen D. Lee.[3]

Thus, on top of its Constitution which guaranteed freedom to citizens and slavery to slave-owners, the growing republic endured under the implication that any state which didn't get along with the rest might go its way. The miracle is not that the nation split in 1861, but that it held together during the decades before then.

To suggest that slavery and secession caused the war may oversimplify. Some historical authorities now view the struggle as an economic conflict between Northern industrialism and Southern agrarianism over high protective tariffs versus free trade. Others see it as springing from states' rights, intersec-

---

[3] General Robert E. Lee is quoted as saying many years after the war, in a conversation with Bishop Wilmer of Louisiana, a staunch Southerner and Episcopalian, that "if it had not been for the instruction I got from Rawle's textbook at West Point, I would not have left the old army and joined the South at the breaking out of the War Between the States." Whether Lee actually said this, or Wilmer actually quoted it, is debatable. Some contend that Rawle's book did not arrive at West Point until after Lee was graduated there in 1829.

tional intolerance, misinterpretation or rejection of the U.S. Constitution, and—fascinatingly—as a natural break between two countries and peoples who were never too strongly attached from the start.

War, however, must have a catalyst. The clashing views that provoked hostilities can be reduced to a sentence:

Slavery was a moral wrong, but a Constitutional right.

From there, extremists of both sides, numbering possibly no more than 10,000 vigorous agitators in a population of 32,000,000, pushed the issue into bloodshed and death for 600,000 men. How could such a thing happen?

A few fanatical propagandists fanned the abolition or anti-slavery movement, which was almost dead in 1830, into a foremost issue of the 1850s. The anti-slavery element captured the new Republican party, with its heavy flavoring of German liberals and Marxists, to the extent that the party pledged to resist the spread of slavery West and North. But ardent abolitionists wanted slavery ended everywhere at once.

This relative handful of Northern abolitionists actively repudiated the U.S. Constitution because of its slavery clauses, even to hanging men who returned slaves under the Fugitive Slave clause. Another relative handful of outspoken secessionists, playing upon emotions, succeeded in leading the South out of the Union.

The secessionists argued that the Union was bound together by a contract between the States, the Constitution; the North had broken the contract regarding slavery; therefore the whole contract was void and the South was released from it.

Any other stand, they added, would leave the South defenseless at the whim of the North. If the North could with impunity violate the slavery clauses, it could ignore any or all of the safeguards in the Constitution for other prescribed rights. The great document would then, for the South, become a halter instead of a shield.

The extremists forced millions of moderate, middle-of-the-road Americans to pick sides. The split was not strictly sectional. So many Southerners sided with the Union—about 300,000 in all—that they, plus some 450,000 foreign-born, formed nearly a third of the Union forces. Numerous Northerners were pro-Confederate.

To most Confederates, including such leaders as Stonewall Jackson, the war was for Southern independence. Not one in a dozen cared an iota for maintaining slavery.

To most Federal combatants, the war was to preserve the
Union. At the start, hardly one in a score burned to abolish
slavery. Some scrupulously returned runaway slaves. A few
surreptitiously peddled them for profit.

The big issue of 1861–62 centered in most minds on
secession.

No part of the world ever received more sinister flattery than
the South, in the North's insistence that the United States
could not get along without it. That was one point on which
the two sections might have agreed.

Northern spokesmen asserted, of course, that secession was
illegal, traitorous, treasonable, because the Constitution failed
to authorize it. Meanwhile 26 Virginia counties beyond the
mountains whetted the issue. By means of a rump legislature,
they seceded from secessionist Virginia—in the name of anti-
secession—and became the 35th state of the Union, West
Virginia. The North welcomed it. Southerners asked why, if
secession was wrong for 11 states, was it right for a fragment
of a state? They are still waiting for a satisfying answer.

For two hard-fought years, the South stayed ahead. "Anti-
secessionism" was hardly the stuff to sustain Federal privates
in combat against dedicated rebels like Jackson's "foot
cavalry." Then the Union war leaders unfurled a new motiva-
tion which sent the secession issue into eclipse. The new
move transformed the conflict into a crusade against slavery.
Its avowed purpose became humanitarian rather than legalistic.
At last privates in blue could tingle with the exalted feeling
of knights in armor. It is possible that the Union actually
was preserved by what today would be termed smart public
relations.

—Ashley Halsey, Jr.

1

Was the War Inevitable?

Abraham Lincoln, elected entirely by Northern votes, assured the split nation, "There will be no bloodshed unless it be forced upon the Government." Jefferson Davis said for the South, "All we ask is to be left alone." But U.S. Secretary of State Seward had expressed the view that the conflict was "irrepressible." Soon it narrowed down to one place and one issue: should Fort Sumter be yielded or strengthened? The fort became a symbol. Lincoln sent an expedition to relieve it. Did his move provoke the war?

Without words first, there can be no war. For decades on end, the words echoed back and forth in a fury like the rising sound of drums. The din filled the land and became constant —until few truly heeded it and expected war. Then it came one April morning. . . .

The words that led to war and warned of it and heralded it are still with us, along with the scars of conflict to the third and fourth generations. On the hundredth anniversary of the firing on Fort Sumter, James F. Byrnes quoted Winston Churchill as saying that it took England 200 years to get over her Civil War of the 1600s. Do Americans heal faster? There is reason to wonder.

Here are the words. . . .

". . . We were embarrassed with more than one Difficulty . . . [among them being] a third Party, which was a Southern Party against a Northern, and a Jealousy against a New England Army under the Command of a New England General. . . ." John Adams, later second President of the United States, speaking of the 1775 sectionalism which led to the appointment of a Virginian, Colonel George Washington, to command the army besieging the British garrison of Boston.

". . . It being among my first wishes to see some plan adopted by which slavery in this country may be abolished by law." George Washington, in a letter dated September 9, 1786.

". . . There never has yet existed a wealthy and civilized society in which one portion of the community did not, in point of fact, live on the labor of the other. Broad and general as is this assertion, it is fully borne out by history." John C. Calhoun, Senator from South Carolina, in the U.S. Senate in 1837.

"The compact which exists between the North and South is a covenant with death and an agreement with hell." Resolution by William Lloyd Garrison, abolitionist spokesman, adopted in 1843 by the Anti-Slavery Society. Garrison burned a copy of the Constitution publicly that Fourth of July because of its slavery provisos.

"Abolitionism . . . is of heaven, not of men. . . . Its scope is not confined to the slave population of the United States, but embraces mankind." William Lloyd Garrison, generalizing.

". . . Abolitionists . . . are atheists, socialists, communists, red republicans, jacobins on the one side. . . . the friends of order and regulated freedom (are) on the other . . ." the Rev. J. H. Thornwell, president of South Carolina College, 1850.

"In this enlightened age there are few, I believe, but what will acknowledge that slavery as an institution is a moral and political evil. . . ." Colonel Robert E. Lee in a letter to his wife, 1856.

"The right of property in a slave is distinctly and expressly affirmed in the Constitution." Chief Justice Roger B. Taney, speaking for the Supreme Court of the United States in the Dred Scott decision, 1857.

"Shall I tell you what this collision means? . . . It is an *irrepressible conflict* between opposing and enduring forces, and it means that the United States must and will sooner or later become either entirely a slave-holding nation or entirely a free-labor nation." William H. Seward, speaking on the Dred Scott decision in 1858, when he was a leading candidate for the 1860 Republican Presidential nomination that Lincoln got.

"I, John Brown, am now quite certain that the crimes of this guilty land will never be purged away but with blood." Among his last words before being hanged in 1859 after raiding the U. S. Arsenal at Harper's Ferry in an anti-slavery uprising.

(John Brown's execution for treason heightened the split in the nation. Many in the North hailed him as a martyr; many in the South viewed him as an ogre seeking to incite slaves to massacre their masters.

(On December 20, 1860, South Carolina became the first state to secede. Significantly, the next were the slave states of the Deep South. Border slave states held back. The Southern secessionist view was not merely a defense of slavery; it claimed provocation by Northern disregard of the Constitution and Yankee grabbing of import tax revenues from the South. Lincoln's election not only inflamed the South, it set off a sectional business decline.

(In vain, moderate Southerners pointed out that Lincoln would be counterbalanced by the Supreme Court and by a predominantly Democratic Congress, 37 to 29 in the Senate, 120 to 108 in the House. Secession spread. So did war talk.

(Southern state militia soon seized 34 U.S. forts, arsenals, barracks, customhouses, even the New Orleans mint, within their states. Some states offered to pay, but said they could not tolerate Federal ownership now that they were out of the Union. Embattled Southerners fired on shipping under the Stars and Stripes twice at Charleston, and at Vicksburg and Pine Bluff, Arkansas, to turn back what they supposed were Federal supplies for forts still in U.S. Army hands. Collection of Federal import taxes in the South virtually ceased.

(Against this alarming background of events, the President-elect spoke moderately at Independence Hall, Philadelphia, on Washington's Birthday, February 22, 1861.)

"There will be no bloodshed unless it be forced upon the Government." Abraham Lincoln.

(And another tall, gaunt, lonely native of Kentucky voiced a similar sentiment at the time of his inauguration as President of the Confederacy.)

"All we ask is to be left alone." Jefferson Davis.

(Mr. Lincoln, from his side of the rising wall, viewed the revenue problem with alarm. Duties on manufactured goods which the agricultural South imported from abroad represented a major Federal income, so much so that Senator Hunter of Virginia protested they "have thrown the burden of Government unequally upon the agricultural States of the South. . . ."

(Now these import revenues shrank. Nobody then had heard of deficit-financing. Mr. Lincoln revealed his concern as early as February 12, 1861, in a speech to the Indiana Legislature quoted in the New York *Tribune*. There he outlined his hard choices.)

"Would the marching of an army into South Carolina . . . without the consent of her people, and in hostility against them, be coercion or invasion? I very frankly say, I think it would. . . . But if the Government . . . but simply insists upon holding its own forts, or retaking those forts which belong to it, or the enforcement of the laws of the United States in the collection of duties . . . would any or all of these things be coercion?" Abraham Lincoln.

(Virginia and other border states held a peace convention in vain. With the same motive, the Rev. Richard Fuller, a Baltimore clergyman, and 30 Y.M.C.A. delegates called on Mr. Lincoln. Mr. Fuller as spokesman urged the President to "recognize the independence of the Southern States . . . the *fact* that they have formed a government of their own . . ."[1]

---

[1] The Rev. Richard Fuller, an Episcopalian by birth and a Baptist by conversion at the age of 27, spent much of his life (1804–1876) seeking to check sectionalism between North and South. He accepted a Baptist pastorate in Baltimore in 1847 largely because that city's location between the sections furthered his objective. Lincoln, however, would hardly have regarded Reverend Fuller as an impartial arbiter. Fuller believed that the Bible sanctioned slavery. In addressing the American Colonization Society, which sought to resettle freed slaves in Africa, he was "so wise, perspicacious and temperate that it pleased nobody," according to the *Dictionary of American Biography*, Vol. VII. Moreover, he was a South Carolinian by birth and his mother was a member of the slave-holding aristocracy, a Middleton. Therefore he was not in the best position to urge Lincoln to recognize the seceded states.

The President's reply, quoted from the Richmond *Dispatch*, April 26, 1861, indicates he was still worried over Federal income.)

"And what is to become of the revenue? I shall have no Government—no resources." Attributed to Abraham Lincoln.

(Meanwhile Fort Sumter, at Charleston, and Fort Pickens, at Pensacola, Florida, became the only strong harbor forts in the South left in Federal hands. Pensacola at the time was a modest port, but Charleston ranked with New Orleans as one of the busiest shipping centers in the South. Thus the Florida port represented less of an issue than Fort Sumter. Regarding Fort Pickens, the ten U.S. Senators from Florida, Alabama, Louisiana, Mississippi and Texas, including Jefferson Davis and Judah P. Benjamin, later holder of three Confederate cabinet posts under Davis, had telegraphed Southern leaders as early as January 18, 1861.)

"We think no assault should be made. The possession of the fort is not worth one drop of blood to us. Bloodshed may be fatal to our cause." Ten Southern Senators.

(That left only Fort Sumter, by now a symbol to both sides. Seldom has a pile of brick on 2 acres of sandbar so greatly altered history. Secretary of State Seward, coiner of the phrase "irrepressible conflict," did his earnest best to repress. He proposed a sort of moratorium on Sumter, pending North-South negotiations over whether to evacuate or reinforce. Then he fell sick. Lincoln's cabinet split on whether to aid the fort. Mr. Lincoln himself was already committed in his inaugural address to hold it. At his orders, a Federal squadron headed by the warship *Pawnee* headed South.

(On receiving word of the expedition, the Confederate cabinet went into emergency session. Acting for President Davis, Secretary of War L. P. Walker on April 11, 1861, telegraphed instructions to Brig. Gen. P. G. T. Beauregard, commanding the Confederate forces at Charleston.)

"Do not desire needlessly to bombard Fort Sumter . . . If Major Anderson [commanding the fort] will state the time at which . . . he will evacuate . . . you are authorized thus to avoid the effusion of blood. If this . . . be refused, reduce the fort as your judgment decides to be most practicable." L. P. Walker.

*So the words ceased and the guns spoke. Sumter fell. Some-
one had started a war.*

"The assault upon, and reduction of, Fort Sumter, was, in
no sense, a matter of self-defense on the part of the assailants."

Thus spoke Abraham Lincoln, President of the United
States, in his message to the Congress. Lincoln continued
in a lawyerly manner:

"They [the Confederates] well knew that the garrison in
the fort could, by no possibility, commit aggression upon them.
They knew—they were expressly notified—that the giving of
bread to the few brave and hungry men of the garrison was
all which would *on that occasion* [italics added] be attempted,
unless themselves, by resisting so much, should provoke more.

"They knew that this Government desired to keep the
garrison in the Fort, not to assail them, but merely to maintain
visible possession and thus to preserve the Union from actual,
and immediate dissolution—trusting, as herein-before stated,
to time, discussion and the ballot-box for final adjustment . . .

"It [this issue] presents the question, whether discontented
individuals, too few in numbers to control administration, according to organic law, in any case, can always, upon the
pretenses made in this case . . . or arbitrarily, without any
pretense, break up their Government. . . . We must settle
this question now, whether in a free government the minority
have the right to break up the Government whenever they
choose."

To accept those statements, as most of Congress and the
North did in the heat of war furor, it is most convenient and
comfortable to believe that Mr. Lincoln in a rustic Midwestern way scarcely knew a fort, harbor, import tax or election result when he saw one. Every word that he uttered may
have been indubitably sincere and literally true—but they
added up to an unrealistic summation. The lawyer, so it
seemed, was trying to make the best of a shaky case. Consider
these points:

1. The fort could not "commit aggression." Obviously,
it could not move off its island and wage a field campaign.
But, sitting athwart the main channel into Charleston with
its heavy batteries, it could strangle one of the South's most
important ports at a word from Washington. One great American grievance causing the Revolutionary War was the ar-

bitrary closing of the port of Boston to commerce by the British. It stood high on the Americans' list of so-called "Intolerable Acts." To Southerners, Sumter was a loaded threat to do the same thing to Charleston. Moreover, one of its heaviest guns, a 10-inch columbiad, was already elevated like a mortar to fire into the city of Charleston. Tested with only a 2-pound charge of powder instead of the usual 18, its mammoth round shot splashed just short of the city's homes. ". . . We knew that Charleston was within range," one Federal gunner recorded.[2] The fort disclaimed any intention —this was before the bombardment—of shelling the city, but its explosive hint got across.

2. Perhaps provisioning Sumter was all that "on that occasion" the Federal Government intended, but the South had already been led to believe by Seward and others that nothing at all would be done pending negotiations. The nature of the Sumter expedition was beclouded, moreover, by the preparations and departure of another similar expedition to Pensacola. And General Winfield Scott, the doughty old Virginia Unionist commanding the U. S. Army in the crisis, plainly referred to the Sumter expedition as intended to "reinforce" the fort with its troops. He hailed it as such.[3]

[2] James Chester, in *Battles and Leaders of the Civil War*, New York, 1887. Chester, an observant artillery sergeant in the Fort Sumter garrison, wrote a vivid account of the opening bombardment in later years while a regular army officer.

[3] For a fresh defense of Mr. Lincoln's Fort Sumter tactics, see "The Confederates and the First Shot," by Dr. R. N. Current, University of Wisconsin, in *Civil War History*, December, 1961. Dr. Current, like Mr. Lincoln, prefers in Midwestern style to overlook the offensive potential of a harbor fort to strangle commerce. He points out correctly that Sumter was built primarily to prevent seaborne invasion—but this fact apparently fails to convey to him a realization that its heaviest batteries pointed seaward and could have sunk incoming cargo ships even more easily than an invasion fleet. He adds that the fort's "weak" side fronted the shore and cites the success of the initial Confederate bombardment as evidence of this weakness. However, if Mr. Lincoln had reinforced the fort as his expedition was prepared to do, Sumter in Federal hands might have held out indefinitely. In Confederate hands, it did. Actually, the fort's weakest side, its gorge wall, faced James Island and Morris Island, not Charleston. In 1863–64, the Federal army planted on Morris Island the heaviest batteries the world had ever known. Still they failed to take the fort.

3. As for "trusting . . . to time, discussion and the ballot-box for final adjustment," Mr. Lincoln had already repeatedly asserted his determination to repossess all 35 Federal forts, customhouses and other property in Southern hands, and to collect taxes as if those states were still part of the Union, when they insisted they were not. After Sumter fell, one of the first "War Acts" of Congress authorized the administration to collect import taxes by military force wherever "unlawful combinations of persons in opposition to the laws of the United States"—in other words, the Confederacy—made it impossible. (This act of Congress, done July 13, 1861, was incorporated in the official U. S. Military Laws, 1776–1863. It empowered the President to set up ports of entry and customs collections anywhere in the Confederacy that U. S. military forces gained a foothold; provided for the seizure and condemnation of vessels and cargoes evading U. S. import duties, and for the blockade and closing of Southern ports.) When it came to adjustment by election, how, from a Southern viewpoint, could a separate nation adjust issues in another nation's ballot-box?

4. In terming secession a "minority" movement, Mr. Lincoln was hardly in the best position to downgrade minorities—he was elected President by one. Only 39.8 per cent of American voters favored him. Out of 4,682,069 popular votes cast in 1860, he received 1,866,542. The majority, no matter which of three other candidates they supported, were against Mr. Lincoln. In the eleven future Confederate States, he got not a single vote in ten and only 1,929 in the Unionist mountain corner of Virginia. His minority popular vote outside the South was so distributed, however, that he received 180 of 303 electoral votes and won a clean, clear victory.

Was Mr. Lincoln right or wrong in his handling of the Fort Sumter crisis? Was Mr. Davis right or wrong? Should the United States have closed its eyes on Sumter and hauled down the Stars and Stripes over U.S. property? Should the Confederacy have ignored an "alien" fort in one of its most important harbors?

One great American prerogative is criticizing those who must make decisions. Baseball umpires, football coaches who lose games, television showmen who lose audiences, Presidents who lose the faith of the man in the street, all are fair targets for the low-level commentator. A politician might term this democracy; a psychoanalyst might call it an escape mechanism.

Making a momentous decision is one of the loneliest, sweatiest measures of self-searching in anyone's life. It is a measure of both inner and outer man. It must have racked both the new presidents involved in 1861—the man elected by a sectional minority to head a split nation, the man chosen against his wishes (he was a West Pointer who would rather have been a general) to head a hopeful new nation.

In retrospect, certain factors stand out.

The Southern batteries around Charleston had already turned back one unarmed ship, the *Star of the West*, January 9, 1861, when it attempted to provision Fort Sumter. With the situation far more acute three months later, was there any reason for Mr. Lincoln to believe they would permit his expedition to carry out its mission?

On the other hand, the *Star of the West* episode had occurred under James Buchanan, an elderly, ailing President who was about to leave office. While it did not result in war, was there reason for Mr. Davis to assume that a second episode of greater magnitude during the administration of a new President pledged to hold the fort also would end without war?[4]

If Mr. Lincoln had not sent his expedition, what then?

If Mr. Davis had not given his "fire-if-necessary" instructions, what then?

[4] Events in history go to the bottom like ships sunk at sea. But bits of evidence rise to the surface later and become flotsam for the eyes of historians to detect. One of these, first made public in 1920, consists of the "Confidential Correspondence" of Captain Gustavus V. Fox, the young Navy officer who organized the Fort Sumter relief expedition and whom President Lincoln later appointed Assistant Secretary of the Navy. In one of his letters, Fox asserts that President Lincoln was eager for it to appear to the world that the Southern forces provoked the war. In Fox's opinion, they did just what Lincoln wished. Fox's letter appears in detail in *Prologue to Sumter*, one of the Premier Civil War Classics by Philip Van Doren Stern (Fawcett Publications, Inc.).

Would a war between the United States and the Confederacy have broken out elsewhere over some other issue?

Or would the two nations, both young and new in the eyes of the Old World, have lived side by side long enough to be re-cemented by economic ties?

2

Who Fired the First Shot?

Ask any two Civil War historians "Who started the war?" and a controversy will almost inevitably result. Getting down to particulars, the question of who actually fired the opening round of the war is, in itself, no mean subject for dispute. "First shot" claims have come under a heavy crossfire of historical argument. In fact, some will contend that the war didn't begin at Fort Sumter at all.

At some time on April 11, 1861, it occurred to Capt. George S. James that he should send for a physician. He was about to start a war the next morning and he thought it might be well to have a doctor on hand.

The captain commanded two Confederate batteries of 12-inch mortars emplaced amid the sand dunes of James Island at Fort Johnson, facing Fort Sumter in Charleston harbor. The doctor who responded to his call, although not needed professionally as it turned out, had a wonderful opportunity to become the star witness in what is now a major historical controversy: Who actually fired the first shot of the Civil War?

With the arrival of the war centennial, there are almost as many nominees for that notable role as there are be-whiskered characters in Cuba. They range from an elderly man to a very small girl. Let us consider the likeliest in order.

Captain James realized that his position was the logical one to fire first, because it was a point of departure and return for Confederate emissaries making an eleventh-hour attempt to negotiate a peaceful surrender at Fort Sumter. James knew that their return without surrender terms would mean war.

The captain, a veteran of the Mexican War of 1846–48, had two good lieutenants, both fresh from West Point. He posted them carefully at the mortars. There had been pre-

Edmund Ruffin

WHO FIRED THE FIRST SHOT?

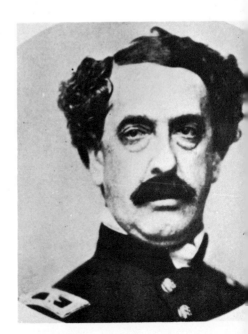

Capt. Abner Doubleday
who aimed the first
Union gun.

E. L. Halsey
(grandfather of the author)

Lt. W. H. Gibbes

H. S. Farley

mature or accidental shots from the batteries surrounding Sumter. James wanted no mistake about his.

Lt. Wade Hampton Gibbes, a newlywed who had served briefly as a United States cavalry lieutenant after graduation from the Military Academy the previous June, commanded at one mortar emplacement. Lt. Henry S. Farley, the first Southern cadet to walk out of West Point without waiting to be graduated, commanded the other. Both were young South Carolinians willing, if not eager, to begin a war in their own back yard.

Both lieutenants later claimed the crepe-draped distinction of having fired the first shot. As a witness, the physician, Dr. Robert Lebby, proved somewhat less than conclusive. He was talking with another doctor, the garrison surgeon, who had been away but returned just in time. Both medical men saw Farley holding the lanyard which set off his mortar and are "of the opinion" that he fired first. In the leisurely way of newspapers of the day, *The Charleston Mercury* got around to this bit of news a week later. "We are informed," it said, "that Lieut. H. S. Farley of Captain James's company had the honor of firing the alarm or first gun of the battle on Friday last."

Whoever informed *The Mercury*, it was not Lt. Wade Hampton Gibbes. That officer stated, "The first shell was fired by Captain James's battery, and, incidentally, by me as his first lieutenant." Gibbes outranked Farley, who was a second lieutenant. In the protocol of starting a war, he held an advantage. He was explicit: "My orders were to fire a shell, to burst high up in the air, as a signal to commence the general bombardment." A shell did exactly that, exploding directly above Fort Sumter. Nearly a dozen Confederate batteries on islands around the fort then opened up full blast at ranges of 1,210 to 2,425 yards.

From a battery at the northern end of Morris Island, near the harbor entrance, there soon resounded another claim to having fired the first shot of the war. Fiery old Virginian Edmund Ruffin served there as a volunteer in the Palmetto Guards. Ruffin turned to war with a distinguished record as an agriculturist. By the experimental use of marl, he had saved thousands of acres of "sour" land. Now he was determined to save his land in another sense.

Ruffin stepped forward, yanked the lanyard of an enormous siege cannon weighing nearly five tons and shouted exuberantly that he had scored the first hit on Fort Sumter, three quarters of a mile away. For a man of sixty-seven, early on a dark and foggy morning, he demonstrated remarkable eyesight. More remarkable still, the feat was confirmed by a strange source —the senior captain of the Federal garrison in Sumter. This was Abner Doubleday, a mustachioed Yankee who fired the first return shot from the fort. Doubleday, who ended the war as a major general and was acclaimed, inaccurately, as the inventor of baseball, reminisced after the conflict:

"Edmund Ruffin of Virginia is usually credited with opening the attack by firing the first gun from the iron-clad battery on Morris Island. The ball from that gun struck the wall of the magazine where I was lying, penetrated the masonry and burst very near my head."

Doubleday surely had ample reason to remember a shell which struck that close to him. But how he could tell, through a solid brick wall on a foggy morning, who fired the shot from behind a distant battlement is one of those little mysteries which make Civil War stories so intriguing. The mystery is heightened by the fact that the Confederates discharged forty-seven cannon and mortars in rapid order after the opening shot. All together, they fired between 3,000 and 4,000 shells at the fort. Some 2,500 registered hits. For Doubleday to single out and glorify the shot that almost killed him as "the first shot of the war" somehow smacks of egotism.

Moreover, Ruffin, by his own statement in writing, was not in the "iron-clad battery" at all, although Doubleday, contemporary Charleston newspapers and other supposedly authoritative sources said that he was. Ruffin's unit, the Palmetto Guards, manned both the "Iron Battery"—so called because the battlement in front of it was iron-plated—and the "Point Battery" at the Cummings Point extremity of Morris Island. The old man, in a letter written only a week later, referred to "the Point Battery in which I was engaged."[1]

[1] One circumstance alone, if correctly reported, would have precluded the possibility that Ruffin's blast was the very first shot of all. It appears that the batteries surrounding Fort Sumter fired in sequence, clockwise. If so, Ruffin's battery, at a hypothetical 10 or 11 o'clock, would have been among the last to open fire. The Official Records quote Capt. G. B. Cuthbert, commanding the Palmetto Guard, in which Ruffin served, as writing from Morris Island on April 17, 1861:

". . . The mortar battery at Cummings Point opened fire on

Ruffin, at any rate, went triumphantly home to Virginia and his 200 slaves soon after Sumter yielded. He felt exhilarated. His beloved South had rebuffed the North without the loss of a single life on either side. Despite the terrific bombardment, the massive brick fort amply protected its little garrison. Only four men were wounded. Ironically, one accidental fatality occurred later when a fort cannon, firing a salute to the Stars and Stripes before the garrison marched out, went off prematurely. It killed a Federal gunner instantly and wounded five others.

Ruffin subsequently wrote a polite "thank you" note to his host of April the twelfth and thirteenth, the commanding officer of the Palmetto Guards, expressing appreciation for the use of his cannon. He also established himself as one of the first souvenir hunters of the Civil War. He asked his comrades to recover a Federal shell which he had seen bury itself in the sand near the Point Battery, and express it to him at Petersburg, Virginia, "as a memento of the occasion."

Before the war ended, Ruffin and his compatriots found more than enough Federal shells coming their way unsolicited. Doggedly shouldering his musket, the old planter made brief, cheer-raising appearances at the Battle of First Manassas or Bull Run, and on return trips to the defenses around Charleston. By 1863 he was dodging from his plantations to avoid Federal troops. As the South went down, the old man sank with it. Two months after Appomattox, he shot and killed himself rather than live "conquered" under "Yankee rule."

Like Ruffin, the lieutenants of the mortar batteries, Gibbes and Farley, survived four years of conflict. Gibbes remained in the artillery, becoming a major. He suffered a grave wound

---

Fort Sumter *in its turn* [italics inserted], after the signal shell from Fort Johnson, having been preceded by the mortar batteries on Sullivan's Island and the mortar battery of the Marion Artillery . . .

". . . At the dawn of day the Iron Battery commenced its work of demolition. The first shell from Columbiad No. 1, fired by the venerable Edmund Ruffin of Virginia, burst directly upon the parapet of the southwest angle of the fort."

Thus Cuthbert apparently makes it plain that Ruffin's was merely the first shell from that battery or gun. He either grouped the Iron and Point Batteries as one unit, or else Ruffin's memory slipped in saying he was in the Point Battery. And if the shell burst "upon the parapet" as Cuthbert states, it seems unlikely that it was the same one which Doubleday said burst inside near his head.

in the Battle of the Crater at Petersburg. In postwar life he became a banker, machinery dealer and senior warden of Trinity Episcopal Church at Columbia, South Carolina. Farley shifted to the cavalry and eventually became a lieutenant colonel. After the war, he conducted a military academy at Ossining, New York. A daughter of his married the late United States Senator E. D. Smith of South Carolina, and a grandson, Farley Smith of Sumter, now heads the anti-integration South Carolina Citizens Councils.

Among those publicized in 1861 as rivals of the three warlike Southerners for the distinction of starting the war was, fantastically, a small girl who happened to have the Czarina of Russia as a godmother. The child, daughter of Francis W. Pickens of South Carolina and his beautiful Texan wife, was born in St. Petersburg in 1859 while her father was United States Ambassador to Russia. Amid much pomp, she was christened Frances Eugenia Olga Neva Pickens. The Czar thereupon nicknamed her Douschka, or "little darling," a name borne today by her granddaughter.

Pickens soon returned to South Carolina and became governor. To be at the center of crisis in 1861, he moved with his family from the state capital at Columbia to temporary quarters in the Charleston Hotel. The more lurid section of the Northern press described in detail how tiny Douschka fired the opening gun of the war while held in the arms of the Confederate commander, Gen. P. G. T. Beauregard. The fanciful story was presented as evidence of the wanton attitude of the South toward bloodshed. Not a single fact can be found to support it. When the war began, little Douschka apparently was asleep at the hotel miles away. She was, after all, only about two. Nor was Beauregard present in the batteries that opened on Sumter. The nearest thing to a Confederate kiddy act occurred at the Iron Battery, where thirteen-year-old Paul B. Lalane, who cleverly picked the occasion to visit an elder brother in the service, was permitted to fire several shells at Sumter.

With the Civil War centennial, all "first shot" claims have come under a heavy crossfire of historical argument. In some places local chroniclers or Chamber of Commerce trumpeters even contend that the war didn't begin at Fort Sumter at all. These place the locale in Florida, Mississippi and Arkansas. Each involves a "first shot" fired before the bombardment of Sumter. Here is the sequence:

At Pensacola, Florida, January 8, 1861, United States troops in old Fort Barrancas, commanded by Lt. Adam J. Slemmer, drove off with a volley of musketry twenty shadowy figures. Presumably the twenty were state troops scouting to see if the fort was garrisoned. The shots were, without doubt, the first discharged in support of the Union.

The next day at Charleston, salvos from a harbor battery turned back the merchant steamship *Star of the West*, out of New York for Charleston with supplies for Fort Sumter. Cadets of the South Carolina Military Academy, now The Citadel, manned the guns. These were the first shots fired at the United States flag.

Within a week rebel shells brought another United States craft to a halt at Vicksburg, Mississippi. Capt. J. F. Kerr's battery from Jackson fired two shots in front of a paddle-wheeler bound from Pittsburgh to New Orleans. Militiamen then searched the ship for supplies for the United States forts around New Orleans, found none and let her go.

In a third incident involving supplies for forts, early in April, the Jefferson Guards of Pine Bluff, Arkansas, rallied at the river bank and diverted a supply transport bound up the Arkansas to Fort Smith. One musket bullet across the bows apparently did the trick. The "sovereign" State of Arkansas then confiscated the military material on board.

The Charleston harbor defenses meanwhile fired on the United States flag a second time. Their target was a little schooner loaded with New England ice for Savannah. The craft blundered up the channel in a fog, without any way of explaining her appearance there. When the guns began to boom, she flew out again like a frightened sparrow.

None of these almost comic performances with artillery scratched a single person, much less set off a gigantic conflict. So the claims of Gibbes, Farley and Ruffin—take your pick—would appear to head the list. Or do they?

When it comes to historical assertions, the Civil War centennial is a "shooting war" in itself. Any statement raised above the parapets whether by Civil War buffs or innocent bystanders, is subject to being drilled full of Minié holes from one direction or another. Here, coming from one of their contemporaries, is a bombshell for Gibbes and Farley.

It fell to Capt. (later Lt. Gen.) Stephen D. Lee, as an aide to the commanding general, P. G. T. Beauregard, to break off the negotiations with Fort Sumter and transmit personally to Captain James the order to open fire. In a statement years later, Lee relates how James in his courtly way invited Roger Pryor, a hotheaded Virginia lawyer and newspaperman who was a sort of younger version of Ruffin, to fire the opening shot. As Lee recalled it, James turned to Pryor and said, "You are the only man to whom I would give up the honor of firing the first gun of the war." Pryor could not bring himself to bear the awesome responsibility. Huskily he declined. At that, Lee says flatly, "Captain James would allow no one else but *himself* to fire the gun."

Lee, however, undermined his own testimony. En route back to Charleston and headquarters, he had his boatmen row him about 800 yards away, where he could witness the effect of the shelling. Obviously he was not at hand to see who first jerked the lanyard. Yet he maintained to the end that it was James.

General Beauregard stated after the war in *Military Operations*, Chapter IV, Page 42: "From Fort Johnson's mortar battery at 4.30 A.M. issued the first shot of the war. It was fired not by Mr. Ruffin of Virginia, as has been erroneously supposed, but by Captain George S. James of South Carolina."

Here was the commanding general's word for it, but the general, like his aide, Stephen D. Lee, was not present in person to see for himself. Another of his aides, Lieut. Edward H. Barnwell, testified that the first shell soared from *"James' east or beach battery."* This raised a point. The general referred to one battery; the lieutenant implied there were two under command of James. And indeed there were, adding to the historical confusion.

A precise account in after years from Dr. W. H. Prioleau (pronounced pray-low), of Charleston, surgeon of the post, who was absent when Captain James summoned Dr. Lebby but who returned before the guns spoke, confirms that the mortars under James were divided into two batteries or sections.

"On the morning of April 12, 1861," Dr. Prioleau stated, "as soon as orders were received to open fire on Fort Sumter, we repaired to our posts, and 25 or 30 minutes after 4 A.M., by my watch, which I held open in my hand at the time, the first gun was fired, this being the righthand mortar in the *battery on the beach.* I cannot recall who pulled the lanyard, but the gun was directly in charge of Lieut. Henry S. Farley, who, as well as I can recollect, sighted the gun, Captain James giving the order to fire."

Dr. Lebby amplified on this and added his own observations in a paper written in 1893 and published in 1911 in the *South Carolina Historical Magazine*. In it, Lebby, a native, resident and practicing physician of James Island, explained that, "having been a college acquaintance of Captain James, (I) was invited by him the previous day, April 11, to be on hand if anything transpired to require my services."

Lebby then bore out his colleague's reference to two batteries. These he identified as "one directly west of Fort Sumter known as the east or beach battery and one northwest of that on a hill near quarantine known as the west or hill battery.

"I was," he continued, "on a bridge that connected the beach and the hill, where I could see the fire of either battery, and at 4.30 A.M. a shell was fired from the east or beach battery commanded by Captain James.

"The second report heard was the blowing up of Greer's house, contiguous to the hill battery commanded by Lieut. W. H. Gibbes, and the second shell was fired from this battery under Lieutenant Gibbes. The firing then became general around the harbor batteries bearing on Fort Sumter. . . .

(The Greer house mentioned as being blown up in the "second report" of the war was a private home which masked the hill battery and therefore was deliberately destroyed. Similar steps were taken on the other side of the harbor, on Sullivan's Island, where the Confederates had erected several batteries, unknown to the defenders of Fort Sumter, behind buildings.)

"As to the question of who pulled the lanyard . . . certain it is that either James or Farley fired it, but as Captain James *gave the order* to fire, it must have been Farley, as James would never have given *himself* the order to fire."

Not content with this deduction, Dr. Lebby wrote to Colonel Farley, then at Mount Pleasant Military Academy on the Hudson River. Farley's reply is incorporated in the doctor's published account.

"The circumstances attending the firing of the first gun at Sumter are quite fresh in my memory," the aging colonel said stoutly. "Captain James stood on my right, watch in hand, and at the designated moment gave me the order to fire. *I pulled the lanyard*, having already carefully inserted a friction tube, and discharged a 13-inch mortar . . . which was at the right of the battery."[2]

All in all, it would appear that Farley's claim was borne out by two physicians and the circumstantial testimony of General Beauregard and two of his aides. It did not, however, silence Gibbes' steadfast statement that his mortar got off the first shot. Nor did it faze the embattled Ruffin in his vaunting at the time.

Much of Ruffin's fame derives from an ambiguous newspaper report. This, a camouflage of facts with words, says that the venerable Virginian "fired the first shot at Fort Sumter from the Iron Battery on Morris Island." All it meant, taken in context, was that he began one battery's part in the bombardment.

To aggravate matters, I, in writing this, must remove another laurel from the grim old secessionist's war record. No matter how close his cannon ball shaved past Abner Doubleday's head, technically it was not the first shell to strike Sumter. The first shot ever landed on the fort hit it much earlier—March 8, 1861, to be exact.

It was during the "cold war" between the Federal Government and the seceding states. Southern artillerymen at Charleston continually tested their guns, usually taking care to aim well clear of the frowning fortress under the Stars and Stripes. To citizen soldiers in the Iron Battery, unaccustomed to heaving about heavy cannon, the toil of endless drills seemed pointless. One night, a twenty-three-year-old private remarked that he was "tired of this nonsense—there will be some fun in the morning."

Shortly after dawn, when the battery went through all the empty motions of firing, an eight-inch columbiad suddenly roared out while aimed at the fort. The solid shot screamed across the water at Sumter. It struck, according to one version, just to the left of the sally port or main gate. The garrison manned its guns—this is a matter of official record—and prepared to reply to further shelling. Instead, the Iron Battery commander rushed over in a small boat under a truce flag to apologize for "the accidental shot."

---

[2] The friction tube was a special copper-encased fulminate of mercury primer which was inserted in a vent or touchhole near the base of the mortar. Farley refers to the piece as a "13-inch mortar." Records indicate it was a 10-incher, but in either case it was a mortar of large calibre.

The shot was no accident. I can say that with certainty, for the man who loaded the gun during the night was my grandfather, E. L. Halsey of Charleston. Grandfather was not the patient type. The explosive gesture seemed entirely representative of his feelings. If action was what he wanted, he soon got it. Transferring from harbor defenses to horse artillery, he became first lieutenant and then captain of a battery which fought in 143 battles and skirmishes from start to finish. Of the unit's original 147 men, only twenty-three answered the final muster. At the surrender they cried as they kissed their cannon good-by. Grandfather broke his saber and kept his revolver.

After the war, with much of the South burned to the ground, grandfather went into the lumber business. He made a small fortune, married a golden-haired young lady eleven years his junior and fathered seven sons and five daughters. He lived out his days totally unreconstructed. My father, as a boy, erected a small United States flag on a pole in the garden one Christmas Day. My grandfather, wordless with anger, got out his revolver, chopped down the pole with three precisely placed bullets and said, "I do not want to see that flag on my premises ever again!" He didn't.

Never, however, did he make any public statement about his attempt to start the Civil War a month ahead of time with the shot that hit Sumter in March. Possibly, having become a veteran soldier, he realized what a breach of discipline his prank represented. When an account of it was published many years ago, my Uncle LeRoy, who lives at Stone Mountain, near Atlanta, recalls that grandfather "was not pleased at it."

As for deciding who actually fired the opening round, Samuel G. Stoney, Charleston's bearded historian, once settled the question facetiously: "Many people believe 'The War' was so big that it was entitled to more than one opening shot."

3

The Forts Come Tumbling Down

General Quincy Adams Gillmore, USA, was a bulldoggish man with pale blue eyes, brushy whiskers, and definite ideas. One of his most definite ideas was that whenever General Gillmore attacked a fort, the place should surrender. An early success in the Civil War gave him an eminent basis for that belief.

The Civil War ended not only a social and economic structure based on slavery, but an elaborate defense structure resting on solid granite. This was the impressive system of pentagon-shaped brick and granite fortresses that girded the American coast from New England around into the Gulf and guarded every major port. These forts, built between 1820 and 1860, represented the ultimate perfection of an era of fortification going back to the classic designs of such seventeenth-century military engineers as the noted Frenchman Vauban, and beyond him to medieval and ancient castles. They were built on the simple premise that masonry could stop any cannon shell. Once, this was true. At the start of the war, American military tradition weighed heavily against attackers of forts. Our strongholds had won notably against British fleets at Sullivan's Island, South Carolina, in the Revolution and at Fort McHenry, in Baltimore harbor, in the War of 1812.

When the war broke out, the mighty fortresses sat as rigid and formal as hoop-skirted ladies at the entrance of Southern ports. Some were among the 17 fortifications which Southern state troops seized in 1861 and busily strengthened. In the military picture of the period, they were as important as missile bases are today. The side that held them, and held them well, could breathe easier.

It remained for Maj. Gen. Quincy Adams Gillmore, USA, an Ohioan of New England ancestry, to bring both tradition and the forts tumbling down. In assaulting supposedly impregnable Fort Pulaski, the key Confederate defense of Savannah, Georgia, General Gillmore revolutionized siege warfare. He employed batteries of heavy *rifled* cannon against a masonry fortress for the first time in history. The result was sensational. Unlike the round shot from smoothbore cannon, which struck like a slow, ponderous blow from a pudgy fist, the sharp-nosed rifle shells punched hard, fast and deep. Gillmore's carefully emplaced batteries smashed Fort Pulaski into submission between 8 A.M. one fine April morning and 2 P.M. the next day.

Gillmore's victory set a pattern of doom for nearly all the Confederate-held fortresses. He proved that the rifled gun, whether on land or aboard ship, could puncture masonry walls.

Although the success at Fort Pulaski was achieved primarily by rifled guns, a variety of things ranging from psychological warfare to Yankee jackknives contributed to it. The subtler side of the siege was related later by Brig. Gen. Horace Porter.[1]

The besiegers knew the general plan and arrangement of the fort because detailed construction drawings existed in the War Department in Washington. But they were eager to learn what the Confederates had done to strengthen the interior of the structure. They learned the answer by playing music.

One of the Federal regiments, the 46th New York, consisted almost entirely of Germans. Their commands, conversation, singing, and cooking all were German. So, with an emphatic "oompah," was their splendid brass band. On hearing of the need for intelligence concerning the fort, a stalwart German soldier made a suggestion: Let the band play nostalgic Teuton airs.

In the tranquil twilight, the band took a position on the river bank below the fort and trilled Deutsch melodies softly enough to make the iciest Prussian weep into his lager. Sure enough, a log came floating down the river. On it perched a homesick German deserter from the fort, probably from Capt. J. H. Steigen's German Volunteers, CSA. In exchange for an earful of tunes, the Federals got from him several earfuls of valuable information.

---

[1] *Battles and Leaders of the Civil War*, Vol. II, and contemporary newspaper accounts.

The night before the Federal gunners were to begin their furious bombardment, a supply catastrophe befell Battery No. 11. This battery consisted of four 10-inch mortars emplaced closer to the fort than any others. Shell fuses arrived for the 13-inch mortars farther back, but none came for the 10-inchers. The battery closest to the fort could not fire a shot.

The missing fuses were simple tapered wooden plugs with a hole drilled vertically through them to contain a thin paper tube of gunpowder. The small end of the plug was shoved into the mortar shell. The fuse was then cut off, if necessary, so that the powder inside would burn for three, four or five seconds—whatever length of time was necessary for the mortar propulsion charge to heft the shell up and over into the fort. By then, the fuse powder would burn down and ignite the explosive charge inside the shell, making a smash-bang blast.

Inspiration suddenly struck Porter, the ordnance officer. He remembered seeing a regiment of Yankee troops lying around whittling during an idle period. Back he went, and located the 6th Connecticut Infantry. They were turned out of their tents that night and ordered to "whittle like mad." By the time they were through, the mortar battery had enough fuse plugs for a two-day bombardment.

The fall of Fort Pulaski struck an ironic blow to Southern morale. The Army engineer responsible for its prewar construction was one Robert E. Lee. When Pulaski faced besieging, General Lee was quoted at Richmond as saying, presumably for morale purposes, that no besiegers could vanquish the fortress. There is evidence that the Confederate high command, Lee included, knew better. Pulaski mounted only 48 of its allotted 140 guns and was not heavily garrisoned. Confederate coast defense strategy permitted its sacrifice in favor of protecting industrial production centers farther inland.

General Gillmore sized up the situation with his pale blue eyes and wrote a report to Washington. He later said, "I reported that I deemed the reduction of the work [fort] practicable with batteries of mortars and rifled guns established on Tybee Island," between the fort and the ocean. Although 10-inch and 13-inch mortars and 10-inch smoothbore columbiads were relatively plentiful, the Army could find only ten rifled cannon of any size for Gillmore in its entire arsenal at that time. Five were new 30-pounder Parrott guns. Five were

James rifles, makeshifts converted from smoothbores by grooving the insides of their barrels. By enabling these to use cylindrical shells instead of round shot, the conversion approximately doubled the weight of their projectiles. Thus Gillmore had a former 24-pounder, two ex-32s and two erstwhile 42s which now fired shells of, respectively, 48, 64 and 84 pounds. They did so under a strain which often threatened to burst the cannon.

At 8:15 A.M. on April 10, 1862, almost the anniversary of the fall of Fort Sumter to the Confederacy, Gillmore's Federal batteries opened up on Fort Pulaski and its graycoat defenders. His ten rifled guns stood only 1,650 yards from the outer wall in Batteries Nine and Ten, the two emplacements closest to Pulaski. "By one o'clock . . . with a glass it could be seen that the rifled projectiles were surely eating into the scarp [lower front of the fort] and adjacent southeast face," Gillmore recorded. After nine and a half hours, "the commencement of a breach was plainly visible." Like good Union men, the gunners quit work for the night. By noon the next day, the rifled shells had smashed open two sections of the crumbling seven-and-one-half-foot-thick walls and were searching out the powder magazine to the rear of them. Breaches aggregating thirty feet in width lay open, with more to come. At 2 P.M., the fort ran up a white flag. The garrison of 385 had lost one killed and three or four wounded. Every parapet gun save three had been wrecked and the moat or ditch surrounding the fort was so filled with masonry debris that it could be crossed dry-footed.

Gillmore's military reputation was made. As one account described it, "his successful use of rifled cannon for breeching masonry walls at Fort Pulaski during the Civil War caused a sensation throughout the world in proving many modern fortifications vulnerable to artillery." Within a few months, General Beauregard penned an official report to Richmond: "The introduction of heavy rifled guns and ironclad steamers in the attack of masonry forts has greatly changed the condition of the problem applicable to Fort Sumter when it was built, and we must now use the few and imperfect means at our command to increase its defensive features as far as practicable."

Beauregard, an artillery specialist who had commanded at the opening bombardment of the war against Sumter, was in a peculiarly apt position to know what rifled guns could do even before Fort Pulaski fell. He happened to have commanded the first piece of rifled artillery used in battle in the United States and the first used against a masonry fort. The outward difference between it and the other cannon was imperceptible, but to a trained observer, its performance spoke volumes.

On April 12, 1861, when 47 Confederate cannon in batteries around Charleston harbor ringing beleaguered Sumter opened the war with a deafening roar, this one small voice of ordnance went virtually unheard. In size and in the weight of its projectiles, it was the least impressive of the awesome array. The larger guns threw shells weighing up to 87 pounds, impelled by as much as 10 pounds of powder. The little cannon pecked away with only a 10-pound shell backed by a single pound of powder. But its shells drilled deeper into the fort than any other. There was good reason. Every other cannon on both sides that day was a smoothbore. The bores or insides of their barrels were as smooth and unfurrowed as a gas pipe. Their round shot pushed through the air much as a basketball does. By contrast, the little rifled cannon discharged a long conical shell which spiraled like a football. The rifling grooves inside its barrel imparted a twist that sent its shell harder and faster than a round shot.

The bombardment continued for 33 hours. Some 2,500 shot and shell battered the brick fort under the Stars and Stripes. Only one, however, drew blood from the Union garrison. It came from the little rifled cannon, which apparently caused the first casualties in the long and bloody conflict. Official U.S. Army records relate that "one shot from the *rifled gun* . . . on Cummings Point . . . struck an embrasure (opening for a cannon muzzle) at the right gorge angle of the fort and fragments wounded a sergeant and three men. . . ."

In a stormy tour that night, officers of the fort dared drenching rain and bursting shells to inspect the damage. They found the five-foot-thick brick walls broadly scarred, but never more than 12 inches deep, where the heaviest round shot had struck. But at the south corner or angle of the fort where the rifled gun had aimed, they discovered a neat tunnel-like hole fully 20 inches deep drilled into the brickwork "with the accuracy of a duelling pistol." It was a sight for military men to behold and study. Using only a small fraction of the powder and shell of the big cannons, the rifled gun had penetrated distinctly deeper. What would a truly huge rifled gun, comparable in size to the smoothbore mammoths, do to a fort like Sumter?

Beauregard, penning his warning, knew the answer. The great irony was that the Confederates, who held and defended the masonry forts, first demonstrated their vulnerability to rifled cannon. And, like so many turning points in the war, that happened by sheer chance.

The 10-pound rifled gun used against Fort Sumter was one man's donation to the war effort. It was a Blakely, made in Great Britain and named after an inventive Englishman who associated himself with Sir George Armstrong, later created a baron for his industrial production. In 1859 Armstrong and Blakely sold the British Government on the first sizable batteries of modern steel rifled cannon, strengthened by layers of metal shrunken over their breeches.

In the tense spring of 1861, with war clouds lowering, a Charleston "merchant prince" residing and doing business in England learned of the novel artillery of Messrs. Armstrong and Blakely. Charles K. Prioleau, of French Huguenot descent, came of an immensely wealthy family. He and his kinsmen were accustomed to making lordly gestures. For heroism in the Mexican War, for example, J. H. Prioleau presented an ornate, silver-mounted bowie knife, specially made at Sheffield, England, to Captain Edmund Kirby Smith, U.S. Army. Kirby Smith, a West Pointer, later became a top-ranking Confederate general. His handsome bowie now reposes in the West Point museum.

Charles Prioleau, enchanted by the Blakely cannon, lavishly surpassed J. H. Prioleau's military gifts. He purchased the cannon complete with accessories and shipped it to Charleston at his private expense to help defend his home. The Charleston *Courier* of April 10, 1861, duly noted that "a rifled cannon arrived in Charleston April 9th from Liverpool. It has been presented to the Sovereign State of South Carolina by one of her citizens residing abroad, in commemoration of the 20th of December, 1860." That was the date on which South Carolina had seceded. The *Courier* noted with satisfaction that the cannon "has been put in place." Then it added circumspectly, "Where that place is, it becomes us not at present to report."

The place was the Point Battery, at Cummings Point on the northeast end of Morris Island, the closest battery to

Sumter, with a range of only about 1,200 yards. Captain John P. Thomas, a professional soldier on the staff of the South Carolina Miltary Academy, now The Citadel, took command of the gun and trained a crew in less than 48 hours. As might be expected, the persistent Blakely ran short of shells during the bombardment.[2] James Eason, head of the largest ironworks in Charleston, immediately began manufacture of 400 "bolts," as the projectiles were called. Eason then went farther. He rifled some smoothbore iron cannon made earlier by the famous Tredegar Iron Works, at Richmond, Virginia. Whether this weakened the barrels too much is conjectural, but one gun burst after being tested with more than 100 rounds.

Another Charlestonian, Archibald Cameron, undertook to manufacture a rifled field piece from scratch. He may or may not have ever seen one beforehand. One of six early Parrott field pieces, made on the Hudson and sold to the state of Virginia before the outbreak of hostilities, turned up in 1959 in an excavation in South Carolina. Apparently Confederates buried it rather than surrender it. So it is possible that Cameron may have glimpsed one of the few rifled guns in existence before he set out to make his. First he melted down the iron remains of the first locomotive of the old South Carolina Railroad for his material, according to the story. Then he fabricated a round barrel with a reinforcing band in the critical breech area, much in the manner of the Parrott gun described below. His rifling followed the style then identified largely with small arms rather than artillery. It consisted of six shallow grooves. The lands or elevated strips inside the bore were twice as wide as the grooves, much as in the famous Kentucky or Pennsylvania rifles. The Cameron gun saw service in South Carolina, although details of its deeds and performance are almost entirely lacking. It is now preserved at Charleston, and bears a bronze plaque stating that it is "the first cannon made in the Confederate States and said to be the first rifled cannon made in America."

---

[2] James Chester, in *Battles and Leaders*, refers to the rifled gun and says it was fortunate for the fort that it ran out of ammunition before breaching the wall—"but a few hours more of that Whitworth 12-pounder would have knocked a hole in our defenses." So the effectiveness of the rifled gun was evident to a smart sergeant, although he confused the Blakely with the Whitworth, another British gun.

While both claims appear debatable, the Cameron cannon undoubtedly was among the first rifled guns made in this country. Among its rivals was the muzzle-loading rifled cannon with band-reinforced breech manufactured by Robert Parker Parrott, a West Point graduate of 1824, at his West Point Foundry (no official connection) at Cold Spring, New York. Parrott supposedly heard of the rifled cannon which Krupp manufactured secretly in Germany in 1849 and years later began experiments of his own. One great problem with all rifled ordnance involved fitting the shell so tightly into the grooves that the powder gases propelling it could not escape through spaces between shell and rifling. Parrott patented an expanding projectile for rifled cannon on August 20, 1861, four months after the firing on Sumter. Its principal characteristic was a brass band soft enough to expand into the grooves. On October 1, 1861, he patented his reinforced breech. He offered both inventions to the United States Government "at cost," and quickly obtained large orders for Parrott guns and shells. The six Parrott guns purchased by the state of Virginia before seceding were soon manned to defend the Confederacy. Other Parrotts blasted away in behalf of the Union in every major engagement in the East from First Manassas, or Bull Run, on. Parrott field pieces were produced in sizes to fire 10-pound and 20-pound shells.

The principal role of rifled artillery in the Civil War was not so much as field pieces—mobile cannon primarily for use against personnel—as it was in battering fortresses or defending them (in the case of the South) against attacks. Parrott, the prime manufacturer in the United States, soon went from field guns into production of 100-, 200- and 300-pound siege guns weighing six to fifteen tons and with barrels as long as 14½ feet. Armstrong, Blakely and Whitworth also manufactured some mammoths. Most of these went through the blockade to the South, and eventually fell into Federal hands. Two of the largest were heavily banded or reinforced Armstrongs, each weighing 27 tons. They fired enormous projectiles, weighing 700 pounds, with a 40-pound charge of powder. To minimize breech pressure and recoil, they were built with air chambers in back of the powder chambers. One burst when, it was said, powder was rammed back too far and entered the air chamber. The big Armstrongs were mounted at Charleston and at Fort Fisher, outside Wilmington, North Carolina. Eighty-pounder Whitworths were placed in the defenses of Vicksburg and Charleston to give added punch to the Southern batteries.

Of all the Southern coastal forts, Sumter, supported by batteries on both flanks on Sullivan's and Morris Islands, put up the stiffest resistance. The Union Navy went it alone.

In the early afternoon of April 7, 1863, nine armored vessels mounting 32 of the heaviest rifled guns ever used in war up to that time hammered the fort for two hours in an intense duel. The Navy soon learned its mistake.

The ironclads got off 154 rounds. Only 34 hit the mark. These breached the right flank wall for a length of 25 feet and dug craters up to 2½ feet deep elsewhere. In a military sense, this was far from enough to punish the stronghold.

The Confederates in Sumter and nearby batteries, able to bring many more guns to bear, hurled 2,209 rounds at the audacious ironclads. One, the *USS Keokuk*, was so hard hit that she sank the next morning—and the Southerners brashly salvaged her guns at night to arm their forts. Four of the remaining eight ships crawled away disabled. Exit the Navy. It was now the Army's turn.

Inevitably, the Army summoned General Quincy A. Gillmore, conqueror of Fort Pulaski. Again Gillmore went slowly and methodically about his business. He landed 11,000 troops on Folly and Morris Islands, south of Sumter, and gradually fought up to Cummings Point and short-range distance of the stronghold.

Expecting Sumter's big batteries "to be silenced sooner or later," as Beauregard had predicted, the defenders removed many of its cannon and reinforced its walls with sandbags and other material.

Gillmore meanwhile carefully set up eight batteries of huge rifled guns at ranges of two to two and a half miles—extreme distances for those days. After some preliminary shelling to test charges and accuracy, the Federal guns roared in earnest on August 17, 1863. A total of 17 rifled Parrotts throwing 200-pound shells crashed projectiles in a steady rain on the fort. Nearly 1,000 fell the first day; nearly 6,000 during the first week.

Then Gillmore added a 13-ton cannon firing 250-pound shells. The world had never seen a bombardment like it. The fort cannon, outranged and outblasted, remained silent. By the end of the week, 39 out of 40 pieces of artillery in the fort had been knocked out. Only one remained serviceable.

An enormous breach in the wall, crumbling into a slope of debris, yawned invitation to attackers.

On the night of September 8-9, the Navy got back into the act with a new tactic. Tugboats towed a landing force of 400 sailors and marines in whaleboats, under Commodore T. H. Stevens, USN, almost to the fort. By then, the Sumter gunners had been withdrawn. The garrison consisted of 320 infantrymen of the Charleston Battalion, a dogged special defense unit. The Confederates held their fire until the attackers began crawling up the debris slope. Then they opened up with muskets, hand grenades, canister from the lone cannon, and brickbats. Fort Moultrie, across the channel, boomed support. The Confederate ironclad *Chicora* came down-harbor firing at the boats. The Navy, having lost 124 killed, wounded and captured, withdrew into the night. To the Army, the success or failure of the attack did not much matter.

General Gillmore claimed victory for his guns by a technical knockout: "The fort was destitute of cannon, could take no part in a defense against a fleet, and as an infantry outpost could be of no value to us if captured."[3]

If the Navy wanted to take Charleston, Gillmore thought it should disregard the forts and sail boldly up the harbor channel as the British had done in their second attack in the Revolutionary War. The admirals thought the harbor defenses, including inner forts and torpedoes or mines in the channel, precluded any such daring.

At any rate, Gillmore appears to have felt that his mission was fulfilled. Fort Sumter, although "heroically held by the enemy," lay battered by his heavy rifled guns "into a shapeless mass of ruins." As a fort, Sumter had been literally pulverized by 3,500 tons of shells thrown into an area of about two acres. Its garrison, seldom more than 400 strong, in 22 months lost 52 killed and 267 wounded. But the rifled monsters that had demolished the mighty structure could not crush the humans inside. Brick, yes; backbone, no. The garrison held out until Sherman's march through South Carolina forced them to evacuate.

Elsewhere along the Southern coast, the forts were less fortunate. Rifled guns aboard ship and on land approaches proved the undoing of most of them. General Banks besieged

[3] See *Battles and Leaders*, Vol. IV, Page 66, for Gillmore's own account.

and seized Fort Esperanza, far down in Texas on Matagorda Bay, in the fall of 1863. The masonry forts guarding New Orleans, Jackson and St. Philip, had already fallen after an earth shaking mortar bombardment of nearly 3,000 shells in April, 1862. A combined land-and-sea bombardment reduced Fort Morgan, on Mobile Bay, in 1864. Another terrific shelling paved the way for the fall of Fort Fisher, near Wilmington, North Carolina, in January, 1865.

Over the broad scene of Civil War operations, the rifled cannon reigned supreme by 1865. The United States furnished them to its armies and fleets as fast as it could. The dying Confederacy made what it could and used the best of British production obtained through blockade running. The old smoothbore was on the way out, as obsolete as cap-a-pie armor. And the elaborate system of brick forts built to turn back wooden ships with smoothbore guns became museum pieces for future preservation by the National Park Service.

4

What They Fought With

More than a decade before the conflict began, a French army officer devised a bullet destined to swell the casualty lists of the Civil War by untold thousands. Yet firearms alone cannot claim the bloody credit for loss of life on the battlefield. Throughout the mournful refrain of war there runs the insistent clangor of cold steel. . . .

Except for their uniforms and the dates on the calendar, at the start of the war most of the infantry on both sides might just as well have been fighting in the American Revolution or any one of scores of struggles preceding it. Nearly all carried as their basic weapon smoothbore calibre .69 muskets, closely akin to Revolutionary flintlocks in their limited range and fire power. The standard infantry attack, "going by the book," called for these men to march ahead literally shoulder-to-shoulder and to fire volleys upon command into opposing ranks of men standing equally jammed together. It was impossible to load and fire volleys of musketry lying down dispersed, so both sides reared up as erect as duelists, with no thought of taking cover. The usual maneuver emphasized blanketing the opposing lines of troops with rapid volleys rather than picking them off individually with aimed shots.

The ineffectiveness of the smoothbore musket is well indicated by a report from a previous war. A British gentleman went along with His Majesty's forces in a Revolutionary battle on Long Island for the fun of it. He tells how redcoats and "rebels" blundered into each other in a fog. They stood only 100 yards apart and ripped volleys from which "very few dropped." Then they plodded forward to the lethally close range of 40 yards and volleyed again. This time, "a number on each side fell." A bayonet charge by the British settled the issue.

The significance of this early account lies in the fact that most muskets of 1861 were little, if any, more powerful or more accurate than those described. Most were fired by the more modern percussion method instead of flints, but a number of Virginia, Tennessee and Midwestern regiments bore flintlock muskets at the time of the Battle of Bull Run, or First Manassas, and for some while thereafter.

An improvement in the killing capacity of infantrymen was already on its way, however, when the conflict broke out. Perhaps several hundred thousand of the 600,000 Civil War dead owed their sad fate to the ballistic tinkering of a French Army officer in 1849. Captain Minié, whose own sad fate was to go down in the Civil War lexicon effeminately as "Minnie," devised a conical, hollow-base bullet which expanded to fill the grooves of a rifle. The United States Army adopted it with refinements in its Model 1855 rifled musket, 40-inch barrel, and shorter rifle, 33-inch barrel. For the first time in American military history, the relatively inaccurate smoothbore was supplanted as the standard infantry weapon by a rifle, that is, a shoulder firearm with twist rifling inside its bore or barrel to improve accuracy. This made a vast difference. The few United States rifles used earlier were mostly special models, for scouts, skirmishers and small picked units. Their deep grooving required a round ball patched or imbedded in cloth to fill the grooves and prevent powder gases from escaping. They were even slower and harder to load than muskets. Now the Minié with its hollow base, which expanded to fill the shallow rifled-musket grooves, eliminated the need for patching. Loading became correspondingly faster, although still a slow process.

The Model 1855 weapons were fired by the Maynard cap lock, an invention of Dr. Edward Maynard, a Washington, D.C., dentist who spent far more time on firearms than on teeth. The Maynard device rotated a roll of waterproof paper caps not unlike those used in boys' toy pistols. A fresh cap popped into place automatically each time the weapon was cocked. The waterproofing, however, proved inadequate and the dismally sodden results disgusted the soldiery.

As a result, United States Army Ordnance evolved the Model 1861-63 rifled musket which was to become the principal infantry weapon of the war. This was almost identical to the Model 1855, except that it was fired by a copper fulminate-of-mercury cap which the soldier placed on a cone or nipple at the breech, above the powder chamber, each time he loaded.

This system, being almost impervious to moisture, worked deadly wonders.

The Model 1861 and subsequent Model 1863, like the Model 1855, fired the conical .58-calibre Minié bullet. The weapons were manufactured by the million by the Springfield Arsenal and a score or more of private contractors including Colt, Remington and Savage. The Confederate version was the Richmond Arsenal product, supplemented by the Fayetteville (North Carolina) Arsenal version of the Model 1855 U.S. short rifle with 33-inch barrel.

All of these pieces had one thing in common—an important thing which commanding generals apparently overlooked until halfway through the war. The rear sights contained two movable leaves with the numbers "3" and "5." The "3" gave elevation to 300 yards and the "5" to 500 yards. The pointblank range of the open-notch, unelevated rear sight was 100 yards. With the improved weapons, it was hard to miss a man at pointblank range and not too difficult to pick off one at 300 to 500 yards.[1]

Yet the generals continued to march their troops in solid masses against these formidable rifles, just as they did when the opposing sides could not shoot effectively much beyond 100 yards. The result, at times, was a fantastic slaughter.[2]

The infantryman armed with the Minié musket could get off three to four shots a minute. His rate of fire was little, if

---

[1] The *Weekly Arizonian* published at Tubac, Arizona, March 3, 1859, and republished in souvenir form for the Centennial by the Arizona Pioneers' Historical Society, contains this interesting little Page One filler apropos of the new weapon's accuracy:

"*The Minié Musket*—G. W. Kendall writes to the New Orleans *Picayune* that in one of Lindsay's recent scouts against the Navajos, one of the latter was killed at a distance of 400 yards, and another wounded, with a shot from one of the new Minié muskets now used by the U.S. troops."

Washington, D.C., papers apparently did not copy.

[2] The author, while an active member of the North-South Skirmish Association in 1954–61, fired some 3,000 rounds of Miniés in target competition and practice. This was far more than the average Civil War infantryman ever shot. Although no exceptional marksman by skirmish standards of the "latter-day Civil War," the author could hit a bullseye the size of a half dollar with every fifth shot or so at 50 yards and one the size of a pie plate regularly at 100 yards. Of course, no one was firing at *him* while he was shooting.

any, faster than with the smoothbore musket. But the accuracy of fire was far greater. The loading process continued to duplicate muzzleloader procedure in past wars. The infantryman pulled a cartridge from his box, bit off one end of the paper casing, poured the powder down the musket barrel, rammed the bullet down on top of it with an iron ramrod. Then he returned the ramrod to the slot under his gunstock, took a copper percussion cap from the capbox on the right side of his belt, and capped the nipple or cone with the hammer at half-cock. Pulling the hammer back to fullcock, he was finally ready to shoot, if not himself shot meanwhile.

Contrary to many stories, the soldier loading with Minié bullets avoided ramming the cartridge paper down on top of the powder. It wasted time in an already time-consuming process and any bits of paper left smouldering in the bore would have set off the next powder charge prematurely in his face while loading. The stories presumably were invented by moderns thinking in terms of shotgun wadding, Kentucky rifle patches, or smoothbore loading.

The military feat of biting through cartridge casing of about wrapping-paper thickness apparently left a lasting impression on the soldierly medical mind. The United States services persisted in demanding good dental occlusion, especially of front teeth, well into World War II. At some point in 1943, the services suddenly realized that it was no longer necessary to bite cartridges or hard tack. They lowered their dental requirements in time to defeat the Axis without perfect occlusion.

Until the Minié musket appeared, the old smoothbores were often loaded with "buck and ball," usually three buckshot packaged with a single large round ball. This was rammed home encased in its paper, to prevent spillage in loading. It scattered like a shotgun load. Actually, this was not surprising. The shotgun saw use into World War I trench fighting. During the Civil War, many Confederate cavalrymen carried double-barrelled muzzle-loading shotguns for close-up fighting or for want of better weapons. They preferred the English Enfield rifled muskets and carbines, calibre .577, firing an English version of the deadly Minié, but these were not always available.

In the infantry, among the many things that a good private avoided was leaving his ramrod sticking in the ground. As his muzzle-loading musket could not be loaded without the ram-rod, abandonment of the rod became a court-martial offense in both armies, although seldom rigorously enforced. At the siege of Petersburg, Union infantry, enjoying a surplus of ramrods, fired them arrowlike out of the muzzles of their muskets into Confederate lines.

Both sides carried leather cartridge boxes designed to contain 40 rounds of paper-encased ammunition. Early in the war, Union boxes bore an oval brass U.S. insignia, later replaced with stamped letters U.S. Confederate boxes mostly were unmarked, unless captured and still marked U.S. In rapid-fire fighting, the box could be emptied in less than 15 minutes. Often it was. Infantrymen time and again ran short of ammunition and groped for extra rounds from the boxes of fallen comrades.

Although casualties scythed down 80 per cent or more of some companies and regiments in big battles, many stand-up fire fights must have been of short duration. One seasoned private in the Army of Northern Virginia spoke disdainfully of any unit which had to fire more than ten rounds to settle a battle. To him and his thrifty comrades in gray, that represented inefficiency, a waste of powder and lead.

Each regiment had its ordnance officer and munitions wagons. The cartridges usually were issued in paper-wrapped packets of ten, plus 12 caps. The extra caps were needed to be "popped" on an unloaded barrel before combat to clear the tiny passage between cap nipple and powder chamber, or to replace those lost by fumbling in battle.

Battlefield issuances of ammunition must have been a chancy thing at best. Units usually left the roads and lanes and struck off through swamps, underbrush and hills where no wagons could follow. Ordnance maintained contacts as best it could. Sometimes pack mules were used. More often, ordnance runners lugged up fresh ammunition on their backs. One well-placed enemy bullet would blow a runner into the next world without trace.

One strong symptom of the effectiveness of the new firearms was the gradual disappearance of the bayonet. The British and Hessians virtually terrorized some patriot units with it in the Revolution, and it played a major role in all clashes of foot soldiers until the advent of the Minié. At that point, the cold steel was gradually relegated to the status of a minor military accessory and was used as a spit over a campfire more often than in combat.

Yet the deadly effect of cold steel, especially during the first half of the war, appears to have been greatly underestimated. Vital statistics of the four-year conflict tell us that more than 90 per cent of the fatalities were inflicted by smallarms fire— "small" being certainly a misnomer for an ounce-weight Minié bullet that flattened horribly when it hit. Only 5 per cent of the casualties sprang from artillery fire, so the figures go, and bayonets, sabers, knives and lances killed off less than 3 per cent.

Statistics were made to be doubted, and these deserve to be eyed skeptically. For one thing, they were based primarily upon the number of wounded treated and the cause of their wounds. Nowhere does the report refer to a battlefield study of corpses or a clinical survey of how the stone dead were killed.

One report that is much quoted to prove the passing or inefficiency of the bayonet covers casualties to the Army of the Potomac in the heavy fighting May 21–June 15, 1864. Surgeon Thomas McParlin, medical director of the Army of the Potomac, lists 33,292 bullet wounds, 2,644 shell wounds, 121 "cannon shot" wounds, and only 37 bayonet wounds or about one one-thousandth of the total. But this came in the latter part of the war, when the bayonet definitely had fallen into disuse. Moreover, it could not and did not take into account the undetermined number of soldiers skewered to death on the spot with bayonets. Only those surviving bayonet wounds were counted.

The continued importance of the bayonet early in the war is emphasized by Harold L. Peterson, National Park Service historian and a leading authority on antique arms, in *Notes on Ordnance of the American Civil War* (The American Ordnance Association, Washington, 1959). Even with the new rifled muskets firing Miniés, Peterson points out, infantry fire was not effective beyond 500 yards. "The bayonet remained an important weapon," he says, "and bayonet charges often decided the outcome of battles." Compact ranks or formations were retained both to give sufficient weight for a bayonet charge and to maintain sufficient depth to resist one.

It stands brutally to reason that a soldier attacking with bayonet or knife in a bloody fury did not cease, unless himself wounded or killed, until he had exterminated his opponent. On the cavalry battlefield in the Gettysburg campaign, the bodies of two opposing cavalrymen, blue and gray, were found in a stark deathlock in a pool of blood. They had hacked each other with their sabers until both toppled from the saddle, then fought on tooth-and-nail at each other's throats. Such was the animal intensity of their personal conflict.

Throughout the mournful bloody refrain of the war there runs an insistent clangor of fatal cuts with sabers. Among the cavalry leaders whose use of the saber was most frequent, Nathan Bedford Forrest, George Custer and Wade Hampton all definitely killed foemen with their blades. The devastating results of their swordsmanship are on record. All three, by coincidence, were large men who favored extra-large sabers. Forrest and Hampton stood six feet or above and weighed over 200 pounds. Custer was nearly as tall and weighed a wiry 170. Where the standard cavalry sabers of both sides averaged about 35 inches in blade length, Hampton's much weightier saber, of the Napoleonic cuirassier or heavy cavalry pattern, extended for 38 double-edged inches. Custer carried a similar straight-blade weapon which he is said to have captured from a Confederate officer. Forrest likewise favored a big, razor-edged saber for himself, although he doubted that the saber was ideal for enlisted men.

It fell to Forrest to perform perhaps the most impressive and certainly the most gruesome feat of swordsmanship of any Civil War general. Late in the war, he and a lone orderly were suddenly confronted by six Indiana cavalrymen and summoned to surrender or be shot down. With one mighty backhand slash, Forrest decapitated the Indiana captain. The head went one way, the body another, according to some accounts, and the Federal survivors fled in confusion.

Altogether, Forrest is said to have killed or wounded 30 opponents with his saber or firearms.[3] Wade Hampton, questioned after the war, revealed that he killed nine opponents with his Colt revolvers and cut down two more with his oversized saber. How many he wounded he did not recall at the time, although he sabered at least one Federal officer and pistoled a Michigan trooper in an individual encounter incidental to the Battle of Gettysburg. (See Chapter 7, Duels and Plain Murder.)

---

[3] Forrest died in his bed in 1877, aged 56. His grandson, Brig. Gen. N. B. Forrest, Jr., a 1928 West Point graduate, was shot down while leading an air attack over Germany in 1943 at the age of 38.

George Custer, by his own account, started the war with a brand new officer's model cavalry saber purchased in July, 1861, from Horstmann's, the noted Philadelphia and New York military outfitters. After the Battle of Malvern Hill, a year later, he shot a Confederate cavalry officer out of the saddle and captured his horse with a silver-mounted morocco leather saddle and long saber attached. From the pattern of the hilt and extreme length of blade, the saber appears to have been the European heavy cavalry model favored on the Continent in the first half of the nineteenth century. Its straight, double-edged blade bore the Spanish motto "*No me saques sin razon, no me envaines sin honor.*" This inscription, meaning "Do not draw me without reason, do not sheathe me without honor," is found on many swords of Spanish manufacture going back as far as the American Revolution. Custer took a fancy to this formidable weapon, which, by coincidence, approximated the length and style of Hampton's and those that Hampton presented to Generals Bradley Johnson and M. C. Butler.

At the Battle of Aldie, shortly before he soared from junior rank to brigadier general overnight, Custer on his favorite black charger, Harry, rode ahead of his men and overtook a group of Southern cavalrymen. The rearmost, according to one biography, "heard him coming, turned in his saddle, and fired his revolver at Custer, missing him. A moment later the long Toledo flashed in the air and the enemy fell from his horse, his left arm nearly cut off."

At that a second Confederate wheeled his horse and rode straight at Custer. This man smartly approached Custer's left side, as Custer had done with the man whose arm he almost lopped off. The tactic was deliberate; it was almost impossible for a righthanded swordsman to reach across his mount and cut down a rival on his left. The Confederate, pressing his advantage, began slashing at Custer. All Custer could do with the "long Toledo" was parry.

". . . The two raced away in the midst of a cloud of dust, one cutting away at his foeman, the other parrying the blows but unable to return them. The wild race lasted for several seconds, both horses at full speed, when they found themselves beyond all the fight and in the quiet rear out of the dust.

"Then Custer suddenly checked Harry and his enemy shot past him. Before his antagonist could stop, Custer was almost up to him, and as he wheeled around they met fairly, on the right front. The fight was short. Two or three mighty blows of the long sword and the Confederate cavalier's guard was beaten down and himself knocked off his horse with a cloven skull."

By then Custer estimated he was a mile behind the Confederate lines, alone. He rode back, halted by only one enemy whom he struck across the face with his saber and knocked from his horse. He later wrote his sister that he owed his escape in large part to his broad-brimmed hat "exactly like that worn by the rebels."

Custer continued to swing his long Toledo blade throughout the war. It now reposes in the Custer Battlefield National Monument museum in Montana. In later years, there arose a strictly Yankee legend that Custer was the only man in the Federal cavalry who possessed an arm strong enough to wield the great sword.[4] If so, it is an interesting commentary on the Federal biceps. A number of virtually identical swords were operated successfully by Confederates, and whole regiments and brigades in Europe carried similar ones presumably without being bowed by their weight. Both the French heavy cavalry sabers used by Confederates and the Virginia Manufactory sabers with their extremely curved blades measured 40 inches from point to guard, although the latter were subsequently trimmed to 36 inches to make them handier. There is in the author's collection a French saber with a straight 38-inch blade, bearing both French arsenal and (dimly) Confederate markings. Granted, it took a real man to handle any of them.

Not all cavalry leaders were blindly devoted to the saber. There was considerable controversy on both sides throughout the war over whether saber, pistol or carbine should be the principal reliance of mounted fighters. The issue was settled at least temporarily late in the war by several developments. The advent of the Spencer repeater in 1863 gave the Federal cavalry such a tremendous increase in firepower that it obviously was more deadly than saber and pistol. The static nature of the war at times toward its close led to increased use of

---

[4] The general's worshipful widow, Mrs. Elizabeth B. Custer, is one source of the "mighty swordsman" legend. She relates her version in *Tenting on the Plains*, New York, 1889, Page 85, in a tone of proper admiration. Custer's acquisition and use of the big saber is related by Harold A. Geer in the *Journal of the Company of Military Collectors and Historians*, Vol. XIII, No. 2, Summer, 1961, among other places.

cavalry as mounted riflemen, who rode to the scene of action and then fought dismounted.

J. E. B. Stuart, the Confederate leader, started the war as an "anti-saber" man. In his Orders No. 3, October 15, 1862, to his cavalry brigade, he defined his views: "In all engagements mounted, the main dependence is placed in the pistol, the fire being reserved for close quarters. The saber is held as a *dernier ressort* for the melee when the fire is exhausted. The thrust should be used in preference to the cut—*en quarte pointe* being the most certain."

A year later Stuart modified his stand to place more reliance upon the saber, less on the pistol. He was killed the following year by a pistol shot. (See Chapter 8.)

Maj. Gen. Franz Sigel, a German professional soldier in the Federal ranks, rated the saber high. Its effective use by Kilpatrick's troopers during the Kilpatrick-Dahlgren abortive raid on Richmond in 1864 was hailed by Sigel as clearly demonstrating "the principle which I have always tried to impress on the minds of our cavalry—that in an attack the sword is mightier than the carbine and pistol."[5]

Nearly all such comments, it should be noted, referred to massive cavalry attacks comparable to the charge of the British Light Brigade in the then-recent Crimean War or the hurling of heavy cavalry units at one another in the Napoleonic conflict. Such tactics did not and could not apply to small-scale or irregular combats. Colonel John S. Mosby, the noted Southern guerrilla fighter, for example, preached to his men that the pistol was far more effective in mounted actions than any other weapon. In his kind of warfare, it was.

An extreme of faith and delight in the saber seems to have been shown by another Virginian, Brig. Gen. W. E. ("Grumble") Jones, a West Pointer tragically become a widower and soured on life, who commanded a cavalry brigade in Lee's army. Jones insisted upon saber-sharpening every Saturday as a military routine, and his brigade encampment could be spotted from afar as the place where portable grindstones whirred and sparked of a Saturday. At least one of his battalions, however, did not share his enthusiasm for the "arme blanche." Its historian, F. M. Myers, noted in later years that

[5] Quoted by Virgil Carrington Jones in Footnote 2, Chapter 4 of his *Eight Days Before Richmond*.

his comrades "had a small opinion of the saber as a weapon to fight Yankees with no matter how sharp it might be."[6]

Whether or not Confederates generally put their trust in extra-sharp sabers, there can be little doubt that many whetted their blades almost to the proverbial razor's edge. The author has owned several hundred U.S. and C.S. sabers and officer's swords. With the exception of medieval Japanese blades, which are notoriously sharp, and some Scottish dirks and broadswords, he has never seen keener weapons than those of the Confederates. Some in his collection reveal traces of having been sharpened and resharpened many times—perhaps every Saturday. Federal sabers, by comparison, he found almost uniformly dull.

In at least two instances of record, however, Federal junior officers wielded sabers with instant deadliness.

The outcome of the Battle of Westport, Missouri, in September, 1864, was decided largely by a man-to-man duel between Col. James H. McGhee, CSA, and Capt. Curtis Johnson, USV, of Kansas. Johnson, although badly wounded, succeeded in cutting down the Confederate leader with a fatal slash. At that, the gray ranks broke.

When Col. B. F. Davis, one of the two regular army officers from Mississippi who remained in the U.S. Army, was shot through the head at pointblank range by a Southern cavalryman in an engagement at Beverly Ford, Virginia, the trooper who killed him was "immediately sabered by one of his staff."[7]

The saber could be embarrassing to the wielder as it was deadly to its victim, however. Saber manuals laid much stress on "recovering" the arm. All they meant was to pull it back into position for a second thrust or cut. The annals of the Jeff Davis Legion, of Georgia, include an instance where recovery was impossible. Two of the Georgia troopers, attached to Wade Hampton's cavalry brigade, rode full tilt at opponents in a furious charge at Upperville, Virginia. Both got their men with the point, ramming their sabers lancelike into them. In the next instant, both were toppled from their saddles while their horses continued the charge. Their sabers being fastened

[6] F. M. Myers, *The Comanches, a History of White's Battalion,* Virginia Cavalry, Page 150.

[7] *Personal Recollections of the Civil War,* by John Gibbon, Brig. Gen., U.S.A.

to their wrists by the usual leather knots, both troopers lay sprawled on the ground beside their victims.

While sabers saw more use than usually realized, another formidable-looking cold steel weapon virtually never got into action. This was one of the oldest known weapons, the spear. In Civil War parlance, it was a pike if carried by a foot soldier, a lance if borne by cavalry. In either case, it was uniformly unpopular with both armies.

Early in the war, especially in the spring of 1862, the Confederacy actually prepared to send *entire regiments of spearmen* into battle. If this plan had been carried out to its fullest, the South would have armed perhaps 25,000 soldiers primarily with spears. These would have outnumbered the enormous Zulu tribal phalanxes in Africa and the noted pikemen of Cromwell in the English Civil War two centuries earlier.

The Southern weapons consisted of pikes with knife-like blades eight to twelve inches long at the end of stout staffs measuring seven feet or so. They were made by the thousands. The Confederate Congress and state governments fully endorsed these primitive tools of war. A resolution in the Congress called for twenty regiments of pikemen, and an enactment in April of 1862 specified that every Confederate regiment should include two companies armed with pikes.[8]

Amazingly, the leading Confederate generals approved the move instead of questioning it. Manpower at the time had far exceeded armament output, and the generals' attitude may have been due in part to a realization of the critical shortage of firearms. J. Thomas Scharf, in his *History of the Confederate Navy*, says the South seized 127,000 muskets and rifles in Alabama, Georgia, Louisiana and Texas arsenals and armories. Most of these were the 117,849 condemned old muskets and rifles sent south shortly before the war, with the Northern states retaining 400,000 others. Former President James Buchanan said all were smoothbore pieces, many of them converted from flintlock to percussion, except for 10,000 "old percussion rifles," probably the Model 1817 common rifle and 1841 "Mississippi" rifle.

The Confederate Chief of Ordnance, Brig. Gen. Josiah Gorgas, a Pennsylvanian by birth, estimated that there were only 25,000 "good rifled arms" in the entire South at the start

[8] See *Confederate Arms*, by W. A. Albaugh, III, and Edward N. Simmons, Stackpole Bros., Harrisburg, Pa.

of the war. The Confederacy produced only about 70,000 more. About two-thirds of the shoulder arms for its million or more soldiers came from battlefield captures or from abroad. Confederate ordnance regularly scoured battlefields for weapons. Even so, Brig. Gen. E. Porter Alexander, Confederate artillery commander, lamented that at Gettysburg in 1863 "many of our infantry still carried smoothbore muskets."

The great Stonewall Jackson requested pikes fashioned "so as to make the arm six inches longer than the musket with bayonet"—in other words, to give his men a half-foot advantage in a jabbing contest. General Lee himself gravely indorsed the request to Col. Josiah Gorgas, chief of Confederate ordnance, with the words, "One thousand pikes should be sent to Gen. Jackson if practicable."

Gen. Joseph E. Johnston objected to some of the pikes that were issued, but not to the weapon in principle. "Those furnished us," he reported, were too heavy and too short, ". . . the shafts should be about ten feet long . . ." He thought such weapons would be far more effective against artillery than sabers, especially in the hands of new troops.

The state governments followed suit enthusiastically. Georgia put some 100 manufacturers to work. They produced an estimated 10,000 or more pikes during the first two years of the war, making Georgia pikes even today almost a glut on the collectors' market. Alabama bought a thousand from a local maker to arm the 48th Regiment of Alabama Volunteer Militia. Nearly every Southern state except the Carolinas fell for the military fad to some degree, so desperate was the need for arms. But the high command appears to have failed to grasp that pikes, largely discarded for more than two centuries, were a sure ticket to suicide against the improved firearms of the 1860s.

There were variations of fancy sorts among these lethal-looking weapons. Some boasted two-edged blades that were said to compare with bowie knives; others, including one in the possession of the author, were clover-leaf in shape, with a main blade projecting straight up or out and smaller blades on either side at right angles to form the "clover"; still others had a curved sickle blade set at right angles to the main blade as a "bridle cutter," supposedly to harass enemy cavalry. Perhaps the weirdest of all was attributed to the inventiveness of a Vermont clergyman turned militant Southerner. It consisted of a hollow staff about five feet long housing a two-foot blade backed by a coil spring. On pulling a trigger, the blade shot forward from the upper end of the staff almost like a gigantic switchblade knife. Examples of this weapon exist in collections, but there is no known instance of any foe standing still long enough for it to be used.

One object of the pike was to defend batteries from enemy attack. It is recorded by author William Albaugh, III, that De Gournay's Heavy Artillery, CSA, were armed with pikes during the Seven Days' Battles around Richmond, but apparently never had a chance to test their points on the enemy.

Even more absurd than the pike was another military monstrosity, "the foot artillery sword." This resembled something left over from the Roman legions. It was a regulation weapon for the foot artillery, the cannoneers who served with the infantry, in both European and American armies from about 1800 through the 1860s. U.S. Army Ordnance solemnly approved the manufacture of thousands beginning in the 1830s. Some were used in the Mexican War in 1846-48. The theory behind these unwieldy weapons was simple and seductive to the military mind.

A major tactic of all set battles—and most battles then were as formally arranged as a small boy's sham warfare with toy soldiers—was to charge and capture the enemy's cannons. The foot artillerymen therefore might find cavalry thundering down on them at any moment. Their short, heavy swords were designed for disemboweling horses, de-legging riders, and chopping back at saber wielders. They were supposed to duck under the gun carriages and caissons and emerge somewhat like sharp-pointed human torpedoes at the moment of attack. As their swords were fully a foot shorter than cavalry sabers, they seldom showed enthusiasm for this form of fighting.

Foot artillery swords went rapidly into the discard. From a Federal viewpoint, however, they had served a purpose. The West Pointers of the Confederacy, slavishly copying everything out of the U.S. Army Ordnance specifications, produced foot artillery swords in quantity in 1861-62 and drained the Confederacy's limited industrial resources by that much more. Nor did this somewhat anachronistic brand of civil warfare overlook the lance. The 6th Pennsylvania Cavalry, equipped with 9½-foot lances with fluted, three-edged steel points and decorated with scarlet swallowtail pennants of heavy twill, charged colorfully into the war as "Rush's Lancers." The lances stuck very little in combat, but the regiment was stuck with the name long after it substituted carbines and sabers for its "fishing poles." Some Confederate cavalry, including DeBray's Texas regiment, originally carried lances, reports indicate. These weapons, if used in the right terrain, might have been deadly. Fifteen years earlier, during the Mexican War, Mexican lancers on their native plains frequently proved effective. One lancer killed Captain Walker of the Texas Rangers, collaborator with Col. Samuel Colt in developing the "Walker Colt," first and largest U.S. Army revolver. But the hills, underbrush, forests and swamps typical of most Civil War battlefields afforded no ground for hard-riding charges of lancers. In the author's arms collection is a Confederate lance (not pike) 8½ feet long. It would be difficult to navigate with it on horseback through many parts of the Southern countryside, much less wage war with it.

The bowie knife fever ran high on both sides early in the war. No common soldier felt fully armed unless he had a knife in his belt. Many of the better ones were imported from Sheffield, England. Others were manufactured in bulk by New England cutlers, and in smaller quantities by Southern blacksmiths and ironworkers. Their blades ranged from half a foot to 20 inches in length and took various shapes, all of them supposedly blood-chilling, according to ample testimony. Stephen B. Oates quotes several descriptions in *Civil War History*, March, 1961. On page 18 of Rose's history of Ross's Texas Brigade, Oates records, a trooper in the 3rd Texas Cavalry asserted the big knives were "heavy enough to cleave the skull of a mailed knight helmet and all." Presumably the trooper's imagination was nurtured on *Ivanhoe*. Another authority quoted by Oates terms the wicked-looking weapons fit to make "a Malay's blood run cold." As there were relatively few mailed knights and Malays around for test purposes, the statements may be taken with reservations. Southern fighting knives survive in numbers, including in the author's collection, but none appear potent enough for armor-slicing or deadlier than a Malay's wavy-blade kris. And little actual evidence of their use turns up between book covers. Southern soldiers were supposed to be especially fond of knives, and one Confederate regiment from Kentucky is alleged to have carried only a single round of ammunition, "after firing which, they charged into battle with their Bowie knives." As the regiment does not appear to have made any great impression on the outcome of the war, it probably was quickly decimated by foemen carrying two or more rounds. Or possibly it ran up against John T. Wilder's Indiana-Illinois "Hatchet Brigade," all of whom, at their commander's insistence, carried hatchets.

Far deadlier than ferocious-looking bowie knives, Romanesque short swords and medieval-headed pikes was another weapon not quite in its prime—the revolver. It probably accounted for more casualties than all of the edged weapons put together, although still in the percussion-cap stage. The Civil War was the first conflict in which revolvers were widely used. Their use in it, in fact, probably never has been exceeded since. Most were loaded with combustible paper cartridges containing powder and ball, then capped on nipples behind the cylinder with a smaller version of the percussion caps used on muskets.

In the course of the war, the U.S. Government purchased 373,819 revolvers from more than a dozen American makers. Colt and Remington models composed about two-thirds of the total. All of these were calibre .44 or .36, corresponding closely to the modern .45 and .38. In addition, individuals in the Union forces purchased their own revolvers by the thousands. Perhaps 100,000 to 200,000 were so obtained. These were often pocket or hideaway models in smaller calibres than the .44 Army and .36 Navy issue pieces. Many were Smith & Wesson cartridge weapons in the relatively new .22 and .32 rimfire calibres. One of the latter was carried by Colonel Rutherford B. Hayes, later President of the United States.

Except for the Smith & Wessons and a few other lesser breeds, all the revolvers in the war were "cap and ball," that is, they relied on caps for firing. Reloading was so slow that many, especially Colts, were issued with extra cylinders that could be loaded in advance and quickly substituted for emptied ones. The Remingtons, Starrs (made in Yonkers, N.Y.) and Colts probably were best, in that order. Large-calibre revolvers capable of firing metallic cartridges were not developed widely until after the war.

On both sides, revolvers were used primarily by mounted men. The cavalry carried them extensively. So did both mounted and foot officers. Many of the smaller non-issue ones were carried by foot soldiers as personal protection weapons.

Among the Confederates, resources for handguns were relatively slim. Nearly a dozen Southern manufacturers attempted to produce revolvers, but their total output probably did not exceed 10,000. A number of single-shot cap-and-ball pistols, already obsolete, found their way to the battle fronts. Included were Virginia Manufactory, Palmetto (South Carolina) Armory and Model 1842 U.S. pieces. The South relied largely on three other sources of supply: prewar weapons already on hand; imports of Adams, Tranter and Kerr revolvers from Great Britain through the blockade; and—largely—upon capture from the Federals, a source more productive of most types of small arms than the Confederate armories themselves. Probably the most awesome, distinctive and awkward-looking Southern handgun was the LeMat revolver, patented by a New Orleans surgeon and produced with several variations in England and France. Under its cylinder it had a single smoothbore "shotgun" barrel for added deadliness. General J. E. B. Stuart carried a LeMat, and was blazing away with it when he himself was fatally shot at Yellow Tavern in 1864.

5

Inventions for Better Killing

The four-year struggle brought into combat use a variety of armaments and techniques unrivaled in military history. Machine guns and aerial reconnaissance heralded the dawn of a new age in warfare. And the murderously effective repeating rifles passed their initiation with flying colors, vindicating the judgment of the Union brigade that mortgaged nearly three months' pay to buy them.

While the advent of rifled muskets to replace smoothbores advanced the killing pace of war on both sides, the appearance of the repeating rifle cinched the victory for the North. For only the North had repeaters. The South, with its limited mechanical means, never produced them. The North, however, had them in sufficient quantity to arm entire brigades during 1864-65. More than a tenth of all bluecoats eventually had them. Their efficiency and terrible firepower awed both armies as if man had suddenly, from on high, been handed lightning.

To appreciate the enormous increase in fighting ability bestowed by repeating rifles, it is best to pause and consider the shoulder weapons used by troops in the Civil War. These varied from antique to obsolete to contemporary to modern, in a scope and variety never rivaled before or since. They extended to almost everything:

1. Smoothbore flintlock muskets, muzzleloaders using a technique of sparking flint against steel into a pan of powder to fire a single round ball or a cluster of ball and buckshot vaguely 100 to 150 yards.

2. Smoothbore percussion muskets, muzzleloaders fired by a copper cap instead of flint, but no more effective than the flintlocks.

3. Rifled percussion muskets, muzzleloaders firing a conical

bullet of .54, .58 or .69 calibre (that is, hundredths of an inch in diameter) accurately 300 to 500 yards.

4. Single-shot breechloading carbines and rifles, still relying upon percussion caps, but with powder and bullet encased in paper, tinfoil, even rubber, and inserted in one relatively quick loading motion.

5. Single-shot breechloaders developed past the point of requiring separate percussion caps by the inclusion of a primer or form of cap in the base of the cartridge—thus eliminating an additional loading motion.

6. The repeating rifle or carbine, which could be shot five times as fast as the muzzleloaders because its cartridges fed fully ready to fire from a magazine tube that held seven to twelve at a time.

The highest that the South attained in this impressive parade of firearms progress was Number Five on the list, and then only in such minute numbers that it made virtually no difference on the battlefields. This single-shot weapon was the Morse carbine, manufactured to the extent of a few thousands at Greenville, South Carolina, by a nephew of the great Samuel F. B. Morse, inventor of the telegraph. Its brass breech mechanism accommodated only one metal cartridge at a time. Underneath was a repeating-rifle type of handle, like the levers used to reload two Federal repeaters and the fabulous Winchesters of Wild West and wild TV—but the Morse lever was immovable and served only as a trigger guard or "window dressing."

By contrast, the celebrated Spencer repeater was a murderously real and effective rapid-fire weapon and so was the Henry rifle, a direct ancestor of the Winchester lever-action guns later made by the millions.

Total wartime production of Spencers is put at more than 230,000 by J. O. Buckeridge in his book on the repeaters, *Lincoln's Choice* (The Stackpole Co., Harrisburg, 1956), but this author feels that distinctly fewer than that number saw service. The U.S. Army and Navy together bought 116,667. Many units armed themselves with others by state or private purchase. Yet these purchases hardly seem sufficient to double the number bought by the government. Altogether, approximately 150,000 Spencer and 10,000 Henry repeaters were used by the U. S. forces during the war.

Except for the few they captured, the Confederates had none and nothing comparable to them.

The largest Confederate ordnance factory, at Richmond, was tooling up to produce Spencer cartridges for captured repeaters at the close of the war, so the story goes; for captured Spencers were of no use without the special rimfire cartridges suited to them and a few other Federal firearms.

Remarkably enough for a weapon which was to work wonders for the Army, the Spencer was first appreciated and adopted by the Navy. It took the Army almost two years, and a change in Chiefs of Ordnance, to get around to what the Navy did June 22, 1861. At that time, Navy Ordnance ordered 700 Spencer rifles with a hundred rounds for each. In ordering only limited ammunition, the Navy either did not expect to do much shooting or else underestimated the rate of fire of the weapons. Before the end of the war, it was to buy a total of approximately 10,000 Spencers with hundreds of thousands of rounds of ammunition.

The Army's first adventure with the repeater represented private enterprise by a colonel. John T. Wilder, an Indiana industrialist and business man without military experience, was unburdened by West Point concepts in waging war. He began by ordering all his men to carry hatchets—they might come in handy. He was charmed by the Spencer, obviously the best mechanical improvement around. Christopher Spencer, the little New England Quaker whose mind and fingertips radiated mechanical genius—he was later to standardize screw-thread making and develop many other contributions to peaceful progress—himself demonstrated his weapon in a forlorn-hope sales effort. Sadly Wilder told him what he already knew: that the Army Ordnance Chief would not buy repeaters for his men.

Then Wilder resourcefully put the question to a vote of his command. The privates and noncoms overwhelmingly favored repeaters. He checked with his bank at Greensburg, Indiana. Yes, they would finance the project. Each of Wilder's soldiers gave his personal note to buy a Spencer at about $35 —three months' pay for a private. Wilder personally endorsed 4,000 notes for his brigade. The bank advanced the cash. The brigade received its Spencers in the spring of 1863 and became the first such unit in any army ever armed with repeating rifles.

At Hoover's Gap, Tennessee, in June, the brigade moved miles ahead of the main army to clear the vital pass of Confederates. The Confederates hurried up reinforcements. The brigade of 4,000 found itself engaged with perhaps as many as 15,000 Confederates carrying old-style muzzleloaders. Solid sheets of flame crashed out from the Federal lines as the Spencers spewed lead at an unheard-of rate. The gray ranks recoiled in retreat, leaving three times as many casualties as Wilder's men suffered. One of their generals later said they believed they were outnumbered five to one. Wilder's troops soon became famous as the "Lightning Brigade." The brigade went on to glory, amid piles of dead Confederates, at Chickamauga, Chattanooga and in the battles around Atlanta. Time and again, it and other units which came to be armed with Spencers exacted a toll of five to ten times their own casualties. Men armed with muzzleloaders simply fell like toy soldiers at the sweep of a gigantic hand.[1]

President Lincoln was so much impressed by the repeater that he tested it himself on the Washington Mall near the unfinished Washington Monument with Christopher Spencer, the inventor, in August, 1863. His secretary, John Hay, noted that it was "a wonderful gun" firing seven rounds in less than half a minute, and that "the President made some pretty good shots." Lincoln gave his blessing to the repeater and the Army began to get them in quantity.

This may have been the making of a famous general, one Philip Sheridan. The cavalry force that Sheridan headed in 1864-65 was not only one of the finest the world has ever seen—it was the first to be armed largely with repeating carbines. No other single factor gave the Federal cavalry nearly the advantage over the once-dominant gray horsemen that the Spencer did. Without it, Sheridan's riders could not have triumphed so easily and might scarcely have won at all.

---

[1] The author first fired a Spencer repeater while in his early 'teens through the kindly indulgence of a father who taught him to handle firearms carefully. The contrast between the .52 calibre repeater and the .22 single-shot rifles of boyhood was startling. From his father's wharf, located on the Ashley River at the old West Point rice mill, now the site of the Charleston, South Carolina, yacht basin, the author shot across the river at wharf pilings of another abandoned rice mill which stood at the water's edge in ranks like soldiers. The big, fat Spencer bullets threw up fountains of water, like miniature naval shells, on near misses and sent splinters flying into the air with each hit on the wooden pilings. The range, now forgotten, must have been at least 350 to 400 yards.

The Spencer carbine was simply a short-barrelled saddle version of the original Spencer rifle with its 30-inch barrel. Actions, loading mechanisms and magazine capacities were the same. The shorter carbine, with its 22-inch barrel, simply proved handier and weighed less. Both fired identical .52 calibre cartridges. The Henry, the other lever-action Civil War repeater, took a .44 calibre.

Both the Spencer and the Henry fed their cartridges into the firing chamber from tubes containing coil springs. The Spencer tube ran from the butt forward through the stock. The Henry tube fitted underneath the barrel and fed backward from muzzle to breech. As this barrel distance exceeded the relatively short length of the stock, the Henry could hold more cartridges. However, it was considered a more delicate mechanism. The exposed tubular magazine might get bent, for example, whereas the wooden stock enclosed and protected the Spencers. Such defects were remedied later when Winchester bought out Spencer and combined the best features of both rifles.

The first Federal cavalry to be extensively armed with Spencers was George Armstrong Custer's Michigan Brigade, consisting of the 1st, 5th, 6th and 7th Michigan Cavalry. It drew some 2,200 of the first 10,000 Spencer rifles received by the Army. The brigade soon became a mainstay of Sheridan's force. After serving at Gettysburg, Custer's troopers were under Sheridan from the Wilderness through the Shenandoah devastation campaign to the end of the war. Other repeater-armed regiments were soon added. The Union troopers with repeaters won for Sheridan at Yellow Tavern, Winchester, Cold Harbor, Cedar Creek, Five Forks and elsewhere. In the most spectacular cavalry operations in the Deep South, youthful Gen. James H. Wilson, not yet 30, led a vast all-cavalry array of 13,000 armed mostly with Spencers on wide, ravaging raids that dismantled both Southern armies and factories.

What could a man who had to stand and ram bullets into a muzzleloader do against demon riders who could fire 15 shots to his three? Courage was not enough.

At least 100 machine guns of two or three patterns added their hideous clamor to the deadly noises of the war. All pre-

INVENTIONS FOR BETTER KILLING

A Confederate Williams gun belches smoke during demonstration in 1961. One of the two known surviving pieces, it belongs to Lt. Col. E. H. Hoffman (right), retired ordnance officer, of Woodstock, Va. D. C. Rosen (center) mans crank. Author Halsey at left.

Saturday Evening Post

Close-up showing the loading of Williams gun. Cartridges are dropped into breech. Turn of crank lowers curved breech-block and closes breech.

Saturday Evening Post

Billinghurst-Requa volley gun crashes into action in 1961 demonstration of U.S. Marine Corps Museum relics. Powder train at rear sets off 25 barrels firing musket bullets. The Union used most volley guns, but Confederates had at least one such gun.

Saturday Evening Post

The Union's fabulous Ager or "coffee-mill" (note hopper, center) machine gun. This specimen from U.S. Marine Corps Museum, Quantico, is fired by CWO H. E. Johnson and Col. W. A. Lee, USMC, Ret. (right foreground) in Civil War Marine uniform.

Saturday Evening Post

ceded the famous Gatling gun, which played a relatively
minor part. They introduced a new, super-rapid rate of fire
into a war begun with slowpoke muzzleloaders. Few, even
today, know that they existed at all, but both sides used them.

The new weapons first went into action in the spring of
1862 in Virginia. One was Union, the other Confederate.
There is a controversy in ordnance circles to this day over
which fired first. Circumstantial evidence points to the Federal invention, but verified fact leaves the Confederate con-
trivance indisputably ahead.

In a spirit of friendly compromise, let it be suggested here
that the honors can be divided. The Federal weapon was undoubtedly the first *light* machine gun used in warfare anywhere. The Confederate piece, of much larger calibre,
unquestionably was the first *heavy* machine gun or rapid-fire
gun to see action.[2]

The Confederate gun was invented by a Captain D. R. or
R. S. Williams—the initials are given both ways—of Coving-
ton, Kentucky. It had a single, four-foot-long iron barrel
mounted on a light wheeled carriage. Three men manned
it. One dropped combustible cartridges into the breech from
above. One fed percussion caps to an automatic firing device
on the left side of the chamber, synchronized with the breech
mechanism. The third turned a handle which loaded and
fired the gun. A skilled crew could get off 60 rounds a minute. The weapon fired either a one-pound shell or "bolt," as
it was called, or a load of big buckshot wrapped in combustible paper. With the buckshot it worked lethally at short
range like a gigantic shotgun.

The Williams gun was first tested by its inventor, then
temporarily attached to George Pickett's brigade, at the Battle of Seven Pines or Fair Oaks May 31, 1862. It killed
Federals so fast that they never knew what hit them. The
Confederacy ordered seven batteries, or 42 guns, made at

[2] In general, "light" machine guns fired the same calibre bullet as
infantry rifles while "heavy" machine guns shot a projectile of larger
calibre and were necessarily weightier to handle the larger projectiles.
Thus in World Wars I and II, light machine guns were .30 calibre
and heavy machine guns were .50 calibre and above. In a corresponding sense, the Union or Ager "coffee-mill" guns were .58 calibre, the
same as the majority of Civil War rifled muskets, whereas the Confederate Williams gun was in most cases 1.25 calibre.

Richmond and Lynchburg, Virginia, and Mobile, Alabama. One battery attached to the 4th Kentucky Cavalry ripped apart a detachment of the 7th Ohio Cavalry in an encounter at Blue Springs, Tennessee, in 1863. Others served with deadly effect elsewhere. Why, then, didn't the Confederacy produce more and employ them widely? The answer apparently lies in the South's acute shortage of high-grade steel. When the Williams gun was fired fast for any length of time, one Confederate officer revealed, its inferior metal heated and expanded so rapidly that the gun could no longer function.

Even so, the Williams gun went down in world military history as unquestionably the first machine gun or rapid-fire gun officially adopted by any army. For the U.S. Army Ordnance firmly repulsed all Northern machine gun inventors throughout the war. That some machine guns saw action with the Federal forces was due, first of all, to others who out-maneuvered Army Ordnance. One of these machine gun-minded non-professionals was a veteran of the Black Hawk War named Abraham Lincoln.

Lincoln cracked the bureaucratic barrier by personally authorizing the purchase of ten light machine guns for test purposes late in 1861. Robert V. Bruce, in *Lincoln and the Tools of War*, says this represented the first recorded purchase of machine guns by any government in history. The weapon that Lincoln chose was the Ager or Union "coffee-mill" gun, so called because its .58-calibre steel cartridges with their percussion nipples fed down into the breech from a hopper shaped like an old-style coffee grinder. Like the Williams gun, it had a single barrel and a crank-operated mechanism. Its cartridges were capped singly in advance of loading, instead of automatically while firing. Using a smaller projectile, the Ager could safely be fired about twice as fast as the Williams gun—120 rounds per minute. Author Bruce deduces from a Union captain's little speech in New York City that the Ager coffee-mill was first used by the 28th Pennsylvania Volunteers at Middlebury, Virginia, March 29, 1862. The captain described how a new weapon "cut to pieces" Confederate cavalry there at 800 yards. However, Col. George M. Chinn, USMC (Ret.), who wrote the Navy Department's authoritative book, *The Machine Gun*, doubts that this performance can "be backed up with solid fact" and regards the Williams gun as the first used.

Certainly the Ager gun went into action soon after the

Williams gun, if not before. By June 27, 1862, North Carolina infantry under Brig. Gen. Isaac Trimble, CSA, captured two "revolving cannon with hoppers into which bullets were poured." Trimble reported that these diabolical Yankee contraptions blazed away for two hours before anyone could get near them.

Meanwhile a North Carolina inventor and medical man who had moved first to St. Louis and then to Indianapolis perfected a machine gun which was to make his name a part of gangster vocabulary many years later. "Gat," the term for any handy automatic weapon, was derived from the Gatling gun developed by Dr. Richard Gatling, a middle-aged M.D. who stayed too busy with advanced mechanical devices to practice medicine. Gatling, whose inventions for farming and industry kept abreast of developments of the day, dreamed up his machine gun after brooding over the heavy battle losses. He envisioned it as a labor-saving device that would expose fewer men to enemy fire and hasten the end of the conflict by its awfulness, or so he stated in a letter years after the war.

Gatling's invention was crank-operated like both the Williams and Ager guns; ammunition in the original model was gravity-fed from above through a hopper like the Ager's. But the Gatling boasted a cluster of six .58-calibre revolving barrels. The heat and strain of rapid-fire was thus divided by six, in contrast to the two single-barrelled weapons. The Gatling in a prime performance could fire 250 rounds a minute—twice the rate of the Ager, four times the rate of the Williams.

Unfortunately for Gatling, fire destroyed the Cincinnati factory where his first six guns were being completed. When he finally produced a number of guns at his own expense, the Federal government proved uninterested. There were broad suggestions that Gatling was mistrusted because of his Southern background. Even Lincoln, the unlocker of doors for ordnance inventors, was occupied elsewhere. Gatling plodded dejectedly around to various Army headquarters, demonstrating his ignored gun and writing irritable letters to those in power.

Finally the inventor hit pay dirt. His gun fascinated a nonmilitary general, a Massachusetts Democratic politician named B. F. Butler. General Butler, imaginative to the point of recklessness, always stood ready to try anything that promised victory. After a demonstration of the Gatlings at Baltimore in 1864, he bought 12 at $1,000 apiece with funds from Massachusetts.

The Army got around to accepting the Gatling gun for the entire service in 1866, and the Navy in 1868. Soon the weapons constituted a formidable part of armaments around the world, even in inventive Russia, where the general responsible for its purchase invented a new name for it—the Gorloff, after himself.

Indirectly and passively, the Gatling proved to be the death of one Civil War general as late as 1876. George Custer's command included four lightweight Gatlings of an improved model capable of firing 1,000 rounds a minute. His troopers at the time were armed with single-shot 45/70 carbines, Model 1873, which the Army had backwardly adopted to avoid burning "too much ammunition" in repeaters like the Spencer.[3] When Custer rode confidently out to what is now famous as Custer's Massacre, he further depleted the firepower of his little command by refusing to drag along the Gatling guns —they presumably held back cavalry. So the ideal means for mowing down the thousands of Indian attackers was absent when the yelling braves swarmed across the open prairie to victory. Single-shot carbines could not stop their mass attacks. The outcome wrote both an epitaph and a military lesson.

During the war, American inventive genius rose feverishly to fantastic heights.

One thing that the United States Army seriously attempted to do was to use the Atlantic Ocean as an offensive weapon. A weird experiment to determine whether the Confederacy

[3] The Army's remarkable self-restraint in firing ammunition is historical. Doughty General Winfield Scott, a capable leader akin to General Douglas MacArthur in calibre and career, criticized the substitution of percussion muskets for flintlocks in the Mexican War. The obdurate opposition of regular Army leaders to repeaters led to a reversion to single-shot arms after the Civil War. And even after World War II demonstrated a need for automatic weapons, certain top Army commanders opposed fully automatic rifles as wasteful of ammunition. Part of the blame, of course, may be laid on the taxpayers who short-sightedly object to financing the military establishment in peacetime—a major American failure until the advent of the atomic age.

could be soaked into submission with seawater was conducted in the Delaware River just off the Frankford Arsenal in Philadelphia. Although cloaked in as much hush-hush as latterday atomic research, it could not be conducted quietly because it involved exploding large quantities of gunpowder.

The object was to learn whether heavy underwater blasts, deliberately set off, would create tidal waves of sufficient size to wash out of existence some of the earthwork forts guarding Confederate harbors.

The reasoning behind the experiment was as elementary as a nursery rhyme. Col. Benjamin Chew Tilghman, of Philadelphia, a white officer commanding the 3rd U.S. Colored Troops, evidently harkened back to childhood bliss beside the sea. Every child knows how the waves of a rising tide demolish his sand castles.

What set Colonel Tilghman to thinking along such novel lines was a military tragedy. In attacking Battery Wagner, a sand-bag fort only a few feet from the ocean near Charleston, South Carolina, the Federal attackers were hurled back with a loss of 1,515 casualties out of 5,000 men. One of the worst-mauled regiments was the 54th Massachusetts, a colored unit brigaded with Tilghman's 3rd U.S. Colored regiment.[4] Although Tilghman and his troops were not in that attack, they sustained casualties later in the same seaside campaign. The total Federal loss ran upward of 15 per cent of those engaged. Battery Wagner ultimately was evacuated by the Confederates, but other Charleston defenses held out.

So on May 21, 1864, Colonel Tilghman took pen in hand, put his offensive concept into words, and sent the letter to the Secretary of War in Washington. The Secretary thought well enough of the idea to refer it to Brig. Gen. G. D. Ramsey, Chief of Ordnance. General Ramsey dutifully sent it through channels to Maj. T. T. J. Laidley, the ordnance officer in charge of Frankford Arsenal. Major Laidley talked personally with Colonel Tilghman, then on leave in his native

---

[4] The regiment headed by ingenious Colonel Tilghman consisted mostly of free Negroes from the Philadelphia area and was recruited through the Union League of Philadelphia. It was officered by experienced white officers from elite units and trained at a special camp north of the city. Such regiments, raised in Philadelphia and Boston, rendered effective service. Some others, raised in the Carolinas, of newly liberated slaves and less adequately trained and officered, naturally proved less effective.

Philadelphia, to be sure that he understood correctly what was wanted. No doubt about it, the colonel wanted whopping big waves. The major approached the experiment with scientific precision and military obedience.

During June, July and August, 1864, fishermen, boatmen and small boys hanging around the Frankford section of the Delaware river became uneasily aware of extraordinary goings-on. Laidley's report, now in the National Archives, was headed, "Journal of experiments made at Frankford Arsenal to test the feasibility of destroying an enemy's earthworks on the sea coast by inundation caused by the explosion of large quantities of powder . . ."

The quantity used on June 15 for the first experiment was 50 pounds of mortar powder, in a sheet-iron keg lowered to the bottom in 34 feet of water. G. W. Beardslee's magneto-electric machine, "which did its work with great certainty," was used to spark this and all subsequent blasts.

At the electric flash, the Delaware h-h-r-r-rumped mildly. A dome of water went up about three feet. "The wave at 150 yards distance was very slight, scarcely appreciable," Laidley noted. So the powder charge was doubled for the next try, in 32 feet of water. It raised a spout about three to four feet high, and at 150 yards distance lapped gently 1½ inches above the river's previous level.

Laidley switched to gun cotton, supposedly more powerful. He tried 30 pounds of it in a sealed wooden box in 34 feet of water. "It made a considerable shock to the land," he recorded. "Threw up a dome of water four to five feet high, and a wave at 150 yards from 1½ to 2 inches."

Later that day, the indefatigable experimenters turned to rifle powder. Of a finer granulation than cannon or mortar powder, it therefore burned faster, gave a quicker blast. Laidley ordered 180 pounds of it in a flat tin case sunk at 34 feet. The dome of water this time reached five feet in height—but the all-important wave that hit the shore 150 yards away was a mere two-inch ripple again. It was maddening.

On eleven subsequent occasions, the Union ordnance soldiers paddled out into the Delaware, lowered powder charges as great as 400 pounds of rifle powder, and set them off at depths as little as 5½ feet. To gauge the results accurately, they could fire charges only in calms. The best of them "threw a spray about 200 feet high," and resulted in a wave at 150 to 200 yards "about 4½ to 5 inches."

Solemnly Major Laidley set forth his conclusions in a formal summation for Washington. The last paragraph got to the heart of it:

"It is not believed that the plan proposed by Colonel Tilghman is practicable. A much larger wave would be produced by exploding a much larger quantity of powder on or near the surface of the water, but the difficulties attending such an undertaking in the presence of heavy [enemy] batteries are so great that the prospects of success are not sufficient to warrant the Government in embarking on the enterprise."[5]

That may have been the end of Colonel Tilghman's idea, but it reads very much like the start or inspiration of Maj. Gen. B. F. Butler's. Whether Butler heard of Tilghman's idea or read Laidley's report on it is not known. An original and unorthodox thinker, he was quite capable of dreaming up an idea for himself.

Confronted by the problem of reducing formidable Fort Fisher, a series of seaside batteries guarding Wilmington, North Carolina, Butler devised a variation of Tilghman's rejected scheme. He decided to let the air, instead of the water, carry his blast. On December 23, 1864, he sent a small ship crammed with 215 tons of powder as close as possible to Fort Fisher. The crew then abandoned ship, and the powder charge—almost 54 times as great as the underground one which blasted a huge crater in Confederate defenses at Petersburg—was set off with a shaking roar. When the huge billows of smoke floated off, there was no ship—but there was a fort. Butler gave up his attack plan with only 15 men wounded and one drowned. Fort Fisher fell to another general three weeks later after a terrific naval bombardment. Neither artificially-created sea waves or air blasts were used in it.

Although no heavier-than-air ship or plane actually participated in the Civil War, inventors of the period took off on

---

[5] Colonel Tilghman's inventive bent extended to his civilian career. With his brother Richard, he developed a sand-blast process for shaping objects of hard, brittle material and manufactured chilled shot for use in blasting machinery. He did not experiment further, however, with seashore sand.

flights of imagination which soared a century ahead of their times. They actually designed and patented such things as rocket ships and helicopters. All their plans and abilities were frustrated, however, by the puny propulsion plants, bulky materials and weighty metals of those days.

Aerial reconnaissance made its debut—the word is peculiarly apropos because of the amount of silk diverted from feminine garments to gas bags—in the form of balloons. The most effective of these were captive rather than free, that is, controlled from the ground by a cable and winch rather than cut loose to wander with the winds. Both sides used them. The Federals, with superior means and organization, managed to spot encampments and troop movements as far as 25 miles away. The Confederates, with proper resentment of this military peeking, loosed what must have been the first anti-aircraft fire on record. They shelled balloons at altitudes as high as 300 to 1,000 feet, sometimes hitting the ground crews and mule teams of the "hauling system" when they missed the big bags in the air. And if some of the mechanical dreams of the 1860s could have come true, the war might have introduced air bombings and combats as well as reconnaissance.

On the same day, June 3, 1862, Northern inventive genius flashed far ahead of the whole world with two aerial patents to further the war. One was nothing less than a jet or rocket plane, the other a form of helicopter. Although the patents were filed within a few hours of each other at Washington, D.C., they came from opposite sides of the continent.

Arthur Kinsella, of Cascades, Washington Territory, obtained Patent No. 35,453 for a rocket aircraft with a balloon body propelled by a gas generator and condenser expelling air through pipes hooked to fan wheels "in such a manner that by the action of the fan wheels the air is forcibly driven out at the stern of balloon, and the latter is propelled in the same manner as a rocket."

L. C. Crowell, of West Dennis, Massachusetts, took out Patent No. 35,437 for what, from his description, sounds like one of the most flexible aircraft ever conceived. It was to consist of "two or more flat, sharp-pointed hinged wings capable of being turned to a horizontal or vertical position, and of one or more rotary hinged propellers, the shafts of which can also be brought to a horizontal or vertical position, or to any desired inclination, in combination with a pyramidal winged steering apparatus or rudder, and with a suitable car, in such a manner that from the said car the motion of the whole machine can be controlled by the position given to the propellers, to the wings and to the rudder."

The sad thing about both of these undeniably farsighted mechanical concepts is that neither apparently took off from the drawing boards. Otherwise the Federals might have been endowed with a rip-snorting air force capable of proving as far back as a century ago that war from the air is hell, too.

The South, even more limited than the North in resources, had its experimenters who looked to the skies. At least two of their flying machines allegedly took shape, odd though the shapes may have been. One is reported to have been flown, glider-like, with the aid of a tow rope from a railroad locomotive. The other failed to survive a high wind while grounded.

The machine that flew, according to the word of its inventor, a Professor Blank, resembled a bird in shape and was known as the "Artis Avis" or "Bird of Art." It consisted of hoop-iron and wire-bound white-oak splints or lathes, driven by a one-horsepower engine. In the body of the bird was space for a number of shells, which the operator, by pressing a release spring with his foot, could dump on the enemy from on high.

Having presented this glowing picture of war made easy except for the enemy, the professor invited the Southern soldiers who heard his spiel at Petersburg in 1864 to contribute a dollar apiece to help him crush Grant's armies from the air. Many did. The professor then moved on—along the ground, not in the air.

Many years later, a newspaperman asked John W. Butler, formerly of the 14th South Carolina Volunteers, whether he had ever heard of the Artis Avis. "I certainly have heard of it," he replied, "for I gave a dollar to it."[6]

The other flying machine was under construction in a Richmond lumber yard at Seventh and Main Streets and Thomas R. Evans of that city later recalled seeing its "extensive framework composed of rectangular bars of light white pine." He saw no wheels but added, "doubtless wheels were sufficiently numerous in the inventor's head."

---

[6] The *News & Courier*, Charleston, quoted in the *Southern Historical Society Papers*.

The war objective announced for the pine-framed machine was to fly over Washington and drop incendiary bombs on the White House and Capitol. President Davis and his cabinet were invited along for the aerial ride and spectacle of the rival capital in flames.

Before the machine's completion, however, a high wind struck it and it took off with a rattle of lumber—in pieces.[7]

Confederate forces in the vicinity of Savannah, Georgia, apparently sent up an observation balloon of their own in 1862 after the fall of Fort Pulaski. It involved the highest raising of women's skirts known in that Victorian age, for it consisted of 980 yards of silk donated from the wardrobes of local ladies. Even minus the hoops, the high-flying skirts must have presented a sight. One account terms the colorful balloon "more variegated than Joseph's coat."[8]

The bag was described as 36 feet high, containing 24,427 cubic feet of gas with enough lift to raise 888 pounds. It measured 46 feet from throttle to valve board and 56 feet from the balloonist's car to the valve. The balloon was in charge of a "Captain Cevor the aeronaut." Beyond that, little appears to be known of it.

In the intensive warfare along the Potomac and elsewhere in Virginia, both armies employed observation balloons. They could take no special credit for originality—Napoleon, too, had used balloons—but they introduced some exciting innovations. One was the towed balloon. The Confederacy, using its Southern equivalent of "Yankee ingenuity," constructed one big gas bag from the silk skirts of Richmond belles, sewed together and made airtight by varnish. As the Richmond gas works seemed to be the best place to inflate the balloon, it was blown up there and towed by a railroad locomotive to the battlefront. Disaster struck later when the Southerners hitched their gas bag to a James River steamer. The steamer ran aground, and Federal forces captured both it and the balloon.

The United States Army soon developed and utilized a full-fledged aerial reconnaissance corps. It used both free and moored or captive balloons. The free balloons cut loose from

---

[7] The *Richmond News Leader*, September 22, 1909, quoted in the *Southern Historical Society Papers*.

[8] A description of the Savannah balloon appears in The Charleston Courier, September 18, 1862.

the ground. Their wicker observation cars were heavily sand-bagged. To rise, the operators dropped this ballast. To descend, they let gas escape through a valve under the bag. The trick was to soar at low altitude over the Confederate lines, then dump ballast and rise high enough for the prevalent westerly winds to sweep the balloon home to Yankee-held territory. This system proved too uncertain for the prompt transmission of information, however. Sometimes it took the balloonists hours to extricate themselves from swamps and cornfields and rush imperative intelligence to headquarters.

The type of captive bag controlled by a long cable from the ground then came into favor. John La Mountain, a former seafarer and adventurer from Troy, New York, pioneered for the Federal army at this time. A ground crew of New Jersey infantry manned the ropes, winches and boilers that inflated his balloons. La Mountain operated as high as 1,400 feet, but he suffered hydrogen burns while experimenting with gas-making to go higher. Worse still, a controversy arose over the accuracy of his reports. His detractors claimed that he inflated not only his bags but his accounts of enemy troops. So his service ended early in 1862.

With La Mountain gone, his principal rival took over and organized balloon observation for the Army of the Potomac literally to a new high point. This was the famous Professor Thaddeus Sobieski Constantine Lowe, an inventive New Hampshire man then not yet 30. Lowe had begun by sending the family cat aloft in boyhood balloon experiments. He made his first personal ascension in 1854 at the age of 22 in celebrating the laying of the transatlantic cable. The connection was peculiarly appropriate; Lowe, through his telegraphic interest, coupled ballooning and telegraphy for military purposes. Running a telegraph line up with his balloon cable, he rose 500 feet above Washington, D.C., and pleased President Lincoln by dictating the first telegram ever sent from the air. It thanked Lincoln for encouraging the aerial demonstration.

Lowe, with Lincoln's backing, developed bigger and better balloons. These ranged in gas-bag capacity from 15,000 cubic feet up to a mammoth 32,000 cubic feet. The largest could carry a crew of five men. In one of these, Lowe is credited with making the first aerial observations to direct the fire of artillery on the ground. When General McDowell's gunners bombarded the Confederates at Falls Church, Va., Lowe hovered overhead correcting the range.

Lowe managed most of his observations at altitudes of 1,000 to 2,000 feet, but once soared as high as 5,000 feet. His telegraphic reports proved especially helpful to Federal commanders at Seven Pines, or Fair Oaks, and at Gaines' Mill. He could spy a large encampment as far as 25 miles away by the campfire smoke, and smaller ones five miles away by the tents.[9]

The generals soon became enchanted at this new viewpoint on war. Fitz John Porter, in particular, made many ascensions with Lowe. Less aerial-minded generals clustered around the balloon's ground control crews. This, however, had its dangerous side.

All of Lowe's balloons bore not only names but vivid insignia such as American eagles and flags, and portraits of great men such as Washington whose names they carried. They made particularly attractive targets for Confederates. The Southern batteries often shelled the bags. Although none were shot down, the shells that came close usually slammed to earth nearby. They are said at various times to have endangered kibitzing Generals George B. McClellan, S. P. Heintzelman and George Stoneman.

Eventually Lowe commanded a corps of seven captive bags and a Navy-manned river boat which was the nation's first aircraft tender. The balloons were towed for miles to strategic observation areas either by the boat or by ground crews with teams.

Lowe worked himself to exhaustion and fell ill, but recovered and survived the war. He held the courtesy rank of colonel while on duty, and drew $10 a day in pay. But his actual designation on the Army rolls gave a vivid clue of the nature of wars to come. It was—Chief Aeronaut.

[9] The most comprehensive account of Civil War aerial operations can be found in F. Stansbury Haydon's Aeronautics in the Union and Confederate Armies (Baltimore, the Johns Hopkins Press, 1941), which won the Mrs. Simon Baruch University Prize awarded by the United Daughters of the Confederacy.

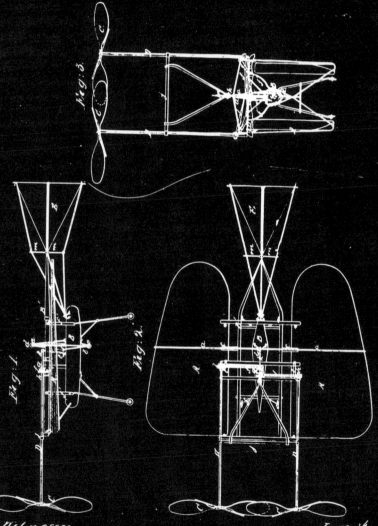

Fig. 3.

Fig. 1.

Fig. 2.

Witnesses:

Inventor

L. C. Crowell

por Munn & Co.

Att'ys

Battle of Pea Ridge, Arkansas (March 8, 1862), from an old Currier and Ives print, showing Indians at left rear with upraised tomahawks.

The Harry T. Peters Collection, Museum of the City of New York

6

The Indians in Blue and Gray

> More than 10,000 Indians—some say as
> many as 15,000—fought as regularly-en-
> listed soldiers on one side or the other.
> Two rose to the rank of brigadier general.
> Their exploits formed a weird background
> to the war west of the Mississippi. Al-
> ways there was that haunting terror of
> frontier fighting: Were the Indians tak-
> ing scalps?

Secretary of War Edwin M. Stanton was emphatic to the
point of rudeness. The Union would win the Civil War with
white troops, he asserted. It needed no help from Indians.

The towering, swarthy man standing before Stanton scarcely
changed expression at the words. Donehogawa, sachem of
the Senecas, had been rebuffed before simply for being an
Indian. After studying law successfully while representing his
tribe in Washington, D.C., for twenty years, he was denied
admission to the bar because he was not a United States
citizen.

Next, he learned civil engineering at Rensselaer Poly-
technic Institute well enough to be appointed superintendent
of a Government project at Galena, Illinois. There, incidentally, he befriended a former Army officer who was so down
on his luck that he worked as a humble clerk.

In 1862 the sachem returned to the tribal reservation in
Genesee County, New York. In accordance with tribal custom,
he obtained his father's permission to go to war. Then he
applied to the governor of New York for a state-militia commission appropriate to his standing. The governor, perhaps
mindful that there were still some voters whose parents had
been tomahawked in past wars, flatly declined to send the
redskin on the warpath even to save the Union. In Washington, Secretary Stanton said the same thing—more impolitely
if possible.

Not until the summer of 1863 did the Seneca chieftain, whose "white" name was Ely Samuel Parker, manage to wangle a commission as a captain of engineers. Quite likely the clerk whom he had befriended at Galena helped him. For by now the former clerk spoke with authority and influence. His name was Ulysses S. Grant, now a major general and the conqueror of Vicksburg. Ely Parker soon joined Grant's staff.

Within a year Parker was a lieutenant colonel and military secretary to General Grant. He rode beside Grant through the death and desolation of the Virginia campaigns, a tall figure on a rangy black horse, known among the troops as "the Indian." At Spottsylvania he is credited with saving Grant from death or capture. The absent-minded general rode straight toward the rebel lines. Parker halted him and guided him back to safety.

Fate reserved a modest place in history for the hawk-faced Indian. At Appomattox, the senior adjutant, Col. T. S. Bowers, felt so overcome by emotion that his hand shook. He could not write. So Parker took the penciled draft of the surrender terms, as set down by Grant, and "transcribed in a fair hand the official copies of the document that ended the Civil War."

Several published accounts of the surrender suggested that Lee, when introduced to Grant's staff, momentarily mistook Parker for a Negro. This Parker denied. In his own words: "After Lee had stared at me for a moment, he extended his hand and said, 'I am glad to see one real American here.' I shook his hand and said, 'We are all Americans.'"

Grant subsequently promoted the big Indian to brigadier general, his commission to date from Appomattox. While President, Grant gave him the postwar distinction of being the first tribesman appointed United States Indian Commissioner. But prejudice persisted.

As late as 1869, Philip Sheridan, then a lieutenant general in the permanent U.S. Army establishment chasing Cheyennes and Arapahoes in the West, was quoted as saying:

"The only good Indian is a dead Indian."

What Brig. Gen. Ely Parker, USA, of the Seneca tribe, thought of this tactful statement is not a matter of record.

Parker was not, in any case, the senior Indian general in the

Civil War. That distinction belongs to a square-jawed fighter, Brig. Gen. Stand Watie, CSA, who held out against surrender longer than any other Confederate general.

As for Stanton's attitude that the Union would win with white troops alone, by 1865 one bluecoat in every ten was a Negro, and the Union ranks were augmented by thousands of Indians.

Unknown to Stanton, nearly an entire company of Tuscarora Indian volunteers served early in the war in the 53rd New York Infantry, otherwise D'Epineuil's Zouaves. Never were redskins better camouflaged. The Zouaves wore gaudy French North African uniforms. Like the rest, the Tuscaroras sported tasseled red fezzes and billowing Oriental trousers. Parker's own tribe, the Seneca, subsequently raised a company of braves who served in a New York regiment. A band of Delawares scouted for Federal armies in the Mississippi Valley area. Some of the Cherokees left in the Carolinas meanwhile served as Confederate scouts in the Southeast.

At least one Indian unit served the Union as sharpshooters in the second battle of Fredericksburg, losing four men fatally wounded who died in "mute agony." A photograph of some of the wounded survivors, one unmistakably a full-blooded Indian, appears in Miller's *Photographic History of the Civil War*, Vol. VII, Page 254. I have not been able to identify the Indian's unit, but it may have been the Seneca company from New York State, as many New York troops were engaged.

All together, more than 10,000 Indians—some put the figure as high as 15,000—participated directly in the Civil War on one side or the other. Most served west of the Mississippi. The Confederacy regularly enlisted at least 5,500 redskin cavalrymen. Some 4,000 Indians are known to have served in the Union infantry. As the figures indicate, the war split the tribes as well as the states. Many were torn by doubts and questions of allegiance.

In the armies, Confederate Indians outnumbered Union Indians at the outset for several potent reasons. The Confederacy promised in writing that, if it won, it would create an all-Indian state or nation in the heart of America, approximately where Oklahoma now stands.

Many Indians in this area, especially the so-called Five Civilized Nations of Cherokees, Choctaws, Creeks, Chickasaws and Seminoles, were originally Southern and owned

Negro slaves. They were deported West years earlier with their belongings, including slaves, under escort of the very same Federal Army arrayed against the Confederacy.

The final and perhaps strongest factor in the redskins' Confederate leaning was a leader—stalwart, full-bearded Albert Pike, a remarkably odd-fish Bostonian turned Arkansan, by background a scholar, teacher, editor, lawyer, orator, soldier, poet and Masonic official.

Pike, bred in the New England hotbed of abolition, negotiated nine treaties with the Indians on behalf of the Confederacy. As one Creek chief related, Pike "tell them ain't no more U.S.—ain't any more treaty—all be dead. Creeks better make new treaty with South and Southern President protect them and pay them more annuity than U.S."

After pausing to write the "fighting words" to *Dixie*, which began as a mellow minstrel tune, Pike became a Confederate brigadier general commanding the Department of Indian Territory, all the redskin lands west of Arkansas and north of Texas. A veteran of the Mexican War, he formed the redskins into regiments and battalions along tribal lines.

Col. D. N. McIntosh and his brother, Lt. Col. C. McIntosh, who were partly Scottish—via a trader ancestor—and partly Creek, headed the First and Second Creek regiments of Mounted Volunteers. The 1st Regiment Cherokee Mounted Rifles, nearly all full-bloods, came under Col. John Drew. Stand Watie, who was a three-quarter Cherokee, commanded the 2nd Regiment of Cherokees, mostly half-breeds. A Seminole battalion formed up under their chief, Hemha Micco, otherwise Lt. Col. John Jumper. The 1st Regiment Choctaw and Chickasaw Mounted Rifles served under Col. Douglas H. Cooper. Except for Pike and Cooper, a former Mississippi planter who had become a Government agent for the Choctaws in 1853, the officers were Indian or part Indian.

Pike promptly made one policy clear to all: "The commissioned colonels of Indian regiments rank precisely as if they commanded regiments of white men, and will be respected and obeyed accordingly."

The regiments were organized to the point of rendering regular fitness reports on their military condition, which often was deplorable by West Point standards.

Like most expert leaders of Indians, Pike let his braves fight in their own way. Nearly all rode wiry plains ponies which they sometimes tethered to the rear while engaged. In at least one battle Pike permitted the Indians to climb trees and fire from that vantage point. Many used shotguns, a favorite weapon of Confederate cavalry generally. Colonel Drew's full-blooded Cherokees, by special authorization, attacked in true Indian style with bows and arrows, tomahawks and scalping knives.

The unconventional weapons of the braves soon led to atrocity stories. Although many Yanks and rebels had armed themselves with enormous fighting knives, and an entire Indiana brigade of white men toted hatchets, the reappearance of the dread tomahawk and scalping blade chilled paleface blood. In vain Pike and his aides pointed out that they were no more barbaric than many other weapons.

The Confederate redskins, originally recruited solely for service in their own territory, first faced enemy fire in a big battle when they followed Pike afield into Arkansas. There nearly 3,500 fought as a brigade in the crucial engagement at Pea Ridge, near the Missouri-Oklahoma line. They formed more than a fifth of the Confederate force in that battle. Cherokees, reinforced by a few Texans, captured a Federal battery despite all Indians' holy horror of artillery in general, but soon let go their prize. When the Confederates, after winning the first day, lost on the second, Stand Watie's mounted men covered the retreat.

Hardly had the war whoops subsided when the Federals, who had no Indians of their own in that battle, accused the rebel redskins of tomahawking and scalping at least thirty Union soldiers. Whatever basis the reports had, they were magnified as they traveled East. The New York *Tribune* of March 27, 1862, referred to the Indian brigade as "the aboriginal corps of tomahawkers and scalpers" and surmised that General Pike in leading them "got himself up in good style, war paint, nose ring and all."

To all indications, the charges were grossly exaggerated and totally unfair to Pike. Indeed, they may stand as a prime example of wartime propaganda. Pike later made a sworn statement that as soon as he heard a rumor of scalping in the Leetown area, where his Indians had charged the Federal ranks, he sent for his surgeon, Dr. Edward L. Massie, of Little Rock. Massie confirmed that he had "been over the whole ground" soon after the charge and found "one body which had been scalped; that it had evidently been done after life was extinct, probably late in the afternoon."[1]

Pike, describing himself as "angry and disgusted", then issued a special order against scalping with instructions that it be "read and interpreted" to every Indian regiment, battalion, and company. Pike stated in the order that he had "learned with the utmost pain and regret that one, at least, of the enemy's dead was scalped upon the field. That practice excites horror, leads to retaliation, and would expose the Confederate States to the just reprehension of all civilized nations.

"If the Indian allies of the Northern States continue (sic) it," the order went on, "let retaliation in kind be used as to them alone, and those who with them may invade the Indian territory and sanction it. Against forces that do not practice it, it is preemptorily forbidden during the present war."

To make certain that his position was clear, Pike sent a copy of his order under a flag of truce to Maj. Gen. Samuel Ryan Curtis, USV, of New York, then commanding the Federal forces. Curtis replied[2] that Pike's action was "fully appreciated" but objected that "the imputation in your order . . . of the use of savage allies on the part of the United States is entirely gratuitous and looks too much like an apology

---

[1] From a sworn deposition made by Pike at Ottawa, Canada, August 4, 1865, in seeking amnesty. The account of Pike's conversation with Dr. Massie comes from the Memphis *Daily Appeal*, April 4, 1867. Both pieces of information were obtained by the author through the courtesy of Ray Baker Harris, biographer of Pike and librarian of the Supreme Council, Thirty-Third Degree, Ancient and Accepted Scottish Rite of Freemasonry, Southern Jurisdiction, U.S.A. Mr. Harris also takes the position that Pike was not really a general in the military sense at all, but received that rank as Indian Commissioner for the Confederacy in order to enable him to maintain his position and negotiations in time of war. This contrasts interestingly with a recent biography of Pike (*Reluctant General*, by Robert L. Duncan, Dutton) which criticizes his generalship, and with a rather vehement review of this biography in *The Civil War Times*, November, 1961, comparing Pike to a "combination Dan Sickles and Jubilation T. Cornpone" and terming him "a rotten general." In any case, Pea Ridge was Pike's only major battle.

[2] *The Official Records of the War of the Rebellion*, Series I, Vol. III, Page 410.

or excuse for what your letter and conscience so strictly condemn. . . ."

The Southern Indians, incensed, repudiated the scalping charges fluently. They asserted that any use of tomahawks and knives was in the heat of battle, legitimately. The Cherokee National Council even passed a formal resolution which would have done credit to a United Nations committee:

"*Resolved*, that in the opinion of the National Council, the war now existing between the said United States, and the Confederate States and their Indian allies, should be conducted on the most humane principles which govern the usages of war among civilized nations, and that it be and is earnestly recommended to the troops of this nation in the service of the Confederate States to avoid any acts toward captured or fallen foes that would be incompatible with such usages."

The resolution may have been well directed, as Drew's full-blooded Cherokees appear to have been the likeliest offenders. The blame, however, never was fixed. The Confederates, in a jab at Franz Sigel's Union command of Germans, countercharged that atrocities had been committed by persons "alleged to be Germans."

The controversy and confusion over scalping was typical of Indian participation in the war. From the start it was a welter of tribal intrigue, military red tape, jealousies and repetitions of the sad story of both white men and redskins breaking promises. Neither the Richmond nor the Washington governments made good fully on their wartime pledges to the tribes. Some braves, on the other hand, switched sides repeatedly and galloped off to whichever army offered the most guns, glory and cash on the line.

Late in 1861 Colonel Cooper's Choctaws and Chickasaws, with the Confederate Creeks and Cherokees and some Texans, attacked a large but unorganized band of pro-Union Creeks. Cooper claimed to have killed or wounded 500 Unionists in a desperate battle. The Union sympathizers then fled up the Verdigris River into Kansas, where many starved or froze to death for lack of Government aid.

Despite much hesitation and some opposition from Secretary of War Stanton, the Union in 1862 raised three regiments of Indians for infantry duty. Many were Cherokees and Creeks.

The Osages volunteered to serve if given flour and whisky. The 1st, 2nd and 3rd Indian regiments, all originally designated as home guards, were brigaded with Kansas cavalry and artillery. Soon they were sent south to recapture from the rebels what is now the upper part of Oklahoma. A description of the redskin soldiers, in the misspelled words of a white Indian agent, survives:

> "The Indians with their new uniforms and small Military caps on their Hugh Heads of Hair made rather a Comecal Ludecrous apperance. They marched off in Columns of 4 a breast singing the war song, all joining in the chorus and a more animated seen is not often witnessed. . . . The improvement the Indians have made in drilling is much greater than I supposed tham capabell of and I think the opinion and confidence of all in the eficiency of the Indian Regements is very much greatar that it was. . . ."

Going to war in their own tradition, the Union Indians invoked "medicine" or magic to ward off enemy bullets. One of their leaders also made a highly practical request for "wagons that shoot," meaning field artillery. They got none, however, and their muskets at the start were of poor quality.

Regularly recruited Union and Confederate Indians first clashed in some numbers at Locust Grove, near present-day Tulsa, Oklahoma. Both sides fought in conjunction with white troops. The Union won. The 1st Indian Regiment, mostly Creeks, surprised the Confederate camp and took 100 prisoners, including a colonel from Missouri. To be on the winning side, many Cherokee enlisted men went over from the Confederacy to the Union. With the next Southern victory they switched back.

During a Confederate effort to recapture the Granby lead mines in southwestern Missouri, an important source of material for bullets, white-led forces of Indians battled near Newtonia. Colonel Cooper's graycoat Choctaws and Chickasaws forced Federal Cherokees under Col. W. A. Phillips to break and run. The loss included many Indian ponies shot down. As at Pea Ridge, scalps were taken. With Federal Indians engaged, the Union made less fuss about atrocities.[3]

---

[3] After Quantrill's guerrillas raided Lawrence, Kansas, in 1863, a number of Indians on the Federal side pursued them. Chief Charles

In two subsequent engagements the Union forces inflicted defeats. A mixed army of whites and Indians caught the Confederate Indians, greatly outnumbered, on the open prairie in the vicinity of Old Fort Wayne, near Maysville. Again Stand Watie and his Cherokee half-breed cavalry covered the retreat. At Honey Springs, near Muskogee, the 1st and 2nd Indian regiments, plus white Union troops, went against the Confederate Indian brigade. Much of the rebel redskins' ammunition proved defective, and they fled.

The general confusion among Confederate Indians was aggravated meanwhile by two breaches—in the Southern chain of command and in the Cherokee Nation.

Picturesque General Pike, his hair flowing to his shoulders and his eloquence pouring forth like passages from the Old Testament, claimed that supplies for his Indians were diverted to white troops in Arkansas. He blasted at Maj. Gen. T. C. Hindman and Lt. Gen. Theophilus Holmes, the Southern commanders in that area. Their subordinates, he asserted, seized 6,500 uniforms, 300 tents and large amounts of munitions and payroll cash, while he personally had to pay $2,000 for 400 pairs of shoes for barefoot Indians.

"While you were . . . robbing the half-naked Indians to clothe other troops," he continued, "the Federals were sending home the Choctaws whom they had taken prisoners, after clothing them comfortably and putting money in their pockets. No one need be astonished when all the Indians shall have turned their arms against us."

Pike resigned his Confederate commission in disgust. His superiors placed him under arrest. Later they released him and accepted his resignation. Another blow befell the Southern cause later on when John Ross, principal chief of the Cherokees, virtually let himself be captured by Union forces with the tribal treasury and documents. Ross, who never had favored secession, was soon reported in Washington dickering to return all his tribesmen to the Union fold.

The secessionist Cherokees called a convention, ousted Ross and elected the doughty Stand Watie as principal chief. The

---

Blue-Jacket a Shawnee, and Chief White Turkey, a Delaware, are said to have led the pursuit with 15 to 20 Delaware braves mounted on wiry ponies. In a footnote to *Quantrill and the Border Wars* (Pageant Book Co., N.Y., 1956), author W. E. Connelley says they no doubt scalped every dead guerrilla they found.

Confederacy made Watie a brigadier general to cinch his status. A miniature civil war broke out within the Cherokee Nation. Many full-bloods switched to the Union side. Watie's half-breeds stood firm for the Confederacy. Each slaughtered the other as opportunity presented.

In the fall of 1864, Watie with some 1,800 of his Indian troopers waged a six-hour battle along Big Cabin Creek to capture an enormous Union wagon train bound for Fort Gibson, Oklahoma. In the end, the gray-clad Indians overwhelmed the 600 Union soldiers guarding the train and seized nearly 300 wagons and 1,300 horses and mules. Watie carried away 129 loaded wagons under the noses of a strong Union rescue party and left the rest in flames. His feat struck a serious blow at the Union in that area and recouped the Confederate war chest.

With the collapse of Confederate strength west of the Mississippi and gradual domination of the region by the Union, Indian warfare degenerated into a series of raids. It was as irregular cavalry that the rebel redskins excelled. Watie and his horsemen specialized in harassing Federal supply trains. In one surprise attack he captured a United States supply ship on the Arkansas River and rode off with ample provisions and other supplies.

Fighting on like die-hards, Watie and Col. Peter B. Pitchlynn, chief of the Choctaws, did not surrender with their men until June 23, 1865, after all other Confederate Army commands had yielded.

The Union Indians rendered equally dogged and determined service, to judge by a terse footnote in an adjutant general's report after the war.

Total Indians in U. S. forces 3,530
Aggregate of deaths, ditto 1,018

In suffering a loss as heavy as one third, the Indians proved themselves something more than "comecal and ludecrous."

THE INDIANS IN BLUE AND GRAY

General Albert Pike recruited Indians for the South and let them fight with arrows and tomahawks.

Brown Brothers

General Grant (left) chose as his staff military secretary Donehogwa (right), a Seneca chief, better known as General Ely S. Parker.

Buffalo and Erie County Historical Society

Colonel Alfred Rhett

Charleston Library Society

Lt.-Gen. Wade Hampton

Library of Congress

7

Duels and Plain Murder

> At least three generals were killed behind
> their own lines in cold blood by fellow
> officers whom they allegedly offended.
> Jackson, Forrest, Sherman and others
> narrowly escaped similar fates. In the
> Southern ranks, especially, dueling took
> a grim toll. What triggered this private
> slaughter?

An obscure aspect of selective killing in the bloody years
1861-65 provides today a psychological clue to the mood that
triggered the Civil War. Now, a century later, it is possible
to subject the conflict to a sort of psychoanalysis. This one
factor immediately rises to the surface. It may explain why
the many efforts to ward off the awful struggle failed.

In a way, the Civil War was sparked by dueling. Time and
again, both before and during the conflict, this becomes
evident. Perhaps more than anything else, it reveals the hair-
trigger temperament of a time in which influential leaders too
often preferred curses to compromise and armed action to
arbitration.

Prewar duelists who figured prominently in the Civil War
included Generals Winfield Scott, Don Carlos Buell and
Philip Kearney, of the Union Army, and President Jefferson
Davis and General Albert Sidney Johnston of the Confederacy.

During the war, personal honor and private anger ran so
high that at least three generals and a number of colonels and
majors were fatally shot by officers on their own side. Some
fell in formal duels; others in quick-tempered circumstances
which had aspects of plain murder.

Through the early years of the republic, dueling represented
more than a politely murderous practice among honor-proud
American gentlemen. It became a quick, deadly means of
resolving all manner of differences. The habit left its impress
upon the thinking of many leaders, especially in the South and

West. The way they thought, in effect, was: "When words fail, shoot it out." Some key secessionists always stood ready to settle political issues with pistols.

The relationship between dueling and the "war mentality" stands out particularly in one grim encounter. Although it occurred in 1839 and had no direct bearing on the war, both the duelists, Louis T. Wigfall and Preston S. Brooks, later played significant roles in bringing on the conflict.

Meeting by arrangement on a sandbar in the Savannah River, the two fiery young South Carolina politicians seriously wounded each other with their second shots in a formal combat over local politics.

Wigfall, moving to Texas, subsequently became a United States senator and such an impatient secessionist that he could not await the surrender of Fort Sumter by its Union garrison in 1861. Being present as a Confederate staff colonel, he took it upon himself to dash out in a small boat during a lull in the firing and demand that the fort yield.

Brooks, the other duelist, while a Congressman from South Carolina before the war, caused a national controversy by cudgeling Charles Sumner, the vituperatively anti-Southern senator from Massachusetts. Brooks felt that Sumner, in a Senate speech, had insulted his kinsman, Senator Butler of South Carolina. As Sumner would not duel, Brooks beat him over the head. The North was outraged.

Dueling became so prevalent during the prewar decades that both future wartime Presidents, Abraham Lincoln and Jefferson Davis, nearly fell victim to the tragic custom in the 1840s. Both were confronted by would-be duelers.

James Shields, a brilliant, peppery Irishman, destined to become a Union general, challenged Lincoln while the two men were lawyers in Illinois. Shields objected to an anonymous letter published in a local newspaper and supposedly written by Mary Todd, later Mrs. Lincoln. Lawyer Lincoln skillfully mollified Shields and bowed out of fighting him.

Jefferson Davis, as colonel of the famous 1st Mississippi Rifles in the Mexican War in 1846 was continually badgered by his rebellious second-in-command, Lt. Col. A. K. McClung. McClung, an unerring shot with a rifle, tried to provoke Davis into challenging him. Under the dueling code, that would have given McClung the choice of weapons, presumably rifles rather than pistols. The duel never took place.

Mexican soldiers seriously wounded both Davis and McClung. That cooled McClung's urge for bloodshed.

The dueling psychology springs into the picture from the very start of the Civil War, and reappears throughout it. It may even have influenced Lincoln, subconsciously or otherwise, in his handling of the Fort Sumter crisis. One frequent move on the part of would-be duelers was to force the other party into the status of an aggressor. Lincoln did exactly that in insisting upon supplying and reinforcing Fort Sumter. To prevent Sumter from being succored and held indefinitely, the South opened fire. Here was the overt act or challenge of the code duello. The North, duly provoked, moved immediately to engage in the huge combat between the sections.

The temper of the times is suggested by two duels which took place in 1861 and involved newspaper editors. The issue in each case arose from friction over North versus South. On Friday, February 8, 1861, Edwin Hart, editor of the Tallahassee (Florida) *Sentinel*, engaged an irate reader named Coleman on the Georgia-Florida state line near Duncansville. The Thomasville (Georgia) *Enterprise* reported the outcome on the 13th: ". . . Both parties were killed. We regret that those gentlemen did not reserve their bravery for the defence of the State instead of throwing away their lives in an affair so trivial."

The second duel was fought in the summer of 1861 at Tubac, Arizona, with the principals using Burnside breech-loading rifles instead of the customary pistols. Edward E. Cross, a New Englander who edited *The Weekly Arizonian*, first newspaper in the state, objected to pro-Southern articles prepared by Sylvester Mowry, a prosperous Tucson mine operator. They quarreled, Mowry challenged, Cross accepted and demanded that they use rifles. At the range chosen, neither man was wounded. Cross was later killed at Gettysburg by a Southern bullet while commanding a New Hampshire regiment. Mowry bought his newspaper, became a territorial delegate to the Confederate Congress at Richmond, and later was imprisoned for six months in Fort Yuma by the Federals for his Southern stand. The imprisonment broke his health and fortune.

Shortly before the war began, two prominent South Carolina politicians dueled over an allegation that one of them, Olin M. Dantzler, of St. Matthews, had aspersed a brother of the other duelist, Lawrence M. Keitt. To avoid possible arrest, the principals and seconds crossed the state boundary into North Carolina. There they shot it out. Keitt's bullet plowed through Dantzler's hat. Dantzler hit Keitt in the shoulder, inflicting a flesh wound. The two men then agreed that honor was satisfied, and became fast friends. To them, the Civil War proved more lethal than dueling. By 1862, Keitt was colonel and Dantzler lieutenant colonel of the 20th South Carolina Volunteers, 1,500 strong. They served together for nearly two years. Then Keitt was killed at Cold Harbor June 1, 1864, and Dantzler was fatally shot the next day near Petersburg in leading a charge against the First Connecticut Artillery.

Upon the beginning of hostilities in 1861, dueling broke out in a rash. Two Confederate officers settled a dispute over their respective roles in the Battle of Bull Run, or First Manassas, by shooting it out with rifles. A subsequent duel sprang from a smoldering argument between South Carolina artillery officers over military conduct in the opening bombardment of Fort Sumter. These encounters cost the South a colonel, killed, and a captain, permanently disabled.

The two armies recognized that the coldly ferocious trend to dueling could lose them valuable officers. The Regulations for the Army of the United States adopted in 1861 specifically forbade duels under penalty of being cashiered, if an officer, or corporally punished, if an enlisted man. The punishments applied equally to "all seconds, promoters and carriers of challenges." The Confederate Army got around to adopting the identical regulations in 1863. For all the effect they had, they might just as well have forbidden the war itself.

As the tension and torment of the conflict grew, two fantastic encounters involving generals lost all pretense of punctiliousness and became sheer shoot-to-kill homicide. One case occurred in the Union Army and one in the Confederate.

The first general to fall victim to a personal feud was a magnificent figure of a man. Maj. Gen. William "Bull" Nelson of the United States Army stood six feet four inches and weighed a solid 300 pounds. A naval veteran of the Mexican War, he never rose above lieutenant in the little postwar Navy. He was, however, a brother of Abraham Lincoln's good friend, Thomas H. Nelson. Lincoln quickly commissioned the seafaring lieutenant as a brigadier general. On July 17, 1862, Nelson was jumped up to major general and sent to organize the Federal defenses of Louisville, Kentucky. His troops consisted largely of raw militia just inducted into the Federal service. In his two-fisted quarter-deck way, Nelson, described as alternately glowing with geniality and glowering with anger, set about hammering his force into a battle unit. In doing so, he rebuked a brigadier general from Indiana for alleged neglect of duty.

On the morning of September 29, 1862, the reprimanded brigadier, accompanied by two friends, called on General Nelson at his headquarters in the Galt House, a noted hotel in Louisville. The brigadier, Jefferson Columbus Davis, born in Indiana in 1828 and named after two great men, was an up-from-the-ranks Regular who distinguished himself in the Mexican War and in the Federal garrison of Fort Sumter during the 1861 bombardment. Presumably he was amenable to discipline if anyone was. Accompanying him were Gov. Oliver P. Morton, of Indiana, already under accusation of meddling with the discipline of Indiana troops in the Federal service, and a Captain Gibson.

The trio arrived before breakfast, a touchy time in anyone's life. Davis and Nelson met in the vestibule. The following conversation was overheard:

General Davis: "Sir, you seemed to take advantage of your authority the other day."

General Nelson (*hand to ear*): "Speak louder, I don't hear you very well."

General Davis (*louder*): "You seemed to take advantage of your authority the other day."

General Nelson (*indignantly*): "I don't know that I did, sir."

General Davis: "You threatened to arrest me and send me out of the state under a provost guard."

General Nelson: "There, damn you, take that!"

Nelson struck Davis across the face resoundingly with the back of his mighty hand. That much was seen. Something else which went before was unseen.

Davis admitted later that he provoked the blow by crumpling up a card and throwing it in Nelson's face. This was the traditional insult to invite a challenge.

The tingling slap that Davis got, instead of a coldly polite response under "the code," made him forget dueling etiquette. In a homicidal rage he walked into the next room, borrowed a pistol from his friend, Captain Gibson, and returned to the vestibule. Without a word he fired a single shot at Nelson, who was unarmed. The bullet struck Nelson in the right breast. He died within half an hour, reportedly after forgiving Davis. At any rate Davis, although indicted, never was called to account for his deed.

Nelson was buried with military honors before a turnout of 12,000 troops, some of whose thoughts on discipline must have been interesting. The war went on, with Davis leading first a division and then a corps under Sherman in Georgia and the Carolinas. Davis later became the first United States military commander of Alaska, but never received a longed-for postwar promotion to major general.

During the Atlanta campaign, a personal feud of long standing between two of the ranking Union generals boiled almost to the bloodshed point. Only the lack of a revolver at the moment of wrath prevented an angry subordinate officer, a much-riled partisan of Maj. Gen. "Fighting Joe" Hooker, from pistoling the commanding general, Maj. Gen. William Tecumseh Sherman.[1]

The basic ill feeling festered between Sherman and Hooker. It supposedly went back some years to garrison duty in San Francisco. There Major Hooker is said to have borrowed a sum from Lieutenant Sherman. Hard words ensued when he failed to repay it on time. After the start of the war, Hooker commanded the Army of the Potomac disastrously at the Battle of Chancellorsville, then was shifted south and placed under Sherman, his erstwhile junior. This naturally did nothing to assuage his feelings.

Hooker's corps suffered heavy casualties in the battles around Atlanta. Sherman jokingly but caustically remarked that the casualties might not really be as bad as reported; Hooker's men had a way of hiding out during battles. The Hooker subordinate grew blazingly ready to kill Sherman on the spot. As he was not wearing a revolver, he strode around trying to borrow one to shoot the "God-damned s.o.b.!" Nobody obliged him, and he cooled down.

The Sherman-Hooker feud kept burning, however. Sherman subsequently passed over Hooker in favor of Maj. Gen. Oliver O. Howard for the important post of commander of the Army of the Tennessee. Hooker soon thereafter asked to be relieved from serving under Sherman because "justice and self-respect alike" demanded it. His wish was granted.

[1] See Walter H. Hebert, *Fighting Joe Hooker;* also J. O. Buckeridge, *Lincoln's Choice,* for a pro-Hooker, anti-Sherman account.

In the closing stages of the war a clash between two hot-tempered Texas cavalry leaders produced a lethal Southern counterpart to the Nelson-Davis case. The details are still scant. What goes on between two enemies behind a closed door is never easy to learn, especially if, when the door opens, one is dead and the other tight-lipped.

Again the killing took place in a hotel, in Houston in the rooms of the commanding general, John Bankhead Magruder, CSA. The two principals were alone at the time. Both had served through four years of war. Now, with the struggle almost over, they argued about reorganization of a cavalry command.

The senior of the two, Maj. Gen. John Austin Wharton, born at Nashville, Tennessee, and educated at South Carolina College, was a Texan by adoption, not yet thirty-seven. He had led a regiment of Texas Rangers, and later a cavalry brigade at Chickamauga. His antagonist, Col. George W. Baylor, was such a red-hot secessionist that he reputedly raised the first Confederate flags in Texas and Arizona. At thirty-two, he commanded the 2nd Texas Cavalry.

On April 6, 1865, the two officers met at the hotel to settle their argument. All that Baylor said later was that Wharton slapped his face and damned him for a liar. Whereupon Baylor whipped out his revolver and killed Wharton. Upon investigation it turned out that Baylor, like Davis, had shot down an unarmed superior officer. Like Davis, he got away with it. Wharton was buried at Austin, the war ended almost immediately, and Baylor, years afterward, became a Texas Ranger major and state legislator.

Unlike the two other slain generals, Brig. Gen. Lucius M. Walker, CSA, managed to get himself killed with due formality. His duel to the death concluded an ill-fated military career which began when Walker, a nephew of President James K. Polk and native of Tennessee, was graduated from West Point in 1850. Two years later he quit the Army to earn a living as a commission merchant. Late in 1861 he became colonel of the 40th Tennessee and led it without luster in several battles. Gen. Braxton Bragg, his commander, a severe disciplinarian, reported to Richmond that Walker and one other high-ranking officer "were not safe men to be entrusted with any command. . . ."

Walker subsequently sought and obtained a transfer to Gen. Edmund Kirby Smith's Trans-Mississippi Department, apparently to start afresh. There he obtained command of a division of Arkansas cavalry. Indirectly it was to prove the death of him.

Also under Kirby Smith was a division of Missouri cavalry headed by Brig. Gen. John Sappington Marmaduke, a dashing six-footer with dainty patrician hands and feet. Marmaduke had attended Yale and Harvard before graduation from West Point in 1857. His father, a former governor of Missouri, pleaded with him to side with the Union. Despite the pleas, he became a Confederate. Only twenty-eight, he soon distinguished himself for leadership at Boonville and Shiloh, although the South lost both battles.

The cavalry divisions of Walker and Marmaduke formed part of a force of 7,600 Confederates under aging Lt. Gen. Theophilus H. Holmes which attempted on July 4, 1863, to capture Helena, Arkansas, from its Federal garrison of 4,100. In the opinion of a private who was there: "Marmaduke was a born soldier, Walker was a martinet, Holmes was uncertain in judgment."

The Federal beat back the attack with 1,636 Confederate casualties and only 239 of their own. It fell to the cavalry, in which Walker was senior to Marmaduke, to cover the dismal retreat. Marmaduke's Missourians bore the brunt of a "fire-and-fall-back" delaying action. Arriving hard-pressed at a point where Walker, according to the story, was supposed to reinforce him, Marmaduke found no one. As one survivor put it, "Marmaduke extricated himself from the situation by a miracle."

Marmaduke later criticized Walker for failing to support him properly and threatened to resign rather than serve further with Walker. When Walker demanded an explanation, Marmaduke said that while he did not impugn Walker's personal courage, he could not forgive his military failure. Walker, convinced his honor was at stake, agreed to a duel. The seconds exchanged notes in the stiff etiquette which surrounded genteel murder in those days.

Although the code duello called for single-shot smoothbore pistols not over nine inches long, it was agreed that in the exigencies of war the opponents would use the more formidable service six-shooters. They were to "fire and advance" until one fell. Out of deference to the fact that Marmaduke squinted and could not see well, the distance was cut short.

The generals met almost in sight of their troops on Septem-

ber 6, 1863, on the bank of the Arkansas River near Little
Rock. Walker fired and missed. Marmaduke, squinting in-
tently, drilled Walker through the body. Walker died a few
days later in Little Rock.

Marmaduke, arrested, was soon released through the influence of highly placed friends and the clamoring of his
Missouri troopers. He rose to major general and became a St.
Louis businessman and Democratic leader after the war. In
1884 he was elected Governor of Missouri, as his father had
been before him.

Walker was the second member of his West Point Class
of 1850 to fall victim to dueling in a year. The first was Col.
W. Ransom Calhoun, a kinsman of the great statesman, John
C. Calhoun. Like Walker, Calhoun quit the Army soon after
graduation. He served as a United States diplomat in Paris.
While there, he undiplomatically engaged "in an affair of
honor with a gentleman from New York, which resulted without blood."

A caprice of fate threw together Captain Calhoun and his
future antagonist, 1st Lt. Alfred Rhett, of Charleston, during
the initial bombardment of Fort Sumter April 12-13, 1861.
Both served in the 1st South Carolina Regular Artillery in
Fort Moultrie, across the harbor channel from Sumter.

Rhett, a son of John C. Calhoun's inveterate political foe,
R. Barnwell Rhett, Senior, fire-eating editor of the secessionist
Charleston *Mercury*, soon clashed with Ransom Calhoun. The
issue was not politics, but what might be termed "West
Pointism."

A third of all Confederate generals were graduates of the
United States Military Academy, as was President Jefferson
Davis. The Confederate secretary of state, Robert A. Toombs,
who almost beat Davis for the Presidency and later became a
general himself, once gibed that the epitaph of the Southern
armies should be: "Died of West Point."

Rhett, who was no West Pointer, apparently first became
irked when the commandant of artillery at Fort Moultrie,
Lt. Col. Roswell Ripley, an Ohioan of the Class of 1843
turned Confederate, appointed his fellow West Pointer, Calhoun, as assistant commandant. Rhett viewed this as a device
"to prevent any volunteer officer" from assuming command if
Ripley became a casualty.

In the bombardment, Rhett and Calhoun commanded
separate batteries. Calhoun, perhaps in his capacity of assistant

commandant, infuriated Rhett by ignoring him and giving orders directly to Rhett's company and by cursing Rhett in the presence of enlisted men. Rhett asserted he was prepared to overlook all this in the heat of the battle, but the day after the shooting ceased, Calhoun again addressed him "in a tone and manner that I felt to be aggressive and insulting."

Because he felt it improper to challenge a superior officer, Rhett informed all and sundry that Calhoun behaved like "a damned puppy." As he expected, word soon reached Calhoun. Instead of challenging, Calhoun went off to Virginia to command a field battery. He afterward explained that he was observing an old dictum that war duty came ahead of private dueling.

Less than a year later Calhoun returned. Now a colonel, he was placed in command of the regiment and of Fort Sumter, which it garrisoned. His second-in-command was none other than Maj. Alfred Rhett. The two enemies were cooped up in a 2.4-acre fortress, with Rhett maintaining an unswerving low opinion of Calhoun and Calhoun ignoring Rhett. The Federal forces, fortunately for the South, did not aggravate matters by bombarding Sumter at the time.

Then in an off-duty moment at the exclusive Charleston Club, Capt. Arnoldus Vanderhorst spoke highly of West Pointers and Calhoun to Rhett. Rhett replied that many West Pointers "were not worth a damn." Pressed, he added that Calhoun was a "damned puppy." Vanderhorst thereupon challenged Rhett. They met at ten paces. Vanderhorst fired and missed. Rhett casually fired into the air. The affair was considered honorably closed. But it caused such notoriety that Calhoun could no longer ignore Rhett. Sixteen months after the original friction, he demanded "that satisfaction which is usual amongst gentlemen" because of Rhett's "offensive language."

The satisfaction took the form of a meeting with smoothbore pistols at 5 P.M.—no early risers, these gentlemen. The seconds, Colonel and State Senator O. M. Dantzler, for Calhoun, Dr. Irvine K. Furman for Rhett, worked out the details. The distance was set at ten paces. Rhett, as the challenged party, is said to have preferred the "drop shot"— that is, to hold his pistol muzzle up and drop the muzzle toward his antagonist at the command "fire"—but he yielded on this point to Calhoun, who asked for the more conventional "rise" in which the duel began muzzles downward. This method was regarded as slightly slower but surer.

Both officers arrived on the field of honor ahead of time. Rhett wore his gray uniform with the insignia of major. Calhoun, who had resigned from the service because of ill health, appeared in civilian garb. The small group of seconds, surgeons and spectators included three state senators, the Speaker of the House of Representatives, a prominent member of the State Constitutional Convention which redrafted state policy, and Captain Arnoldus Vanderhorst. Rhett and Calhoun dueled, and the seconds punctiliously reported the outcome in a signed statement:

"The challengee with his friends arrived on the ground 20 minutes before 5 o'clock and found the challenger with his friends already there.

"The seconds proceeded at once to select and measure the ground, which being done, they tossed for the choice of position or word. Col. O. M. Dantzler, the second of Col. Calhoun, had the word, and Dr. I. K. Furman, the second for Major Rhett, the choice of position. The principals were posted at a quarter past 5 o'clock. Col. Dantzler read the terms of meeting, and twice repeated the word in the manner in which it was to be given. The pistols were then placed in the hands of the principals, and the word given, both parties fired almost simultaneously, Colonel Calhoun firing first. Colonel Calhoun fell. Dr. Furman then asked leave to remove his friend, and permission being granted, the party retired.

"The friends of the challenger were Col. O. M. Dantzler, second, Hon. James Simons and Cdr. Catesby ap Roger Jones, CSN, advisers, and W. T. Wragg, Surgeon.[2]

---

[2] Catesby ap Roger Jones was, of course, the noted Confederate naval officer who as a young lieutenant commanded the CSS *Virginia* or *Merrimack* in the famous battle with the *Monitor*. Jones took command the previous day when Commodore Franklin Buchanan, CSN, was wounded. After serving in the *Virginia*, Jones, promoted commander, ultimately became director of the Confederate naval gun factory at Selma, Alabama. A 7-inch rifled gun bearing his initials on the right trunnion now stands in Battery Park, Charleston, South Carolina, with a brass plate saying it formerly was in the harbor defenses at Fort Johnson. The author believes that it may be one of two 7-inch rifles at Fort Johnson commanded in 1863-64 by his great-uncle, Lt. Michael Halsey, CSA, 2nd South Carolina Regular Artillery. If so, it rendered considerable service in support of Fort Sumter, by flanking fire.

"The friends of the challengee were Dr. Irvine K. Furman, second, Hon. F. D. Richardson and Hon. Charles Alston, Jr., advisers, and John D. Burns, Surgeon.

"The above is an accurate statement of what occurred on the field, and we declare the duel to have been fairly and honorably fought."

Rhett's bullet caught Calhoun in the middle of the body. The round ball of soft lead drilled him through, apparently expanding itself and enlarging the hole as it went. The surgeons could do little. He died in an hour or so.

The Charleston newspapers maintained a strange silence. The *Mercury*, owned and published by the Rhetts, covered a multitude of other subjects but printed not a word of the duel ever. The rival *Courier* came out reluctantly, without referring to Rhett, eight days afterward. On page two of its issue of September 13, 1862, it explained that it refrained because of its "unwillingness to do anything to aggravate rumors." Then it reported that Colonel Calhoun "fell mortally wounded on the afternoon of Friday, 5th inst., near this city, in a hostile meeting . . . a victim added to the list of victims that our State and City have lost in deference to the so called 'Code of Honor.' . . ."

Actually, the encounter created such a furor that there were, according to a Charleston correspondent of the Mobile (Alabama) *Advertiser*, demands that the city courts make their first legal investigation of dueling in twenty years. The *Advertiser* correspondent did not suggest that there was anything technically raw or wrong about the duel. On the contrary, he wrote, "the arrangements of the meeting were conducted throughout with the nicest regard for the etiquette of the 'code' and I have heard of several of those who were on the ground who express their belief that a more fairly-fought duel never occurred."

When news of the duel belatedly reached the Confederate capital at Richmond, G. W. Randolph, then Secretary of War, called for the prosecution of Major Rhett under the Articles of War. Apparently proceedings against Rhett were started "through official channels," but soon got nowhere. The Confederacy was too much in need of fighters to try one of the best for a personal and—as many thought—entirely legal and gentlemanly killing.

Instead of being court-martialed, Rhett became colonel of the regiment and succeeded the man he killed as commander

of Fort Sumter. He held the fort during a period of furious
bombardment, during which one shell burst on a group of
officers at dinner and broke off Rhett's table-knife in his hand,
cutting his hand but leaving him otherwise unscathed.

Rhett and his regiment garrisoned Sumter during two con-
centrated Federal attacks in which 6,878 shells struck it and
virtually reduced the walls to rubble. When the garrison was
relieved, Rhett was officially commended on August 27, 1863,
with these words:

"The Commanding General has witnessed with genuine
pride and satisfaction the defense made of Fort Sumter by
Colonel Rhett, his officers, and men of the First Regiment of
South Carolina Regular Artillery. . . . *In the annals of war,
no stouter defense ever was made.* . . ."

After the war, Rhett became chief constable of the state of
South Carolina and wrote a 40-page unsigned pamphlet
in defense of the "Code of Honor." Dueling, he asserted,
"stands upon the principles of nature and principles of
Christianity, precisely as public war."

Devotion to the precise formality of the dueling code in
battle against the Federals nearly cost the Confederacy one
of its best cavalry leaders and in a sense did sacrifice its most
famous sea raider.

During a lull in the Battle of Gettysburg, Maj. Gen. Wade
Hampton, CSA, rode off alone to investigate random
firing. He found a Michigan cavalry private, dismounted and
atop a fence, taking pot shots. Hampton engaged the private
with his revolver. When the private's gun fouled, Hampton
chivalrously withheld his fire, so the story goes, until the
private cleaned his gun. Then they resumed. Hampton
winged the private. Just then a Michigan major totally un-
acquainted with the code of honor rode up and sabered
Hampton across the head from behind. Hampton angrily
chased him into a woods.

An extreme quirk of the dueling mentality apparently led
to the sinking of the famous Confederate commerce raider
Alabama. There is evidence that Capt. Raphael Semmes of
the *Alabama,* a mustachioed Southerner reared in the code-of-
honor tradition, took as a personal challenge the appearance
of the USS *Kearsarge* off Cherbourg, the French port in
which the *Alabama* sought overhaul. French officers, it is said,

fostered Semmes' notion that he was honor-bound to engage the *Kearsarge*. So the *Alabama*, although badly in need of repairs, steamed out to sea for single combat with the *Kearsarge* and was sunk within two hours.

A fabulous wartime duel behind the Confederate lines pitted the field officers of an insulted North Carolina regiment against the staff captains of a South Carolina general. Rather than use conventional dueling pistols, the principals selected double-barrelled shotguns in one case and Mississippi or U.S. Model 1841 rifles in another. They arranged to fight with these deadly weapons at only 40 yards.

The fantastic affair sprang from a clash and jangle of wounded military pride after a minor Federal victory on April 19, 1863. A force of bluecoats made a twilight landing unopposed on the bank of the Nansemond River near Suffolk, Virginia, and surprised and overwhelmed old Fort Huger there. Among the Confederates, the blame clearly lay on whoever failed to guard the river bank.

A report to headquarters filed by Brig. Gen. Evander M. Law, a South Carolinian, suggested that Colonel J. K. Connally and his 55th North Carolina Regiment were derelict. Connally and his officers, on the other hand, retorted that Law's troops were supposed to be holding the critical area.

Within 24 hours, Connally rode over to Law's tent and demanded pointblank to know whether it was true that Law had "reported that my regiment acted cowardly last night and fled before the enemy without fighting and in violation of orders." [3]

Law, although utterly fearless in battle, apparently sensed that Connally was spoiling for a duel. He replied with exactitude that he based his criticism of Connally and the 55th North Carolina on what two of his staff, Captains Terrell and Cussons, "reported to me."

"Well, it's a damned lie," Connally snapped, and went in search of the two captains. He had no difficulty finding them.

Terrell promptly said that he made the statement and could not retract it because it was true. Cussons, a long-haired

[3] See *Lee's Lieutenants*, Vol. II, by Douglas Southall Freeman, Charles Scribner's Sons; *The War Between the Union and the Confederacy*, by Col. W. C. Oates; *Histories of the Several Regiments and Battalions from North Carolina in the Great War, 1861-65*, edited by Walter Clark; *The Civil War Dictionary*, by Lt. Col. M. M. Boatner, III.

Englishman, replied tongue-in-cheek in a tone of great politeness that while he had made no such statement, "If you gave
your men orders to retire when the enemy appeared in their
front last night, they obeyed damned promptly."

At that the duel was on. Connally and Major A. H. Belo
of his regiment challenged Captains Terrell and Cussons. The
first pairing, Connally and Terrell, agreed to use double-
barrelled shotguns loaded with round ball—equivalent of the
so-called "punkin ball" in modern hunting. It was Cussons
who selected the even deadlier Mississippi rifles for his meeting with Belo. Connally added a proviso that if he and his
major were killed off, the captains of his regiment would
take up the dueling in sequence to the last man.

Both General Law and his immediate superior, Maj. Gen.
John Bell Hood, apparently knew of the startling arrangements
in violation of Confederate Army regulations against dueling,
but both, being "gentlemen of honor" themselves, looked the
other way. Nearly every other officer around assembled to see
the spectacle.

Belo and Cussons fought first. Belo's bullet drilled a hole
through Cussons' hat. Cussons missed. The seconds reloaded
the rifles. Belo missed. Cusson' bullet ripped his opponent's
coat collar and drew blood from his neck. But Belo persisted in
fighting on. The seconds rammed home fresh loads. Just as
they handed the rifles to their principals for a third and
perhaps deadly round, there came an interruption. Colonel
Connally and Captain Terrell, it developed, had settled their
quarrel. Belo and Cussons thereupon shook hands. All further
shooting was to be directed at Yankees.

Nathan Bedford Forrest, the Confederacy's almost legendary
cavalry leader, was nearly cut down in the middle of the war
by an irate subordinate. At Columbia, Tennessee, on June 14,
1863, a Lieutenant A. W. Gould, CSA, furious at his
commanding general, fired a pistol shot which nearly dropped
the massive Forrest in his tracks.

Again, the personal friction went back to a question of battlefield performance. Less than a month earlier in an engagement at Day's Gap, Alabama, Lieutenant Gould had
audaciously run his two field pieces up to within 300 yards of
the Federal lines. The Federals charged and captured both
guns complete with caissons. It was a point of honor with both
armies never to yield cannon. The loss of two valuable pieces
made Forrest furious. He subsequently ordered Gould trans-

ferred to another battery. To many, this appeared to be a form
of reprimand or punishment. Gould, high-spirited and not
much past 21, felt entitled to an explanation. Forrest disdained
to discuss the matter with the young lieutenant, so Gould
sought him out. He found Forrest in his temporary headquarters at the Masonic Hall in Columbia, Tennessee. Several
small boys, tagging worshipfully after the great leader in the
manner of small boys of all centuries, were the only witnesses
to what ensued.

Forrest happened to be toying with a penknife. Gould, with
his hand on a small pistol in his pocket, demanded an explanation, but got no satisfaction from Forrest. As Forrest started
to turn away, Gould fired the pistol through his pocket almost
against Forrest's left side. The wounded general clamped an
unshakable grip on the lieutenant with his mighty left hand,
opened the penknife in his right hand between his teeth, and
stabbed the younger man in the abdomen. Gould broke loose
and ran. Forrest unholstered a cavalry revolver and pursued.
Gould, who had taken refuge in a tailor shop, ran out the back
door. Forrest fired and missed, but Gould collapsed in some
high grass.

Someone told Forrest the boy was dying. Doctors who meanwhile came up assured the general that his own bullet wound
had missed the vitals and would not prove fatal. Immediately
Forrest ordered them to take care of Gould first. The medical
men tucked both officers into bed. Forrest was up and about
in a week and a half. Gould, fatally stabbed, died before the
general recovered. Forrest, who had fully relented by then, is
said to have wept bitterly.

For a variation on the theme of pistols for two, the two top
Southern cavalry leaders in the Mississippi Valley area nearly
had it out with sabers. It happened at Spring Hill, Tennessee,
during the last meeting between Generals Earl Van Dorn and
N. B. Forrest before Van Dorn was slain by an irate husband.
The two generals, both tense and hot-tempered, are said to have
argued over a Chattanooga newspaper account giving Forrest's
forces credit to which Van Dorn felt entitled.

Van Dorn was quoted later as saying he confronted Forrest
and charged him with "treachery and falsehood." Then Van
Dorn took his saber down from the wall, where it was hanging,
and proposed that they have it out then and there. Forrest,
"his face aflame with feeling," half-drew his own saber. Van

Jefferson C. Davis

Library of Congress

Stonewall Jackson

Library of Congress

General William Nelson

Library of Congress

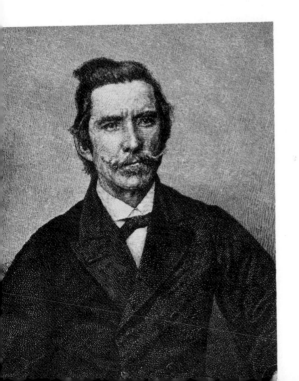

Rear Admiral
Raphael Semmes,
Captain of the *Alabama*

Library of Congress

Dorn bared his blade and advanced. But as he did so, Forrest steadied himself and with deliberate slowness sheathed his saber. With a restraint that must have reflected enormous effort after being insulted, Forrest said, "It would never do for two officers of our rank to set such an example to the troops. I remember, if you forget, what we both owe to the cause." His action left Van Dorn in mingled shame for himself and admiration for Forrest.

Van Dorn met a fate both untimely and unseemly at Spring Hill, Tennessee, in May, 1863. A local physician named Peters walked up behind him as he sat writing at his headquarters desk and fired a bullet into his head from a stubby derringer pistol. The wound proved fatal. Dr. Peters pleaded the "unwritten law," asserting Van Dorn had been overly attentive to charming Mrs. Peters.

The strain and personal rivalries in the Confederate high command nearly led to a war-within-a-war in the hot summer of 1862. Two conflicts arising from the conduct of the Seven Days' Battles before Richmond involved four generals in gray: James Longstreet and A. P. Hill, D. H. Hill and Robert Toombs.

Longstreet, the iron-willed old "warhorse," and his red-haired Virginian subordinate, Ambrose Powell Hill, differed over the roles taken by their commands in combat. The two, who had been on ill terms for some time, reached the point of exchanging terse notes through their staff officers. Formal details of a duel were being discussed when General Robert E. Lee heard of it and promptly halted it.

The second clash occurred over the conduct of the same campaign. It pitted Daniel Harvey Hill, a hot-headed South Carolinian with a cutting tongue, against Robert Toombs, heavy-drinking Georgia politician. In charging up Malvern Hill against intense Federal fire, Hill's division suffered heavily. Hill, a professional soldier who later rose to lieutenant general, felt Toombs' brigade nearby was to blame because it broke ranks and retreated. He rode over, assumed command, and rallied Toombs' troops for a time.

Toombs later wrote Hill a hot note defending the valor of his brigade. Hill replied that his criticism was directed at Toombs personally—"it is notorious that you retired from the field." In a rage, Toombs challenged Hill to a duel. Hill declined on grounds that "we have a country to defend and enemies to fight." Toombs soon quit the army and returned to politics.

Meanwhile, behind the Confederate lines in Tennessee, beetle-browed Braxton Bragg, one of the South's eight full generals, came perilously close to personal combat with Maj. Gen. John C. Breckinridge, CSA, former Vice President of the United States. At the Battle of Stone's River, or Murfreesboro, Bragg insisted that Breckinridge's division do what its commander termed "an impossible thing"—drive superior Union forces from a strong position on higher ground. The division dutifully charged and lost 1,700 of its 4,500 men before its attack collapsed. Breckinridge, in tears, cried: "My poor orphans!" Bragg wrote a caustic report criticizing Breckinridge and his men. Stung, the survivors urged Breckinridge to resign and duel Bragg. Breckinridge placated them by saying that after the war "he would not forget their request to call the commanding general to account. . . ." After the downfall of the Confederacy, however, he took refuge abroad.

While the war raged on, no high-ranking commander, especially on the Southern side, could feel immune to the constant threat of a challenge from subordinates. Stonewall Jackson died under the shadow of one. If he had survived the war, he might have had to face hard-fighting, hard-swearing Col. Andrew Jackson Grigsby.

Grigsby, after Jackson's rise to higher command, led the old Stonewall Brigade at Harper's Ferry and Sharpsburg and fully expected promotion to be its brigadier. Instead, Jackson appointed his staff officer and fellow-townsman of Lexington, Virginia, E. F. Paxton, better known as Frank, or "Bull". Grigsby, swearing mightily, resigned from the service and announced that he would duel Jackson as soon as the war ended.

Ironically, being passed over for command of the brigade probably saved Grigsby's life. "Bull" Paxton was killed leading the brigade at Chancellorsville less than twenty-four hours after Jackson himself was fatally wounded. Succeeding Paxton in command came youthful Brig. Gen. James A. Walker, and here again was irony. Walker, as a cadet at the Virginia Military Institute in 1852, took offense at a very strict professor and challenged him to a duel. The professor was T. J. Jackson, later famed as Stonewall. Jackson soberly considered whether a professor ought to duel a student, decided not and had Walker expelled. One of Jackson's final decisions while lying fatally wounded eleven years later was to promote young Walker to command the Stonewall Brigade.

As for irate Colonel Grigsby, he lived to be seventy-seven. Evidently he forgave or forgot his grudge against Stonewall, for one of his last public acts was to participate in unveiling the Jackson statue at Lexington in 1891. With pride and pleasure, Grigsby and Walker led the parade of veterans honoring the leader they had threatened to shoot.

Eight of the 318 Confederate generals who survived the war were shot to death later in personal encounters. Their assassinations—for that is what most were—reflected their political roles in the postwar South or animosities amounting to feuds. Four former Confederate brigadiers were shot down in Mississippi between 1870 and 1888. Four other generals were killed during approximately the same period in North Carolina, Tennessee, Arkansas and Missouri, respectively. The shootings are recounted in Ezra Warner's *Generals in Gray* and elsewhere. Brig. Gen. James H. Clanton, CSA, Warner says, "was assassinated at Knoxville, Tenn., Sept. 27, 1871, by a drunken ex-Federal officer, the son of a former Union Congressman from East Tennessee, who provoked a quarrel with him." Brig. Gen. W. F. Brantley was shot dead while riding in his buggy near Winona, Mississippi, in 1870, in the course of a long feud which took other lives. Brig. Gen. William W. Adams, whose younger brother D. W., also a Confederate brigadier, had killed a man in a duel before the war, was fatally wounded in a street shooting in Jackson, Mississippi, in 1888. Brig. Gen. St. John Liddell was slain aboard a river steamboat in 1870 by a former Confederate colonel over personal differences. That same year, an unknown assassin cut down Brig. Gen. R. V. Richardson, a wartime and business associate of Gen. Nathan Bedford Forrest, with a load of buckshot in the back from ambush at Clarkton, Missouri. Lt. Gen. Thomas C. Hindman was killed at Helena, Arkansas, in 1868 by an unknown slayer, probably because he opposed the carpetbag regime. Brig. Gen. W. F. Tucker, incapacitated by war wounds in 1864, was murdered by two men at Okolona, Mississippi, in 1881, reputedly at the instigation of a third party whom Tucker had charged with misappropriation. A hired assassin killed Maj. Gen. Bryan Grimes in 1880 near his North Carolina plantation.

8

The Stealthy Snipers

Seldom have so many ranking officers been slain by the calculated fire of expert marksmen. Continuing a tradition which cost the British commanders dearly in the Revolution and War of 1812, both sides picked off victims at long range. How did they manage it?

A sniper must be a cold man. He personifies war reduced to its iciest thin stab. To him, humanity is a target. He should have no conscience about killing, or else be able to freeze his conscience like meat in cold storage. He should love his rifle better than he loves people. If he does, it will help him immeasurably in his work.

The work of a sniper is to sit back, usually in comparative safety and from a considerable distance, and kill people who do not know of his existence or realize his menace. He is most efficient if he functions as impersonally as a housewife with a fly swatter. To him, the men across the line—the exuberant boys, the married men worrying about their families at home, the higher officers burdened with the gravities of war—are so many flies. He gently squeezes his trigger. Swat! Another is dead. He reloads and begins looking for another man—or is it a fly?

Sniping has been like that in every war. Leonardo da Vinci, the colossal genius of the Italian Renaissance, was a sniper. When his city was besieged, Leonardo, as inventive with firearms as with most else, perfected a long-range rifle and picked off besiegers from the walltops.

Sniping played its stealthy part in the American Revolution; the Napoleonic period, during which Tyrolean chasseurs killed two French generals of note; in the War of 1812, which concluded with a triple British thrust that riflemen helped to choke off by killing two of the three British generals and wounding the third (Pakenham slain at New Orleans, Ross

shot dead at Baltimore, George Prevost wounded at Platts-
burg), and in most wars since.

Although not peculiarly an American military institution,
sniping reached a high degree of exactitude and exercise in
American wars. The frontier environment of the nation produced riflemen, and snipers are essentially riflemen—armed
with a precision weapon, able to operate as individuals.

Around Boston, from the very start of the American Revolution, the British protested bitterly at the colonial penchant
for shooting down redcoat officers of high rank. They suggested that it was another low form of barbarianism developed
in the uncouth New World. Before the end of the Revolution, and in the Napoleonic Wars, they had their own riflemen
sniping away.

Inevitably, the Civil War proved a heyday for snipers or
sharpshooters. Both sides were American and both sides
contained frontiersmen; firm-nerved farm boys accustomed to
hog killing; mathematicians who could plot the velocity and
trajectory of a lead slug; and plain men who could shoot to
kill. All types had their innings.

The Union made more noise about it, with Col. Hiram
Berdan's sharpshooters demonstrating before President Lincoln
and the elite of Washington, and getting their pictures in the
illustrated weeklies of the day. The Confederates, less publicized, made the biggest single day's killing of the war on July
2, 1863, at the Round Tops at Gettysburg, a long rifle-shot
from where ex-President Eisenhower's farm now stands.

The statistics of sniping or sharpshooting in the Civil War
are especially unclear. So many bullets flew that it became
difficult to tell which of the many dead bore the sad distinction
of having been individually marked out by a sniper. Yet the
record of that deadly day at Gettysburg was sharply etched on
the casualty lists and on the minds of those who were there.

The second day of the climactic battle hinged largely on
action south of the town of Gettysburg. There the Confederate
right wing and Federal left wing opposed each other across
simple farming ground which has now become unforgettable
as The Peach Orchard and The Wheat Field. Through the
area trickles a little creek, Plum Run. It runs approximately
north to south. Just east of Plum Run are two knobs or
hillocks, Little Round Top and Big Round Top. On July 2,
1863, they were at the southern or lower end of the Gettysburg battlefield. Whoever controlled them had the field under

his guns and the outcome of the battle under his arm. Nobody realized this at first; then suddenly everybody realized it. Both sides hurled troops at the Round Tops. The Federals got there first.

At that point, Confederate sharpshooters went to work. Just across Plum Run from the Round Tops stands a rugged jumble of rocks. Whatever its name before that day, from then on it has been known as the *Devil's Den*. There the Southern riflemen played the devil with Northerners on the Round Tops. Conditions and location were ideal that day for long-range killing. It was hot and almost airless; no moisture to affect gunpowder, no strong wind to deflect bullets. Moreover, the light—as important to a sniper as to an artist or photographer—was just right. Devil's Den lies west of the Round Tops. Most of the sharpshooting was done after noon. Therefore the sun was at the backs of the shooters, shadowing them and illuminating their targets to the east across Plum Run.

For once, the usually ill-armed Confederates came properly equipped for their deadly task. They bore heavy-barrelled target rifles especially built for accurate shooting at extreme ranges. These pieces were too heavy to be fired offhand from the shoulder, with the piece supported by the shooter's arms. As a rule, they were used with special benches for rests. If the roughness of terrain prevented use of benches, they were rested on convenient rocks or tree limbs, always with something soft under the barrel. One sniper rifle picked up in Devil's Den after the battle is said to weigh 36 pounds. It is now preserved in a Gettysburg museum. Like most such weapons, it bore a long telescopic sight mounted on top of the barrel. With these weapons, the Confederates took the Round Tops under fire.

The first Federal officer to recognize the vital importance of the two Round Tops was the chief topographical engineer of the Army of the Potomac, Maj. Gen. Gouverneur K. Warren, a West Pointer and native of New York State. Warren quickly sized up the situation with a trained eye. He realized that if he waited to send a message to a corps commander, requesting troops be placed on Little Round Top, the Confederates would take the position while the Federals were fighting out their paperwork. So he led the nearest Federal troops personally in a scramble up the craggy, bush-covered sides of the hillock. Warren saved the position for the Federal Army, but a Confederate sharpshooter tumbled

him from his perch, wounded. At that, he was luckier than
the next two Federal generals on Little Round Top.

Acting Brig. Gen. Strong Vincent, a lawyer from Erie,
Pennsylvania, was not yet twenty-seven and never would
be. Although no professional soldier, he led his troops so well
that he, a colonel at twenty-six, had already been assured of
promotion to brigadier. Vincent, taking his cue from Warren,
put his brigade to climbing Little Round Top. While he
cheered his men on, one of the huge rifles in Devil's Den
cracked. Vincent crumpled. He died the next day, July 3,
1863, the same date that someone in a Washington bureau
penned out a commission as brigadier general for Strong
Vincent.

The grim job of holding Little Round Top under a hail of
Confederate artillery and small arms fire fell to Brig. Gen.
Stephen H. Weed. Weed, a New Yorker, was twenty-nine
and had been graduated from West Point nine years earlier.
The war catapulted him up to brigadier. Now it cut him down
to mortal sod. A bullet from Devil's Den killed him on the spot.

As he lay dying, General Weed attempted to murmur some
instructions. First Lieutenant Charles E. Hazlett, of the 5th
U. S. Artillery, leaned over the fallen figure in blue. He remained in that position just long enough, it would seem, for
the sniper on Devil's Den to reload. Another shot barked out
amid the battle din. Lieutenant Hazlett fell dead across General Weed's body, presumably killed by the same marksman
who shot the general.

One of the senior officers, Col. Patrick H. O'Rorke of
the 140th New York regiment, then assumed command in
the immediate vicinity. In the furious clamor of battle, taking
command necessarily involved becoming conspicuous. It was
a calculated risk of the day. The colonel took it—and lost.
The snipers cut him down, too, dead in his booted tracks.

As dusk ended the fusillade from Devil's Den, the score
stood: two generals killed, one general wounded, one colonel
killed, several lesser officers including Lieutenant Hazlett
killed. And that, necessarily, was only part of the story.

Nobody knows exactly how many Confederate snipers
populated Devil's Den. There may have been one or two or a
half-dozen. Probably there were no more than that in all, for
trained sharpshooters with special rifles were as rare in 1861-65
as astronauts in 1962. A Civil War photograph exists of a
Southern "sniper" killed in Devil's Den. It shows an infantry-

man armed with an ordinary rifled musket of the Model 1861 made at both Springfield and Richmond. From his arm, it is quite evident that he was not one of the special snipers. He was simply a foot soldier who contributed his lead to the hail.[1]

Apparently it was a regular infantryman such as this, and not a specially armed sniper, who killed Maj. Gen. John F. Reynolds, the senior Federal field commander at the time, on the first day of the battle west of Gettysburg. Reynolds, like Warren next day, paid the price of exposing himself to avert a Union defeat. He reinforced and rallied the first Federal troops to feel the shock of the Southern attack. While the battle was still fluid, a bullet struck and killed him.

From the situation at the time of Reynolds' death, it seems almost certain that he was shot by a soldier in the ranks. At that time, there had been no opportunity to settle down to the cool, calculated business of sharpshooting. The bullet which killed him, moreover, is said to have been .58 calibre, the standard infantry bullet.

Most special sniper weapons used in the Civil War ranged in calibre between .45 and .56. This did not necessarily mean that the bullets were lighter than the .58, which weighed almost an ounce. The sniper projectiles were of a different shape, often much longer and a little narrower than the .58s. Where the .58 Minié bullet relied upon a cavity in its base to expand on firing and fill the rifle grooves inside the barrel, the sniper bullet often was patched with paper or cloth like the older, round "Kentucky rifle" bullets in order to fill the grooves snugly and prevent escape of the propellant powder.

Both the standard Civil War rifled musket and the usual sniper rifle loaded from the muzzle. The powder was poured in first, and then the bullet was rammed down with a ramrod. The infantryman loaded his musket hastily and casually, thrusting the bullet down upon the powder with an iron rod.

---

[1] The fallen private was later identified by a cousin, Governor J. Hoge Tyler, of Virginia, as 18-year-old Andrew J. Hoge, 4th Virginia Infantry, a line regiment rather than a sharpshooter unit. In *The Civil War Times* of October, 1961, CWT Art Director Frederic Ray cites evidence that Alexander Gardner, the Northern photographer who took a famous picture of the slain infantryman after the battle, carefully rearranged the body between exposures for composition and dramatic effect.

The sniper loaded carefully. Often his heavy rifle had a special "false muzzle" which fitted on the front. This took the wear and tear of starting the bullet into the rifling. Then it was removed before firing, so that the rifling at the real muzzle remained sharp, true and unworn.

Where the infantry musket bore only a rudimentary front sight and usually an open-notched rear sight with leaves marked for 100, 300 and 500 yards—the latter seldom used, by the way—the sniper rifle usually was equipped with elaborate sights that could be adjusted to allow for the deflection of bullets sidewise by cross winds, and the like. The front sight was hooded, or shaded by a hood of metal. The rear sight was an adjustable peep sight. In many instances the sight took the form of a tube-like telescope running almost the entire length of the barrel and giving 8- to 24-power magnification.

The big sniper rifles were fitted to long, narrow, four-legged benches which themselves sometimes held apparatus for elevating the rifle barrels to obtain greater ranges. The sniper sat beside or behind the bench on a little seat like a milking stool. Obviously, this equipment, including a rifle weighing 25 to 50 pounds, was not an outfit to be carried around by one soldier on the double in infantry charges and rapid field movements. Snipers as a rule moved with more leisure and deliberation than field artillery. They were usually a detachment in themselves and a law unto themselves. They commanded the respect given a specialist in any trade, although the common soldier sometimes held them in extreme distaste even when they were on his own side. He felt that their form of warfare was too cold-blooded.

Perhaps the most notable long-range shot made with a sniper rifle is attributed in official Army records to Capt. John T. Metcalf, III, U. S. Army Engineers. It was made with the impersonal deliberation and computation of a surveyor laying out a playground. That it was a mathematical success, Q.E.D., is beyond question. It killed a man.

Metcalf, a West Point graduate, was attached to forces under Brig. Gen. James W. McMillan in the Red River campaign in Louisiana in 1864. He combined a devotion to mathematics with a fascination for firearms, as is often the case. It was his thesis that a proper sniper rifle could kill at a mile or more.

To prove his point, Captain Metcalf obtained a weighty

muzzleloading rifle [2] complete with twenty-four power telescope and bench rest. He tested it thoroughly at ranges of a mile or more. Then his great opportunity came.

The Confederate forces, so the story goes, occupied a strong position on a hillside across a mile-wide valley from the Union advance lines. The Federal general pondered whether to attempt a direct assault, and decided his losses would be too heavy. The Confederates, on the defensive, were satisfied to sit tight on their hillside.

For Metcalf, the situation was made to order—battle lines static, ample leisure for setting up a sniping point, range approximately one mile. Behind the Union front line, a hill nicknamed Bloody Top offered a convenient position. Metcalf took a detail of men and had them scoop out a rifle pit for his mammoth gun. They floored the pit for steadiness, cut underbrush to conceal it, and set up the bench rest.

The big rifle was emplaced on the bench, loaded. Metcalf set up a surveyor's transit. Sweeping the opposite hillside with binoculars, he located the Confederate headquarters tent. With his transit he computed the distance from his rifle muzzle to the headquarters. It came to 5,467 feet, or one mile and 187 feet. He figured his bullet velocity with the black powder load he used. It would take the bullet five seconds or more to travel the distance. Next he began watching for the moment when some ranking officer, preferably the Confederate commanding general, would stand or sit still outside the headquarters for more than five seconds.

At this point, the story varies and it gets more romanticized with every telling. One of the most fascinating versions crowns Captain Metcalf with personal credit for a great victory. It goes like this:

The tent fly of the headquarters tent opens, and a bearded general in Confederate gray steps out and looks up at the morning sunlight with a smile. Metcalf sighted carefully,

---

[2] According to one published account, the rifle weighed 30 pounds. However, Maj. Ned H. Roberts, a famous muzzleloader authority, says in his book *The Muzzle Loading Cap Lock Rifle*, page 80, that Captain Metcalf's rifle weighed between 50 and 60 pounds. Roberts says he saw the rifle many years later, and that it was a .50 calibre piece made by Abe Williams, of Oswego, New York, and firing a long, cylindrical paper-patched bullet. Williams is known to have made a heavy, octagon-barrel target rifle weighing 28 pounds and to have made big sniper rifles for the Union Army.

squeezed the trigger, and the big rifle roared. A lieutenant ticked off the seconds. At the count of five, the general spun and fell. With the Confederate leader down, the Federal army swarmed across the valley and won a quick victory.[3]

Two earlier accounts are only slightly less remarkable. One injects a fantastic touch. The name of the maker of the captain's rifle, it says, was W. G. Langdon. There was a man of that name. He was a Boston watchmaker and gunsmith who contracted in 1862 to make twenty heavy-barrel sniper rifles for the Federal army at $150 each, complete with scope sights. Many of his rifles saw use. But, the fantastic part of this story is that the rifle bearing the maker's name W. G. Langdon killed a Confederate general of the identical name, W. G. Langdon. There was no such general, so far as the records go.[4]

Whatever else Captain Metcalf may have done, he proved that he could hit a man at a distance of more than a mile. The identity of the Confederate whom he shot remains indefinite to this day. So does the question of whether he was a general or a lesser human.

Federal snipers did kill at least six Confederate generals beyond doubt or dispute, however, in the course of the war. Their victims were Generals Branch, McCulloch, Green, Doles, Tyler and Pegram. They were shot at ranges varying from nearly a mile to as little as sixty yards. Their deaths followed the stolid pattern of sniping in almost every instance: static warfare, or at least a pause in movement, made the killing shots possible.

Brig. Gen. Lawrence O. Branch, a 41-year-old North Carolinian, was one of the first to fall. He was at Harper's Ferry on September 17, 1862, conferring with other Confederate generals. They formed a cluster of gold braid across the valley from the Union lines: A. P. Hill, Archer, Gregg and Branch, four generals in all. The target was too inviting for an unknown Federal marksman to resist. He fired at the group of four. Branch happened to be the one hit.

[3] TRUE magazine, January, 1961, "Mile-Long Shot to Kill."

[4] Charles W. Sawyer, *The Rifle in America*. A more factual account, without the far-fetched anecdote about the coincidence in names, is given in Roberts' authoritative *The Muzzle Loading Cap Lock Rifle*, which pictures some sniper weapons.

In contrast to the long-range shot which killed Branch, Brig. Gen. Martin E. Green, CSA, a Virginian, fell prey to a sniper close by. Green, commanding a unit in the defense of besieged Vicksburg, Mississippi, peered over the parapet to study the advance of a Federal sap or undercover trench being dug toward his defense lines. The Federals were only sixty yards away. One of the snipers sent out to cover the digging operation caught the Confederate general's braided kepi in his gunsights and fired. Green tumbled down from the parapet, a bullet through his head.

Under somewhat similar circumstances, Brig. Gen. George P. Doles, a 34-year-old Georgian, was "instantly killed by the bullet of a Federal sharpshooter" [5] while supervising the entrenching of his troops near Bethesda Church, Virginia, on June 2, 1864.

Another Confederate brigadier, Robert C. Tyler, a long-mustachioed career soldier who had filibustered in Nicaragua before the war and had risen from the Confederate ranks, met his end in Georgia nearly at the close of the war, April 16, 1865. The doughty fighter's name had been given to a small earthworks, Fort Tyler. Federals attacked Fort Tyler in overwhelming numbers. Recklessly directing the defense, General Tyler exposed himself too long to enemy snipers. One got him.

Tyler's death in Georgia at the close of the war had a tragic parallel in Virginia. There young Brig. Gen. John Pegram, older brother of the vaunted boy artilleryman of the Confederacy, Colonel Willie Pegram, turned to rally his men in battle at Hatcher's Run on March 28, 1865. As he did so, a Federal sharpshooter's bullet tore through the back of his head. His brother Willie was killed a few days later.

One of the most colorful Southern generals to fall to a sniper bullet was Ben McCulloch, a former Texas Ranger, Indian fighter, and pal of Davy Crockett. Bewhiskered Ben disdained to wear a regulation uniform. On the day of his death, as on most days, he rode attired head to foot in black velvet. The funereal costume proved peculiarly appropriate. McCulloch led his Texas fighters into the battle of Pea Ridge, Arkansas, largest pitched engagement west of the Mississippi in the entire war. A bullet from a marksman hidden in a thicket tore through his right breast and toppled him from his mount.

[5] Ezra Warner, *Generals in Gray*, Page 74.

Tradition has it that the fatal bullet was fired by none other than the famous frontiersman, Wild Bill Hickok, later a law officer and more recently a television mainstay. Hickok did indeed scout for the Federal army and he is said to have taken part in the battle of Pea Ridge. It is claimed that his sniping killed 32 Confederates. There is no reason to doubt that he did his share of slaying on that occasion. As a scout, he almost certainly would have fired from cover.

Probably the senior general to fall victim to sharpshooters was on the Union side. At the time of his death at the Battle of Spottsylvania, Maj. Gen. John Sedgwick, an old-line regular, commanded a Federal army corps. He apparently was slated for greater things, had he lived. Brig. Gen. John Gibbon, USA, tells of Sedgwick's last hours in his *Personal Recollections of The Civil War.*

"That afternoon being near Gen. Meade's Headquarters, I paid him a visit and was invited to remain and take dinner in company with Gen. Sedgwick. It was the last I ever saw of this honest-hearted, brave old soldier, for the next day whilst in his own line observing the enemy's, he was shot in the head and instantly killed, it was supposed by a sharpshooter, numbers of whom were very busy endeavoring to prevent any closer observation of their lines. His death was universally regretted in the Army where his character was held in very high esteem."

Not all of the casualties of sharpshooting, however, were officers of rank. Privates would do if no better targets presented themselves. Sharpshooters or snipers took a regular role and it often called upon them to fire on privates on the other side. One function, as General Gibbon indicated, was to prevent opposing officers from observing troop movements and dispositions. Another was to cover fortification digging and other exposed activities by one's own troops. Yet another took the form of counteroffensive—firing back at snipers on the other side to "keep their heads down" so they could not shoot. It was in this deadly game that privates swapped shots and lost lives. One of them, Pvt. George M. Kirkpatrick, 42nd Indiana Veteran Volunteer Infantry, left a vivid account of it after serving in Georgia.

"I was commissioned as a sharpshooter and on the 11th of August was sent out on our picket line, to keep down some [Confederate] sharpshooters a mile away on a hill. . . . It was terribly hot, 110 in the shade and no shade to be had. I went along the line of pickets to find a place of shelter to shoot from . . . and was in a rifle pit talking to a buddy. . . .

"A sharpshooter from the First Georgia Regiment came down as near as fifty yards. . . . When I got out of the rifle pit, he plugged me, aiming straight for the heart. It broke two ribs and shot nine holes in a silk handkerchief that was around my neck. He shot me with a Whitworth rifle. . . ."

Whether or not the wounded man's companions got a sufficient glimpse of the rifle to identify it, it could be recognized as a Whitworth by the distinctive bullet. Unlike the ponderous bench-rest sniper rifles, the Whitworths were no larger or heavier than many rifled muskets. Their barrels ran only 26 to 33 inches long as a rule. But their bores were rifled hexagonally and their bullets had a special shape to fit this rifling.

Both Whitworth rifles and Whitworth field pieces or light artillery were manufactured in Great Britain and run through the blockade into the South. The rifles were especially accurate and were prized accordingly. Unlike the mammoth American-made pieces, they could be carried around handily.

One account of their use has been left us by Maj. John Johnson, CSA, the engineer officer who was in charge of Fort Sumter for fifteen months during its terrific siege by Federal forces. The Federal cannoneers established heavy batteries on Morris Island, gradually edging on until they reached the end of the island nearest to Fort Sumter, a sand spit known as Cummings Point. At that stage, Confederate marksmen stationed on Sumter began picking off the bluecoat artillerymen. Johnson reports, in *The Defense of Charleston* (page 173) that:

". . . (Four) very fine Whitworth rifles with telescopic sights . . . obtained through the blockade . . . were found to be quite effective . . . although the range was fully 1,300 yards to Cummings Point."[6]

[6] Jac Weller, of Princeton, New Jersey, one of the leading researchers with antique and modern firearms, tested 27 shoulder arms used by the Confederacy and reported the results in *The American Rifleman*, magazine of the National Rifle Association. Weller, a conscientious and careful experimenter, ranked the Whitworth rifle first of all. He rated its accuracy at 1,000 yards as "first class plus" whereas the Sharps rifle, Model 1863, ranked "poor" at that distance and below the Whitworth at closer ranges. Weller and his fellow shooters fired at silhouette or torso-sized targets. At 100

The rifles, some of them fitted with telescopic sights extending nearly the length of their barrels, were credited with being accurate up to 1,800 and even 2,000 yards. They reputedly accounted for at least two Union generals—Maj. Gen. Sedgwick, killed at Spottsylvania, and poetic Brig. Gen. W. H. Lytle, of Ohio, who was fatally wounded by a sharpshooter while leading a charge at Chickamauga.[7]

Probably not more than 50 to 100 of the special sniper Whitworths were imported by the Confederacy. A dozen arrived early in 1863. Eagerly sought, they were rationed out two to an army corps, east and west. The Confederacy also doled out heavy-barrelled bench-rest rifles by such Georgia makers as J. P. Murray, of Columbus, and D. C. Hodgkins & Son, of Macon. The author owns a similar rifle, in fact, one larger and weightier than those attributed to either Murray or Hodgkins. This piece, marked in script on the left side of the barrel "N.D.L. * C.S.A. * 1862," and otherwise devoid of identification, weighs 26 pounds and appears to be almost identical to the heavy Southern sharpshooter rifle picked up at the Devil's Den at Gettysburg after the battle and now on display at the Gettysburg National Museum, Inc.

Like the Whitworths, the heavy-barrelled special rifles were not handed around casually nor were they the arms most used by sharpshooters. At least two Whitworths were in the hands of sharpshooters under Maj. Gen. John Gordon, however, in the grim, forlorn-hope Confederate attack on Fort Stedman, near Petersburg, in March of 1865. Their effective marksmanship is recounted in *Battles and Leaders*, Vol. IV, by a Union artilleryman whose battery suffered from it. George L. Kilmer, Company I, 14th New York Heavy Artillery, tells how the snipers riddled the gunners as they attempted to repel the Southern attack. A lieutenant attempting to sight the angle or end cannon lost an arm. The captain commanding the battery then sighted it himself. "He then left the piece with a corporal, the highest subordinate fit for duty, with instructions to continue working it on the elevation just set, while he himself went to prepare another gun for closer quarters," Kilmer re-

yards, he reported, "the fellow firing the Whitworth had nine shots in a group about the size of two hands in the lower chest. . . ."

[7] See *Confederate Arms*, by W. A. Albaugh, III, page 274, and *The Civil War Dictionary*, by M. M. Boatner, III, page 917.

lates. "The corporal leaped upon the gun-staging and was brained by a bullet before he could fire a shot. The Confederate column was preceded, as usual, by sharpshooters. . . ."

A classic use of sharpshooters to cover an attacking force by keeping down enemy fire is related in connection with the Federal assault on Fort Fisher, North Carolina, January 15, 1865. Sixty sharpshooters of the 13th Indiana armed with Spencer repeating rifles, and 40 men from Brig. Gen. N. M. Curtis's brigade, with shovels, rushed forward "and dug themselves in within 175 yards of the fort. When the sharpshooters had gone into action to cover the parapet Curtis moved his brigade . . . and took up a position 50 yards to their rear. . . . At 3:25 P.M. Curtis's brigade led the assault. . . ."[8]

Both sides employed special sharpshooter units as skirmishers or loosely strung advance lines. The Confederates' basic organization of such units appears to have been at battalion strength, while the Union organized its snipers into regiments in at least two instances.

By 1864, the Confederacy is known to have had at least ten battalions specially designated as sharpshooters, in addition to miscellaneous units of "riflemen" who may have served the same military purpose. Nearly every Southern division apparently had a battalion of sharpshooters attached to it. Some had several.

At the Battle of Cedar Creek, Virginia, Oct. 19, 1864, Lt. Gen. Jubal A. Early's army used at least two special units, the 30th Virginia Battalion of Sharpshooters and the 1st North Carolina Battalion of Sharpshooters. Earlier that year in Arkansas, the 9th Battalion of Missouri Sharpshooters figured in fighting by Brig. Gen. M. M. Parson's Missouri Division, CSA.

No fewer than seven sniper units are identified in the 1864 Atlanta campaign on the Confederate side. The 1st, 2nd and 4th Georgia Battalions, commanded respectively by Majors A. Schaaf, R. H. Whiteley and T. D. Caswell, all served in Maj. Gen. W. H. T. Walker's division. The 17th Alabama Battalion, Capt. J. F. Nabers, and the 9th Mississippi Battalion, Maj. W. C. Richards, were in Maj. Gen. T. C. Hindman's division; the 14th Louisiana Battalion, Maj. J. E. Austin, in A. P. Stewart's division, and the 1st Mississippi

[8] Lt. Col. Mark M. Boatner, III, in The Civil War Dictionary, Page 294.

Battalion, Maj. G. M. Stigler, in W. W. Loring's division.

The Union meanwhile organized at least two regiments totalling eighteen companies as sharpshooters. The Union riflemen continued a tradition as old as the U. S. Army. The first peacetime units, in 1792, were riflemen. Four regiments of riflemen were authorized late in the War of 1812. Others figured prominently in the Mexican War, including the 1st Mississippi Rifles led by a former West Pointer, Col. Jefferson Davis.

To head the sharpshooters of the Civil War, the Union selected Col. Hiram Berdan, a New York City mechanical engineer who had won almost every formal shooting match in the East for fifteen years. Berdan, an experimenter and inventor in the firearms field, became colonel of the 1st U. S. Sharpshooters. His opening battle was with the army commander-in-chief, old General Winfield Scott, and Brig. Gen. James W. Ripley, Chief of Ordnance. They wanted to issue the sharpshooters standard Springfield muzzleloaders. Berdan insisted upon Sharps breechloaders. He won his point after appealing personally to President Lincoln and presenting a spectacular demonstration of the Sharps before the President.[9]

Berdan's sharpshooters hailed from upstate New York, Michigan, New Hampshire, Vermont and Wisconsin—places where they still knew how to draw a steady bead. Their original uniforms, according to their historian, Capt. C. A. Stevens, were "a dark green coat and cap with black plume, light blue trousers (afterward exchanged for green ones) and leather leggins. . . . The appellation of 'Green Coats' was soon acquired. . . ." At the start of the Civil War Centennial, a New England unit of the North-South Skirmish Association was regularly wearing replicas of the Berdan green uniform, complete with black plumed caps. In appearance they resembled somewhat the Italian, Austrian and other European chasseurs or jagers—Alpine troops of World War I—whose uniforms also stemmed from the traditional "rifleman's green."

Applicants were rejected, according to the old *Harper's Weekly*, unless they could put ten consecutive shots within five inches of the bullseye at 200 yards. The same publication reported a spectacular demonstration of marksmanship which

---

[9] Details of the organization, arms and uniform of Berdan's Sharpshooters may be found in the *Journal of the Company of Military Collectors and Historians*, Washington, D.C., Vols. VI, No. 3, and XIII, No. 2.

Colonel Berdan himself gave before a crowd of spectators at Weehawken, New Jersey, August 7, 1861. Berdan was armed with a special target rifle of .48 calibre, weighing 32 pounds and having a 31-inch barrel, false muzzle, bullet starter and telescopic sight. The target was the figure of a man, nicknamed "Jeff Davis," at slightly more than 200 yards.[10]

Firing from rest, Berdan put nine consecutive shots through the head of "Jeff Davis." He and spectators sometimes called the shots, as "eye," "nose," and so on. On the tenth shot, for variation's sake, he put his bullet through the "heart." The account concluded: "In this manner, the Colonel proceeded to shoot at buttons on the coat, the left or right arm, or wherever directed by the spectators until the entire heart and chest region of the image was well riddled with bullet holes."

On first taking to the battlefield, however, Berdan's regiment carried regulation muzzleloader Springfields. Their colonel improved the sights and devised a special bullet to aid marksmanship. Then he began his campaign to obtain the Sharps breechloading rifle with President Lincoln's aid. These, of the model 1859, were issued during the Peninsula campaign in the spring of 1862. With them, Berdan's men effectively picked off Confederate gunners and silenced several batteries. Some of these Sharps rifles (including one in this author's collection) were equipped with double-set or hair triggers to aid accuracy. Otherwise they resembled regular military rifles.

Meanwhile, the 2nd U. S. Sharpshooters was organized from Maine, Minnesota, Michigan, Vermont, New Hampshire and Pennsylvania woodsmen, with only eight companies instead of ten. Like the First Regiment, it served in most major battles in the East. As long as the battles were fluid, with the opposing lines moving and changing, Berdan's Sharpshooters usually fought as skirmishers in a loose, thin rank

---

[10] If the range of "slightly more than 200 yards" reported by *Harper's Weekly* happened to be 220 yards, or 40 rods, it was and is a standard distance for target competition with heavy bench-rest rifles. Without minimizing Hiram Berdan's performance, it can be said that there are a number of men and women living today, members of the National Muzzle-Loading Rifle Association, who might have tied or beaten Berdan's performance that day. Mrs. Walter F. Grote, of Canton, Ohio, in a competition at 220 yards in July, 1940, put eight of ten shots in a two-inch wide bullseye with the other two touching it. She, and others equally accurate, could easily have qualified for Berdan's Sharpshooters.

ahead of the main body. In this role they suffered their heaviest casualties. The 1st had 546 out of 1,392 men killed or wounded, and the 2nd 462 out of 1,178, according to William F. Fox in *Regimental Losses in the Civil War*. Fox adds, "They undoubtedly killed more men than any other regiments in the Army. . . ."

Berdan's sharpshooters once intervened in a long-range duel between Confederate and Federal artillery and tipped the scales in favor of their side. It was in the Peninsula campaign in 1862. Four Federal batteries opened up on a strong Confederate earthworks mounting heavy naval guns from Norfolk. The Confederates replied with 32-pound roundshot and punished the bluecoat gunners severely.

At that point, a skirmish line of Berdan's men equipped with long-range rifles with telescopic sights crept forward to within half a mile of the Confederate position. There they dug rifle pits and began sniping. Whenever a Southern gunner showed himself in loading, a rifle cracked. Man after man went down.

For fully an hour, according to reports, the Confederates were unable to continue their cannonade. Then they brought up light artillery of their own to pick off the sharpshooters. One piece, described as a rifled gun of 1-inch bore, apparently was a Williams machine gun or rapid-fire gun.

Five of Berdan's men soon fell, killed or wounded. But the Federal artillery, during the interval allowed them by the sharpshooters' daring, silenced three Confederate guns.

Perhaps the most sensational individual achievement by Berdan's Sharpshooters and certainly the most costly to the Confederacy came late in the war and was crowned by irony. A Private John A. Huff, after winning a target medal for the highest accuracy while serving a two-year enlistment under Berdan, apparently decided he was too old to reenlist in a walking, foot-aching infantry outfit. So the 48-year-old Huff enlisted this time in the 5th Michigan Cavalry. He rode to battle in style until toppled from his saddle in the cavalry clash at Yellow Tavern, May 11, 1864. Looking up from the dust in the melee of horses, riders and gunsmoke, Huff spied a plumed Confederate general prancing by. For an instant, he was again Huff the sharpshooter. Lying on the ground on one elbow, he took careful aim with his pistol. His bullet sent the general reeling. Seventeen days later, Huff himself was mortally wounded in another cavalry engagement in Virginia. By then, the Confederate general whom he had shot was stark dead and much mourned—and Huff had learned his name, J. E. B. STUART.

9

What Is a Massacre?

Quantrill's guerrillas killed nearly every man and boy in Lawrence, Kansas. Forrest's cavalry shot down most of the Negroes in garrison at Fort Pillow. Both casualty lists made for Northern retaliation. But similar slaughters went almost unobserved. Who ever heard of the "Fort Gregg massacre" of Confederates?

The technique of surrender is delicate. It is also precarious. A soldier literally gambles his life on it. At one moment you are doing your hot-blooded damnedest to exterminate the faceless enemy before you. The tide of battle turns against your side. You realize it. In the next moment, the enemy has a face and you are begging that enemy to forgive and forget. You watch the face. Your comrades behind you may be still firing at him. His officer, with drawn pistol, may stand ready to shoot him from behind if he falters in his machinelike function of killing you. It is a moment for politeness, diplomacy and prayer.

Such moments come to soldiers in all wars. They came darkly to Americans in World War II at Malmédy, on Bataan and elsewhere. Others had come earlier at the Alamo, and still earlier, in the Revolution, at hamlets like Paoli, Pennsylvania, and Hancock's Bridge, New Jersey, where the bayonets kept thrusting despite pleas for quarter.

There were such dark episodes in the Civil War, too, when pleas and cries of surrender went unheeded. Several are well-known because they befell Federal troops and, to paraphrase "God is on the side of the greater battalions," history is on the side of the bigger printing presses. There are others, less well known, which happen to have victimized Southerners.

The wholesale killings of Federals in the confused process of surrender have gone down as massacres, which some were and some were not. The indiscriminate slaughters of Confederates are less clearly labeled. They have been glossed over where known at all.

Some of the most brutal episodes of the entire war barbarized the conflict in the Missouri-Kansas area. Formal hostilities signalled the resumption of what would now be termed a limited or local war between Missouri and Kansas. This had begun six years earlier over whether Kansas should be a slave or free state. Missourians insisted that the U. S. Constitution gave them the right to move into Kansas with their slaves. Kansas abolitionists resisted. New England abolitionists sent the latest in firearms. John Brown of Ossawatomie cut his fighting fangs in the resulting butcheries.

East of the Mississippi, the Civil War got off to a start as formal as a tea-party, with truce flags, amenities and politeness. West of it, the old antagonists whipped their revolvers and knives out of their boot tops and lunged into the first total warfare waged in the United States.

Missouri rapidly became more fought-over than any other state except Virginia and Tennessee. Eleven per cent of all the war's engagements, 1,162 by count, bloodied her soil. The state was caught in a peculiar conflict fought at two levels. The uniformed regular armies combated each other. Guerrillas, many of them non-military brigands, campaigned against the civilian population to further feuds and personal gain. Some of their deeds would have shamed vultures.

On both sides, volunteer militia and home-guard units tended to degenerate into banditry. The farther they got from home and the more the war inflamed them, the worse their acts became. Among them were some volunteer militia companies organized in Kansas under Federal authorization. These units were recruited from free-staters and abolitionist veterans of the prewar fighting. Some seized upon the war as an opportunity to pay off old grudges.

Kansas bands known as Jayhawkers or Kansas Freebooters raided and burned Missouri communities in pro-Southern areas. Soon irregular Confederate troops and pro-Southern bands retaliated. Some went further and, in the name of "self defense," indulged in the same brand of atrocities against Unionists.

Regular Federal forces, during interludes between battles with the Confederate armies, resorted to extreme measures to curb the guerrillas. After a Confederate raid on the town of Palmyra, Missouri, in September, 1862, an elderly Unionist named Andrew Allsman was carried off by the raiders. He never reappeared.

Col. W. R. Strachan, U. S. Army provost marshal for northeastern Missouri, a heavy-drinking firebrand, carried out a grim retaliation. Strachan persuaded Maj. Gen. John McNeil, commanding the district, to authorize him to select ten Confederate hostages from among military prisoners held at Palmyra and Hannibal and execute them unless Allsman was immediately returned.

There is doubt that the message warning of this retaliation ever reached the proper Confederate officers, but there is no doubt of what ensued. The ten prisoners, chosen at random, were taken to the nearby fair grounds on October 18, 1862, seated on their coffins, and shot by a Federal firing squad of 30 riflemen. The firing squad was so upset by the horrible unfairness of the deed that its volley killed only three prisoners outright. The others had to be shot repeatedly to end their agonies. When a relative claimed one body, Colonel Strachan is said to have replied: "Take the whole goddamned lot of them if you like. They're good for nothing but fertilizer now and poor stuff at that."[1]

The executions created a brief national flurry. Strachan was court-martialed for exceeding his authority and executing prisoners in violation of the Articles of War. He argued in his own defense that strong measures were necessary to halt the border raiders. Many pro-Union Missourians professed to endorse his stand. Sentenced to a year in prison, he never had to serve a day of it.

Soon the pendulum of public disgust and horror swung in the other direction.

For utter ruthlessness against the broad prairie background of burned homes and slain civilians, nothing surpasses two massacres committed by a flamboyant guerrilla band nominally serving the Confederacy. Their leader was William C. Quantrill, an Ohio-born former school teacher and abolitionist baiter with a reputation for cold-eyed sadism. Quantrill's "battalion," wearing distinctive long guerrilla shirts of brown homespun with colored trimmings, soon embarked on its own violent career of plunder and murder.

[1] For a full account, see *Quantrill and His Civil War Guerrillas*, by Carl W. Breihan (Sage Books, Denver, 1959), and other reports on the war in the West.

Less than a year after the executions which were supposed to check guerrilla warfare, Quantrill and his horsemen made a lengthy foray through Federal-held territory against Lawrence, Kansas, known as the "abolitionist capital" because anti-slavery forces founded it. Thundering down on the hapless town on August 21, 1863, the guerrillas struck by surprise.

The first onslaught enveloped two puny military objectives, recruiting centers or camps for the 14th Kansas Regiment and the 2nd Colored Regiment. Eighteen of the 20 young white recruits at the 14th Kansas camp were killed in quick order. Most of the score or so of Negroes at the other camp, some distance away, heard the firing in time to flee.

The guerrillas then turned upon the civilian population, many of them known as staunch Unionists. They slaughtered more than 150 men and boys in the streets, in yards and in doorways. Contrary to some reports, no women or small children were killed. But at least one husband was murdered in his wife's arms, while she sought to protect him. The killer is said to have fired his pistol past her head. After widespread looting, 185 buildings were burned.

Within four days, the Federal commander of the "Border District," Kansas and western Missouri, put a "scorched earth" policy into effect. Brig. Gen. Thomas Ewing, Jr., an Ohio-born Kansas lawyer, issued his sweeping Order No. 11 on August 25, 1863. It prescribed a calculated devastation unknown in the war until then. The entire civilian populations of pro-Southern Jackson, Bates and Cass counties, and part of Vernon county, all in western Missouri, were given 15 days to evacuate their homes and farms. Those who tarried were driven out at the bayonet point. Then every building in the area was burned to ashes to deprive raiders of shelter and sustenance. Inevitably, the mass depopulation was accompanied by pillage and murder. The despoiled area was long known as "The Burnt District."[2]

A wagon train passing through this wasteland in 1865

[2] R. S. Brownless, *Gray Ghosts of the Confederacy*, and other sources. The Missouri "Burnt District" should not be confused with the "Burnt District" of Rockingham County, Virginia. There, after Major J. R. Meigs was killed allegedly by bushwhackers, Gen. Philip Sheridan ordered every building within a five-mile radius burned. After the flames were kindled, it developed that Meigs was killed in a fair fight with bona fide Confederate soldiers. So the remaining buildings were spared.

paused. Like a ghost in the distance, a frightened small boy flitted away. Some of the party overtook him. He was grimy, almost naked, speechless with fear, and nearly starved. He had lost his home, parents, friends, contacts in the depopulation. Asked what he lived on, he mumbled, "Grasshoppers and bugs."

One unanticipated result of Order No. 11 was the damage it did to the postwar career of the man who signed it. General Ewing, a brilliant lawyer, was the son of the first U.S. Secretary of the Interior. He had moved with his bride from Ohio to Leavenworth, Kansas, before the war. There he became an anti-slavery leader, and was the first chief justice of the Kansas supreme court after that territory was admitted as a state.

Ewing's arbitrary disregard of the constitutional rights of civilians in his military district led George Caleb Bingham, a famous artist, to paint his powerful "Order No. 11" portraying the ravages of forcible evacuation, plundering, burning and killing. Bingham, a strong Unionist who was state treasurer of Missouri at the time, witnessed the carrying-out of Ewing's order.

"I can affirm from painful personal observation that the sufferings of the unfortunate victims were such as should have elicited sympathy even from hearts of stone," he wrote later.[3] "Barefooted and bareheaded women and children, stripped of every article of clothing except a scant covering for their bodies, were exposed to the heat of an August sun and struggling through the dust on foot. [Nearly] all their means of transportation had been seized by their spoilers. . . .

"It is well known that men were shot down in the very act of obeying the order, and their wagons and effects seized by their murderers. . . . Dense columns of smoke arising in every direction marked the conflagrations of dwellings. Many of the ruins can be seen yet, the chimneys standing scarred and blackened, the monuments of a ruthless military despotism which spared neither age, sex, character nor condition. No aid or protection was afforded to the banished inhabitants by the heartless authority which expelled them from their homes and their rightful possessions."

After the war, Ewing lived for five years in Washington, D.C. Then and later, his friends claimed that he had issued

---

[3] The *Republican*, Jefferson City, Missouri, February 22, 1877, quoted by Carl Breihan, 1959.

Order No. 11 upon instructions from the War Department via his commanding general at St. Louis, Maj. Gen. J. M. Schofield. Schofield disclaimed responsibility and indicated that Ewing originated the order. He did, however, uphold Ewing's decision as "an act of dispassionate wisdom and humanity" to check guerrilla raids by laying waste the countryside.

Ewing returned to his native Ohio in 1870 and ran for Governor on the Democratic ticket in 1879. Bingham, who was just completing a term as Adjutant General of the state of Missouri, where he lived most of his life, stumped Ohio against Ewing with his painting "Order No. 11" as an exhibit. Although Ewing campaigned vigorously, he was defeated in no small measure by Bingham's tactics and two years later quit Ohio for New York City.

The devastation of the "Burnt District," far from halting Quantrill, simply led him to shift his operations into Kansas. Six weeks after the Lawrence raid, he found an opportunity to further his vengeance in a way which particularly appealed to him. The Confederate Government had flatly refused to commission him a colonel or lend further countenance to his roughshod campaigns. So he whipped a Federal general who had been instrumental in beating two Confederate generals. To Quantrill it showed the world that, colonel or not, he was a leader to be reckoned with.

The victim of Quantrill's attack this time was Maj. Gen. James G. Blunt, a fiery abolitionist from Maine who had settled in Kansas before the war. For his role in previous Federal successes, Blunt had been promoted and given a new assignment. Apparently bent on impressing the world with his military importance and prowess, he set out across the prairie to his new post with fanfare. He recruited a band of musicians, formed a military entourage, and rode in a buggy with the lovely young wife of a military contractor at the post at his side.

Near Baxter Springs, Kansas, stood a log-and-earth Federal fort. Blunt approached it just as Quantrill prepared to raid it. The Federal general apparently mistook the raiders for a guard of honor coming out from the fort to greet him. While Quantrill quickly formed his men in two ranks, one along the road and the other out of sight in the woods to the rear, Blunt and his fancy procession rode right into the trap. His band played and his brand new flag blew crisply in the breeze.

But his men sensed that something was wrong. Within 200 yards of Quantrill, ten of his troops broke and fled. Quantrill roared "Charge!" Thirty out of 40 men in the foremost Federal company were shot down, most of them dead. Blunt and his lady traveling companion hastily mounted saddle horses, the lady astride without pausing to adjust her attire in the absence of a genteel side-saddle. Both galloped safely away.

Quantrill, bent on proving that he could whip General Blunt even though two Confederate generals couldn't, kept his men after the Federals in a bloody running fight across the prairie. A Federal teamster, recognizing one guerrilla as an old friend, is said to have surrendered and handed over his pistol—only to be fatally shot by his ex-friend. A Negro with the Federal force saw his former master in the Quantrill ranks and ran forward joyfully to greet him—but was met with a bullet through the heart. A woman and child among the civilians attached to the Federal force were shot down with male relatives. Another victim was "Pony Johnny" Fry, noted Pony Express rider.

Before the slaughter ceased, 80 of the Federal party lay dead and a score more were wounded. Among these were a number of civilians. Quantrill reported losing three men killed and three wounded, either in the bloody pursuit in the open or in attacking the little log fort in another phase of the engagement.

Was it a battle or a massacre? Actually, it was both. Like the attack on Lawrence, which began at the Army recruiting camps, it started with a semblance of a military objective. Then it turned into a merciless mass murder. Certainly at the outset, with both sides lined up in the open 200 yards apart, it was almost as formal as a set combat in the days of knighthood. Just as certainly at the end, with civilians who yielded their arms being shot down, it was a massacre.

Undoubtedly the "Fort Pillow massacre" was the most widely known episode of its kind in the war. Because it made splendid Union propaganda in 1864 and makes sensational reading even now, it has been re-examined in current times. Some of the conclusions have smacked anew of smear-the-South campaigning. The undisputed facts are these:

Fort Pillow, originally a Confederate earthworks, stood on a bluff overlooking the Mississippi River some 80 miles north of Memphis, Tennessee. It fell to the Federals in 1862. The

Confederates recaptured it on April 12, 1864. Its garrison at the time of the Confederate attack consisted of 262 Negro troops of the 6th U.S. Heavy Artillery and 295 of the 13th Tennessee Cavalry, USA, composed of white Unionists from East Tennessee. The fort mounted six cannon. Further artillery support was provided by the Federal gunboat *New Era*, Capt. James Marshall, stationed nearby in the river.

Forrest invested the fort with 1,500 hard-riding troopers under the immediate command of Brig. Gen. J. R. Chalmers. They dismounted and opened a hot musketry fire about 5:30 A.M. The firing continued until late afternoon. Sharpshooters on both sides proved deadly. A Southerner soon killed Maj. L. F. Booth, veteran commander of the fort, and his adjutant was shot down shortly afterward. When Forrest galloped up to direct the attack in person, having ridden 65 miles in a day, Federal riflemen nearly hit him repeatedly. A bullet killed his mount. He took a second horse. It fell shot. His third horse that day also was hit. He himself suffered severe bruises as the animals toppled over.

The Federal gunboat, darting busily back and forth in the river, meanwhile shelled both Confederate flanks near the water's edge with 282 rounds. Early in the afternoon, the gunboat withdrew a short distance to cool and clean its guns. A brief truce was established. It ended abruptly when the Confederates spied two Federal steamers approaching laden with troops, as if to reinforce the fort.

The final Confederate onslaught drove the garrison back toward or into the river. Afterward, 229 Negroes and 131 whites were listed as killed or missing.

At that point, the stories diverge. The Northern ones almost without exception recount unspeakable atrocities: hatred unleashed against anti-Confederate Southerners and former slaves with arms in their hands; crawling wounded shot dead on the ground; tents containing wounded burned down, and, in several reports, Negroes nailed to logs and set afire. The Southern versions tell of wild Federal confusion, of failure to surrender and persistence in firing, of Federal gunboats rushing to support the garrison and continue the fight, of provocation by disorganized resistance.

One of the latest and most temperate Northern recitations [4]

---

[4] See "The Fort Pillow Massacre: A Fresh Examination of the Evidence," by Dr. Albert Castel, U.C.L.A. history professor, in *Civil War History*, published quarterly by the State University of Iowa,

reaches the conclusions that there was no widespread, organized slaughter of the surrendered; that the only burned bodies were those of men killed earlier and seared by accidental fire; but that the Confederates slaughtered a large number of more or less helpless Federals in a battle fury spurred by racial animosity.

Two Confederate generals stated the case for the South immediately after the battle. Forrest, on April 26, attributed the extremely high Federal casualties to the fact that two Confederate detachments worked around to the rear of the retreating Federals and caught them in a murderous crossfire at only 30 to 100 yards. "As it was, many rushed into the river and were drowned. . . ." He reported capturing 164 Tennessee bluecoats and 73 Negro troops, including 14 wounded Negroes who were delivered to a U.S. gunboat the next day.

Lt. Gen. Stephen D. Lee, CSA, commanding that department, replied to an inquiry of the Federal district commander that "our officers, with all the circumstances against them, endeavored to prevent the effusion of blood," but found it difficult because "your colors were never lowered, and your garrison never surrendered, but retreated under cover of a gunboat with arms in their hands and constantly using them. This was true particularly of your colored troops, who had been firmly convinced by your teachings of the certainty of slaughter in case of capture. Even under these circumstances, many of your men, white and black, were taken prisoners. I respectfully refer you to history for numerous cases of indiscriminate slaughter after successful assault, even under less aggravated circumstances."[5]

Reading between the lines, Lee virtually admitted that a great many men got shot down in short order amid confusion. The final assault took only 20 to 30 minutes.

March, 1958, pages 37-50. While this author cannot agree with some of Dr. Castel's deductions, pro and con, he bows in respect at the objective and dispassionate presentation.

For an all-out exposition of the most sickening details reported, see "The Fort Pillow Massacre," by Dr. Lorenzo J. Greene, of Lincoln University, Jefferson City, Missouri, in *Battles of the Civil War*, a *Pictorial Presentation*, 1961, Pioneer Press, Little Rock, Arkansas. Its intensity rivals much in the Northern press in 1864.

[5] See *Battles and Leaders of the Civil War*, Vol. IV, page 418, for Lee's letter of June 28, 1864.

In considerable measure, the Fort Pillow massacre may be blamed on the demon rum. Both attackers and survivors told of barrels of whisky standing open inside the fort with dippers handy for anyone who wanted to renew his "courage." Confederate officers, once inside, knocked over several barrels. But many of the garrison and some attackers undoubtedly battled on under the influence of liquor.

The evidence that it took drunkenness, as well as racial and sectional animosities, to whip up the blood fury is borne out by circumstances six months later. Forrest's forces took two Federal strong points with garrisons identical to that of Fort Pillow—West Tennessee Unionists and Negroes. In neither case was there any report of widespread liquor drinking or of butchery.

When Forrest bluffed 125 Tennessee cavalry and 450 Negro troops into surrendering the Union's strongest defensive position on the Nashville and Decatur Railroad, near Decatur, Georgia, not one of the surrendering soldiers was harmed. A day later at Sulphur Branch, the Federal commanders of a fort and two blockhouses manned by 1,000 bluecoats, including 400 Tennessee cavalrymen and 400 Negroes, rejected Forrest's demand for surrender. His artillery shelled the stronghold until Federal corpses littered it. Then he checked his guns and renewed his surrender offer. It was accepted, and not another shot was fired.

At Fort Pillow, by contrast, there is much evidence that the defenders were prepared psychologically as well as alcoholically to make a last-man stand. The fort's commander, Major Booth, assured his commanding general that he could hold out "at least 48 hours" until aid arrived. Booth even worked out a plan which would enable Federal reinforcements to land and counterattack the fort if he lost it. He arranged special signals with Captain Marshall of the New Era by which the gunboat could be beckoned close to the bluff. There it could support with its naval guns a beachhead stand by the garrison from the fort. Captain Marshall testified later[6] that "we had

---

[6] Report No. 65, 38th Congress, 1st Session, House Committee on the Conduct of the War, Washington, 1864, "The Fort Pillow Massacre." (A Congressional investigating committee of pro-war Republicans heard, chronicled and printed every word of damning testimony that they could rake up from survivors. Some 40,000 copies of their report were circulated before the 1864 election for political effect.)

agreed on a signal that if he had to leave the fort, they would drop down under the bank and I was to give the rebels canister."

Except for the canister, that is approximately what happened. The circumstances fit perfectly with the fact that the Federals, retreating from the fort proper, failed to haul down their flag in an admission of surrender. According to plan, they weren't surrendering. They were simply withdrawing to be reinforced for a comeback. When the Confederates finally swept over the inner parapets with 1,200 muskets belching volleys, most of the garrison drew back to the river bank. Booth's successor in command, Major Bradford, signalled to the gunboat to move inshore and open fire.[7] But the Navy took no chances of being trapped and sunk by the fort's cannon in Confederate hands. Being short of ammunition anyhow, the gunboat steamed away. Desperation and panic appear to have swept the Federal ranks ashore. Just then, the two Confederate flanking detachments mentioned by Forrest approached along the river bank and raked the disordered Union ranks from both sides at short range.

In a somewhat reversed situation, the Federal Army refused to give up the ship after the Federal Navy had hoisted a white flag. The unexpected resumption of firing on that occasion led the Confederates to renew their shooting. Federal casualties aboard ship mounted above 30 per cent. Was it a "massacre"? Hardly, and nobody called it such.

That engagement pitted the ironclad CSS *Virginia*, ex-USS *Merrimack*, against the old wooden-hulled USS *Congress* off Newport News, Virginia, in 1862 the day before the *Monitor* arrived for the immortal clash of ironclads. The *Congress* soon caught fire. Her crew ran the blazing ship aground and hoisted a white flag about 4 P.M. The *Virginia's* ten big guns ceased firing. Her captain, Commodore Franklin Buchanan, sent a tug to the *Congress*. The tug crew received the surrender and sword of the acting captain of the *Congress* and other officers. Just then a blast of rifle and artillery fire from the shore toppled Confederates on the tug. Another Minié bullet from a Federal rifle tore into the thigh of Commodore Buchanan aboard the *Virginia*, seriously wounding him. What had happened?

"I ordered Brown of the 20th Indiana Regiment to send two rifle companies to the beach," Brig. Gen. Joseph Mans-

---

[7] The same.

field, USA, reported later, adding that the Confederate approach was "beaten off with loss."[8] Mansfield also stated: "The *Congress* surrendered but aground at Signal Point. . . . We had driven off from her the gunboats."

Reports of both Federal and Confederate Navies concur that the Federal Army continued fighting over the *Congress* after the Navy had given up the ship. Lt. Arthur Pendergrast, USN, executive officer of the *Congress*, said that when the Confederate tug came alongside, "a sharp fire with muskets and artillery was maintained from the troops ashore upon the tug, having the effect of driving her off. The *Merrimack* again opened on us, although we had a white flag at the peak. . . ." From the *Virginia* or *Merrimack*, the shooting appeared to come from the *Congress*, to judge by the report of Lt. Catesby ap Roger Jones, who took command when Buchanan fell wounded. "We drove the *Congress* ashore, where she hauled down her colors and hoisted the white flag," Jones said, "but she fired upon us with the white flag flying, wounding Lieutenant Minor and some of our men. We again opened fire upon her and she is now in flames."

The situation at Newport News, and at Fort Pillow two years later, raises a fine technical question of whether a branch of the service which yields a ship or fort surrenders it outright for the nation it represents or only insofar as its own branch of the service goes. There was no sharp aftermath of the naval battle, but the gory reports from Fort Pillow inflamed the North and made strong wartime propaganda. Pvt. Robert Hale Strong, of the 105th Illinois Volunteer Infantry, vividly describes one tragic consequence of it.[9] In storming a Confederate earthworks near Atlanta about a month after Fort Pillow fell, Strong's regiment captured a red-haired Southern artilleryman with "Fort Pillow" tattooed across one arm— or so it read in the heat of battle. Although the artilleryman pleaded for mercy, Strong relates that "as soon as the boys saw the letters on his arm, they yelled 'No quarter for you!' and a dozen bayonets went into him and a dozen bullets were shot into him."

[8] For this episode, see *Official Records of the War of the Rebellion*, Naval, Series I, Vol. 7, which contains numerous reports and detailed information.

[9] See *A Yankee Private's Civil War*, by R. H. Strong, edited by Ashley Halsey, Jr., Henry Regnery Co., Chicago.

Several sobering facts make this tale especially painful in retrospect. The Confederate units which stormed Fort Pillow consisted principally of McCulloch's and Bell's brigades of cavalry and they were not present at the later engagement near Atlanta. Furthermore, the red-haired victim of vengeance was not a cavalryman or horse artilleryman like the captors of Fort Pillow. He was a garrison gunner, such as manned Fort Pillow during the inactive period when the Confederates first held it. Therefore it seems fair to ask:

Did the slain gunner pause during a month of fighting—between the Fort Pillow massacre and his own individual massacre—to be tattooed with a bloody boast? Or, as appears much more likely, was he one of the original garrison who had the tattooing done during the spare time and *ennui* of garrison duty? Did "Fort Pillow" on his arm have no more significance, when put there, than a post office address? Whatever the case, "A dozen bayonets went into him and a dozen bullets were shot into him."

Another Federal soldier's war diary published in 1961 reveals a similar incident on a greater scale, instigated by the Fort Pillow reports. Pvt. John F. Brobst, of the 25th Wisconsin Volunteer Infantry, stated darkly in a letter written in 1864 that "we take no prisoners" in the absence of officers to check the slaughter.[10] After the Fort Pillow capture, Brobst related, Federal troops shot and killed 23 Confederates who attempted to surrender in a body.

Heavy casualties among Negro troops occurred elsewhere than at Fort Pillow. An instance verging on "massacre" proportions—in terms of casualties only—was reported by Maj. Gen. J. R. Hawley, USV, at the Battle of Olustee, Florida, in February, 1864. There the 7th New Hampshire, a white regiment, and the 8th U.S. Colored Troops were sent around to strike the left flank of the Confederate line. The New Hampshire infantry encountered a heavy fire at 250 yards, their colonel apparently misunderstood an order, and they broke and fell back, losing 209 men. The 8th then received the brunt of the Confederate fire. They refused to run, General Hawley said, although they were green troops who scarcely knew how to fire a musket. Before retreating, more than 300

---

[10] See *Well, Mary: Civil War Letters of a Wisconsin Soldier*, the University of Wisconsin Press, Madison, Wisconsin.

out of 550 were killed or wounded. Two other Negro regiments also lost heavily in the Confederate victory.

Negro infantrymen serving as shock troops in the assault on Fort Wagner, South Carolina, and in the Battle of the Crater took heavy punishment of a sort which might have shaken or broken any units. High casualties did not in themselves spell a massacre. Just as often, they bespoke unyielding bravery.

In two isolated instances in the closing weeks of the war, the ruthlessness and casualties might compare with Fort Pillow.

One clash, the very last of the conflict, arose when a superior Federal force set about capturing Confederates garrisoning Palmito Ranch, on the Rio Grande below Brownsville, Texas. The Confederates met the attacking bluecoat infantry and cavalry with artillery and horsemen. Of 111 Federal troops killed in a running fight, many drowned in the Rio Grande. Yet no one cried "massacre"—the war was over.

Nobody cried "massacre," either, in the capture of Fort Gregg, an earthworks defending Petersburg, only a few days before Appomattox. History, in fact, scarcely records the incident. What it does tell is a story of heroic, obstinate resistance against 10-to-1 odds that undoubtedly infuriated the Federal attackers. The text of *The West Point Atlas of American Wars*, Vol. I, Map 142, relates:

"The main Federal attack swept ahead, up to the line of Confederate earthworks protecting the western face of Petersburg. Two detached forts—Whitworth and Gregg—checked the advance here. Both were stormed, but it was now too late . . . a pause to regroup was necessary. Furthermore, the gallant stand of the garrisons of these two forts had given Longstreet time to bring troops south across the James River to reinforce the Petersburg defenses."

Infantrymen, mostly of the 12th and 16th Mississippi, under Lt. Col. J. H. Duncan, held Fort Gregg. The entire garrison numbered about 300. The Federals attacked the fort with three strong columns, each 1,000 or more. The Confederates fired until the trench in front of the fort was filled with blue forms. The Federal loss is given officially as 674 killed and wounded, more than double the strength of the defenders. The Confederate casualties are put at 55 or 57 killed, 129 wounded, more than 100 captured.

Brig. Gen. Horace Porter, USA, describes a bloody hand-to-hand combat which raged for half an hour after the at-

TECHNIQUE OF LOADING

Two men in front of the muzzle are "ramming home" a projectile. The man at right has his thumb or index finger over the vent, or touch-hole, at rear of cannon. This was to keep the process from fanning any lingering spark inside the cannon, for, if that happened, the cannon discharged prematurely and killed the gunners around the muzzle. Man just to left of the two

A HEAVY SIEGE GUN

rammer men holds a powder scoop. Before projectile was put into cannon, he shoved powder down the cannon barrel into chamber inside scoop, then turned it over to dump powder into chamber for firing. Other gunners, including the man at left with handspike or heavy pole, elevate and traverse gun to correct range.

tackers succeeded in swarming over the parapet into the fort. He makes no mention of Federal troops refusing to give quarter to surrendering Confederates. This account was widely published and generally accepted.[11]

Yet a Confederate survivor left a revealing story.[12] When the Federals rushed over the parapet, he said, "the cry was to kill, and but for their officers, who with cocked pistols made the men desist, all of us would have been murdered. . . . *We lost about 40 men killed in the fort after it was captured.* . . . It was ten minutes before the shooting could be suppressed."

If this account of the unknown "Fort Gregg massacre" surprises anyone, let them consider the case of a Confederate general who surrendered in good faith. Brig. Gen. Thomas Benton Smith, then 26, put up a stiff fight with his brigade at the Battle of Nashville in 1864.[13] Captured and disarmed, he was being led to the rear when a Federal colonel whose regiment his troops had mauled rode up angrily. The colonel beat the captive "over the head" with a saber so badly that the blows exposed his brain and nearly killed him.

[11] *Battles and Leaders*, Vol. IV, page 717.

[12] Account of Capt. A. K. Jones, 12th Mississippi Infantry Regiment.

[13] Publication of the District of Columbia Civil War Round Table, November, 1952, and Ezra Warner, *Generals in Gray*.

10

Whose Prison Camps Were Worse?

Despite the anti-Southern propaganda that has focused on Andersonville for nearly a century, Northern prisons were no less deadly. They reflected all the brutality, hunger, cold and oppression of the worst in the South. And then there was the Yankee hellship cruise. . . .

One summer day at the height of the war, a highly observant and humane physician visited an overcrowded prison camp where men daily died like flies. Returning, he lamented:

"Twenty deaths a day of dysentery and the living have more life on them than in them! Thus a Christian (!) nation treats the captives of its sword."

The prison was not Andersonville, in the bare woods of Georgia, but Fort Delaware, on Pea Patch Island in the Delaware River below thriving Philadelphia and Wilmington. Its victims were not Federal but Confederate.

Long before Andersonville was established, the deadly war jail in the Delaware ran up a monthly death rate which is said to have exceeded that of Andersonville at its peak. Its military reputation as a hellhole went back in official records some 35 years, yet the Federal Government confined Confederates there from the summer of 1862 into the summer of 1865. And horrified Delaware citizens who sought to relieve the suffering were at one point jailed by a Federal provost marshal.

Dr. S. Weir Mitchell, of Philadelphia, a well-known author, reported of his visit to the place on July 26, 1863, that it was "an inferno of detained rebels—a thousand ill, 12,000 on an island which should hold four."

The Federal Army medical director for the district, Dr. G. R. Suckley, voiced a similar feeling: "I think mere humanity should cause us to select a more healthy place for prisoners of war."

Robert Ould, the Confederate commissioner in charge of

the exchanges of prisoners conducted during the first part of the war, protested that soldiers redeemed from Fort Delaware emerged as "living wrecks" although they entered it "hale and robust . . . inured to almost every kind of hardship and proof against everything except the regimen of that horrible prison."

When an exchange of prisoners was delayed, Ould amplified his protest. "They have been promised to us time and again, and yet are drinking the poisonous water that has sent so many of their fellows to the grave. In the name of that common humanity to which we all, though enemies, belong, I beseech you to use every power of influence you have to change the place of confinement of our soldiers."

To which the Confederate Government added a letter addressed directly to President Lincoln and sent under flag of truce, imploring: "Can nothing be done to stop the fearful mortality of Fort Delaware? Is it intended to fill our land with mourning by such means of subjugation?"

As the letter could not be totally ignored, Secretary of War Edwin M. Stanton requested an explanation of the brigadier general in charge of the fortress prison. Back came a point-blank denial of all charges and criticism.

Yet the records of Stanton's own War Department bore witness to the deadly effect of Fort Delaware even on free and well-nourished human beings. As far back as the summer of 1826, Maj. A. C. W. Fanning, commanding the then-incomplete brick pentagon fortress, wrote a protest that it was "one of, if not the most, sickly station in the whole nation." He said the July and August heat made it murder to keep troops stationed there. The Adjutant General in response authorized Fanning to take his troops down-river almost to Cape May, New Jersey, a summer resort, "for the duration of the sickly season."

The imprisoned Confederates, of course, got no such consideration. Crowded mostly into wooden barracks north of the fort under the muzzles of some of its 131 heavy cannon, they slept in three tiers on rough planks, tormented by mosquitoes and intense heat in summer and nearly frozen in winter. Although their rationed drinking water was supposed to be hauled from above Philadelphia by waterboats, they often had to dip and drink river water polluted by the cities upstream.

In a single month alone, the mortality from cholera alone

ran as high as 331. Other illnesses and occasional shootings by guards swelled the total. The island proved too marshy to bury the dead; indeed, if they could have been interred there it might scarcely have left room for the living. So the Delaware that George Washington of Virginia once crossed on a mission of freedom became the River Styx for 2,436 dead Confederates. Their bodies were ferried across and buried at Finn's Point, New Jersey.

By October, 1863, with hundreds of soldiers captured three months earlier at Gettysburg already dying, the monthly toll at Fort Delaware is said to have reached 12.5 per cent of all those confined there. This rate is stated to be about 3 per cent higher than the worst month at Andersonville, although the statement is disputed.[1]

By the following fall, the only change in prisoner status took the form of a reduction of the already meager rations on order of Secretary Stanton to retaliate for the scant rations served Federal prisoners at Andersonville. The order came after the commandant of the prison himself pleaded in vain for fresh vegetables for his prisoners. Heeding his plea, Delaware citizens obtained permission to hold a benefit picnic to provide food. But the provost marshal broke it up with 60 soldiers of the 114th Ohio Regiment; two young men who argued with him were jailed for more than a week in Fort McHenry.

In general, the deadliest place to be in the Civil War was in a prison camp on either side. By one authoritative estimate, 204,070 Federal and Confederate soldiers died or suffered mortal wounds in battle. More than 50,000 lost their lives in prison camps. If one accepts these figures and takes into consideration the far larger forces involved in combat, the

[1] For a comprehensive recent account of "Fort Delaware—Northern Andersonville," see *The Civil War Times*, November, 1960. In it, W. Emerson Wilson, a Wilmington journalist and historian who had forebears in both armies, sums up the deadly effect of the island prison. Wilson was highly instrumental in the preservation of Fort Delaware as part of the Delaware State Park system. Names of the 2,436 Confederates who died there were listed by unit and state in 1960 in a 47-page publication of the Civil War Round Table of Wilmington entitled, "To Those Who Wore the Gray."

death rate in battle runs below 6 per cent while that in prison goes above 10 per cent.[2]

One of the highest monthly death rates of any prison camp may have been reached in February, 1863, at Camp Douglas, a swampy drill ground outside Chicago. Of 3,884 Confederate prisoners held there in the muck, ice and misery, 387 or 10 per cent died in the one month. Official records reveal no higher rate. U.S. Sanitary Commission officials urged that the camp be abandoned. Instead, more prisoners were sent to it.

Of all the ghastly confinement places on both sides, there can be no doubt that Andersonville grasps the public imagination as the most awesomely horrible. Yet it was only a larger statistic in the general nightmare of abuse. It had no vicious feature that was not duplicated in Northern prison camps holding Confederates. Food was scarce, water almost undrinkable, overcrowding unendurable, shelter inadequate or lacking, disease rampant, and guards at times brutish in most of them, North and South.

Andersonville, the bigger statistic, killed in misery more than 13,000 Federal privates and noncoms, over three times the Union combat toll at Gettysburg. But Camp Chase, near Columbus, Ohio, took twice as many Confederate lives as the Battle of Shiloh; the vast PW jail at Point Lookout, Virginia, killed double the number that fell to Union arms at Chancellorsville; and Camp Douglas, near Chicago, counted nearly twice as many Confederate victims as died on the bloody field of Antietam.

The great crime of it all then was that prisoner-of-war deaths on both sides were often avoidable and sometimes unforgivable. The pity of it since is the manner in which the blame and brunt has been foisted upon the South and used for a century to shame Southerners with the implication that they, alone, are brutes.

Andersonville has become a word of indictment of the South, a brand to burn into the back of a whole section. The war was no sooner over than it became a political issue; "waving the bloody shirt" meant echoes of Andersonville, and

[2] We are speaking here of well men, fit for combat. According to one source, the Federal hospital death rate ran above 14 per cent but it inevitably included far-gone men whose deaths could be expected.

in the halls of Congress it stirred acrid debate. In the 1960s it became the subject of a prize-winning book and play entitled, of course, *Andersonville*.

As recently as 1961 the play was produced in Germany with a preliminary which compared the Confederate prison with Dachau or Belsen and by inference likened Southerners to Nazis.[3] A national magazine, in a bellicose criticism of the South and the Civil War centennial observances, actually used the phrase, "*concentration* camps were established. . . ."

From all the indictments and damnations, past to present, a stranger to the United States might conclude that the South was viciously addicted to mass murder and that Northern prison camps were health resorts.

Actually, the proportion of Confederate prisoners who starved and froze and sickened to death in Northern detention camps in the midst of plenty runs higher than that of the Federals who died imprisoned in the hungry, war-scarred South. The North even had its prison hellship, with the half-starved and thirsting victims crowded and sweated below decks.

The official records themselves are so much a confirmation of the Federal Government's abuse of Southern captives that Northern historians have gone through contortions to this day to give a different picture.

On July 19, 1866, Secretary of War Edwin Stanton made public an official count and made a great political mistake. Stanton reported that:

Of 270,000 Union soldiers captured by the Confederacy, 22,576 died in prison.

Of 220,000 Confederates captured by the Union, 26,436 died in prison.

On that basis, the Southern death toll came to 9.3 per cent compared with 8 per cent for the Northern, and Captain Henry Wirz, of Andersonville notoriety, should have been pardoned, presumably, rather than hanged.

Stanton's report was made after the war when there should

---

[3] Special Berlin dispatch to the *New York Times*, November 24, 1960, quoted by J. B. Blackford and others. Judge William M. Beard, a past commander-in-chief of the Sons of Confederate Veterans, formally protested network plans to broadcast *The Andersonville Trial*. Beard asserted, "The two men primarily responsible for Andersonville were Abraham Lincoln and Ulysses S. Grant," because they declined to exchange prisoners.

have been time to substantiate the facts. Yet it was not allowed to stand. Its implications were intolerable to a Government intent on fixing most or all of the blame on the
South.

In 1885, the Adjutant General of the United States issued a report revising the total of Federal deaths upward
to 24,866.

In 1908, a subsequent Adjutant General added and re-
calculated and discovered that the total came to 33,218.

Thus the public was asked to believe that only two-thirds
of those who died in prison camps were counted among the
known dead one year after the war, and that nearly 11,000
others were verified as deceased twenty or more years later.

By some remarkable form of statistical resurrection, the
Government meanwhile computed the total of Confederates
who died in Northern camps at a *lower* figure than ever
before. This may explain why contemporary Northern writers refer to only 1,200 Confederates dying in the Point Lookout stockade while one Southern author reports counting
3,384 names on the memorial to the Confederate dead there.[4]
Or why the Northern figure for deaths at Elmira, New York,
in a usually healthy and well-fed sector, is given as 775 while
the Southern count of Confederate dead there is 3,020.

The Elmira death count occasioned fiery debate in the
Congress of the United States in 1876 between Representative Hill, of Georgia, a former Confederate Senator, and
Representative Platt, of New York, in whose district the
prison lay. Hill read from the report of a Federal prison surgeon, as published in The New York World, assertions that
Confederate prisoners at Elmira were forced to drink polluted water, were starved amidst plenty, and were at times
inadvertently infected with syphilis in administering smallpox inoculations. Hill quoted the surgeon:

"The winter of 1864-65 was an unusually severe and rigid
one, and the prisoners arriving from the Southern States during this season were mostly old men and lads, clothed in
attire suitable only to the genial climate of the South. . . .
This alone was cause for an unusual mortality among
them. . . ."

Then there was confinement in tents amid the snows, in

---

[4] Lt. Col. Willard Jones, AUS (Ret.), of Silver Spring, Maryland,
and others.

"narrow, confined limits but a few acres in extent, and through which slowly flowed a turbid stream of water, carrying along with it all the excremental filth and debris of the camp; this stream, horrible to relate, was the only source of supply, for an extended period, that the prisoners could possibly use for the purpose of ablution and to slacken their thirst from day to day.

"The tents and other shelter allotted to the camp at Elmira were insufficient and crowded to the utmost extent; hence smallpox and skin diseases raged through the camp. . . . Owing to a general order from the Government to vaccinate the prisoners, my opportunities were ample to observe the effects of spurious and diseased matter, and there is no doubt in my mind that syphilis was ingrafted in many instances; ugly and horrible ulcers and eruptions of a characteristic nature were, alas! too frequent and obvious to be mistaken. Smallpox cases were crowded . . . so adjacent that the simple movement of one would cause his neighbor to cry out in an agony of pain. The confluent and malignant type prevailed to such an extent and of such a nature that the body would frequently be found one continuous scab.

". . . Out of the number of prisoners . . . over 3,000 now lay buried in the cemetery located near the camp for that purpose . . . the range of mortality was no less at Elmira than at Andersonville."

At that point, Representative Platt could contain himself no longer. He asked and received permission to interrupt.[5]

"I desire," the New Yorker said, "to say that I live within 36 miles of Elmira and that those statements are unqualifiedly false."

To which Hill replied ". . . I believe the statement of the surgeon in charge before that of a politician 36 miles away. . . . More than 12 per cent of the Confederates in Federal hands died. . . . Sir, it appears that Confederates (who survived) came from Elmira, from Fort Delaware and from Rock Island and other places with their fingers frozen off, with their toes frozen off, and with their teeth dropped out."

Under questioning by Representative James A. Garfield, of Ohio, later President, Hill read into the Congressional Record General U. S. Grant's reputed refusal to exchange prisoners in 1864 because such reinforcements to the Con-

---

[5] *Congressional Record*, January 11, 1876, page 348.

federacy "would insure Sherman's defeat and would compromise our safety here." Garfield, a former Federal officer, questioned this. Hill then quoted Grant as testifying February 11, 1865, before a Congressional committee on the exchange of prisoners that "I did not deem it advisable or just to the men who had to fight our battles to reinforce the enemy with thirty or forty thousand disciplined troops at that time. An immediate resumption of exchanges would have had that effect without giving us corresponding benefits."

> On November 10, 1865, the post-war Federal Government, accepting the verdict of a military commission of seven generals and two colonels after a much-publicized three-month trial, hanged one man: Captain Henry Wirz, the war-crippled Swiss soldier of fortune who commanded at Andersonville.

The annual report of Secretary of War Stanton for that year cried out in vain for more blood. His obvious aim was to get Jefferson Davis, Mexican War hero (on the side of the U.S.), former U.S. Secretary of War, more lately President of the Confederacy, then a frail man past middle age confined in irons in Fortress Monroe. Said the report:

"The barbarities of Wirz . . . were clearly shown to have been but the revolting features of a system, doubtless devised at Richmond, for the destruction by starvation and fatal cruelties of all Federal prisoners of war who should come into the enemy's hands. . . . The administration of Wirz, though atrocious in the extreme, was but a striking example of the general system of treatment by the enemy of prisoners of war. . . . For the result . . . the chiefs of the rebel Confederacy, the instigators and leaders of the rebellion, should be held responsible. . . ."

Significantly, Henry Wirz went to the gallows after calmly asserting "Jefferson Davis had no connection with me as to what was done at Andersonville. I would not become a traitor against him or anybody else even to save my life." He remarked to the major ordered to direct his hanging, "I know what orders are, Major—I am being hung for obeying them."[6]

[6] *Harper's Weekly*, November 25, 1865, and *Congressional Record*, 1876.

That Andersonville was a massive overdose of sheer hell on earth, through chance circumstances or through some-one's fault, nobody could deny. Within seven years after Wirz was hanged, the Northern presses poured forth 48 books of "personal experiences" and testimony on the horrors of Andersonville. By 1910, the total was up to some 150 books and articles.[7]

Typical of the accounts is a privately printed 30-page pamphlet written in letter style by Calvin S. Engle, of Randolph County, Indiana, who served in the 5th Indiana Cavalry while still a teen-ager. Captured, Engle was imprisoned for ten months at Andersonville and Charleston. He left a vivid picture, including "old Captain Wirtz," as he called him, getting furious because the newly captured cavalrymen failed to obey his infantry-drill commands on being marched into the prison.[8]

"One of these small piles [of cornbread], about three inches long, two inches thick and two inches broad, was a man's ration for 24 hours," Engle wrote.

"The guards did not tell new prisoners what the dead line was for. . . . One evening some prisoners came in late and did not know about the line, the next morning one of them was laying [sleeping] under the dead line. The guard shot him while asleep—they got 30 days furlough for every Yankee they killed.

"There was a little stream of water running through the center of the pen and on both sides of the stream was a swamp . . . the swamp was used as a necessary by the well ones and the filth was two or three inches deep . . . carrion flies were as thick over the swamp as bees are when they are swarming, and the whole swamp was working with maggots and the carrion flies was a great plague.

". . . The guards kept constantly shooting somebody. There was a man who reached under the dead line to get some clean water and the guard shot his brains out. He fell into the water. There was a man that stayed close to me who had both his legs off. . . . The prisoners thought he was too in-

---

[7] W. B. Hesseltine in "Andersonville Revisited," *The Georgia Review*, Spring, 1956.

[8] C. S. Engle, *Andersonville and Other Southern Prisons*, a first-person account privately printed by his youngest daughter, Mrs. Jennie Engle Staudt and quoted by permission.

timate with the rebs . . . and threatened to kill him. He got on his crutches and hopped outside the dead line. It happened to be a man on guard who did not want to shoot him, so he called to old Capt. Wirtz [Engle's spelling] and told him that there was a man over the deadline. 'Yes, shoot him,' was the response. The guard did so immediately, the charge taking effect in the lower jaw. He lived eight hours and his suffering during that time was terrible. The guards loaded their guns with a ball and three buckshot.[9] A man hung his blanket on the deadline in the evening, and when he came to get it the guard shot at him and hit two other men laying in their tent and their cries and groans were heard all over the prison for two hours.

"About the fifth of August I had the scurvy very bad in the mouth. The doctor looked at my mouth and said, 'You have got the scurvy, all you need is a little acid, go back.' That evening, the Sergeant of our ninety [unit] brought me about two mouthfuls of shoemack berries. I said if that was all there was for me . . . I would not go to sick call any more. My mouth got so bad my gums turned black and came loose from my teeth and swelled and bled. . . . It stunk so I could hardly bear my own breath."

A soldier friend bought Engle some Irish potatoes, and he survived. He was transferred to prisons at Charleston and Florence, South Carolina, then freed at the war's end. Back home, he lived out his years a staunch Republican because "every officer that had charge over Union prisoners are Democrats."

While Engle suffered for want of medicine, a Confederate negotiator said he sought medicine from the unresponsive Federal Government for its prisoners in the blockaded South. Dr. R. R. Stevenson is quoted in *The Dixie Book of Days* (by M. P. Andrews, J. B. Lippincott Co., Philadelphia, 1912) as relating:

"In the summer of 1864, in consequence of certain information communicated to me by the Surgeon-General of the Confederate States as to the deficiency of medicines, I offered

---

[9] A ball and three buckshot was a recognized and regulation U.S. Army load for approximately 50 years, beginning with the War of 1812. Both sides used it widely in early Civil War battles. Hence its use at Andersonville should not be taken as extra evidence of Southern brutality.

to make purchases of medicines from the United States authorities, to be used exclusively for the relief of Federal prisoners. I offered to pay gold, cotton or tobacco for them, and . . . gave assurances that the medicines would be used exclusively in the treatment of Federal prisoners; and moreover agreed, on behalf of the Confederates States, if it was insisted on, that such medicines might be brought into the Confederate lines by the United States surgeons and dispensed by them."

War has a wanton way of making the most routine human functions an ordeal. Minor habits are transformed into herculean efforts. Undoubtedly one of the worst horrors of most prison camps was simply—going to the toilet. The Victorian accounts of the survivors on both sides prudishly skip the subject almost entirely. Yet no phase of prison camp life rankled more. Along with eating and sleeping, it became a prime problem of survival. The complications besetting this elementary human need cost thousands of prisoners their lives.

At the outset, both Federal and Confederate regimes erected their prison "sinks"—the official term—over the nearest running water. This was an ancient camp decency dating back to the Roman legions and derived from common sense. Running water washed away the impurities. At least, it did so for small bodies of troops in an uncluttered world. The inadequacy of this primitive arrangement became ripely apparent in stockades confining thousands of men. Engineers and surgeons of both armies eventually recognized its dangers, but their arguments for change came too late to save lives.

The situation was aggravated throughout Northern and Southern prisons by a lack of basic utensils of all sorts, but notably the pre-plumbing standbys, the chamber pot or more delicately, the commode. Only hospitals had such conveniences. Prisons seldom had sufficient cups, plates, pots, pans or buckets, much less the rarer refinements of living.

Under the "running water" doctrine of camp sanitation, sinks or latrines consisted of frameworks, sometimes open and sometimes dignified to the status of row outhouses, erected flimsily over any stream or lake.

The Elmira, New York, stockade for Confederates and the piney slope of Andersonville both harbored brooks. Andersonville's, ironically, was a branch of Sweet Water Creek. These rustic brooks became latrines and open sewers. As the prisons grew overcrowded, their pollution, filth and germs menaced everyone forced to go near them, and spread over the whole area. Similar poisonous situations arose at other places of confinement North and South.

Both sides favored islands for prisoner detention. Their watery locations deterred all but strong swimmers from attempting to escape. The largest Confederate stockade for years was on Belle Isle, in the James River near Richmond. The North penned Southern captives on Pea Patch Island, in the Delaware; Rock Island, in the Mississippi between the Illinois city of that name and Davenport, Iowa; and Johnson's Island, in Sandusky Bay off Sandusky, Ohio.

Sinks at such island prisons were constructed out over the water. This placed them, logically, away from the center of the camps. Soon, however, the masterminds of this sanitary plan discovered that many prisoners who went to the sinks were answering a higher call of nature—escape. Skin divers and others exploring the Delaware River off Pea Patch Island recently discovered quantities of Civil War Minié bullets underwater. From their location, they appear to have been fired at escaping prisoners.

While escape never became an acute problem at places like Johnson's Island, some two and a half miles offshore in a rough bay, it kept the prisons in the Delaware, Mississippi and James Rivers in a constant uproar. The far shore beckoned only a few hundred feet or yards away. Prisoners going to the sinks at night had a knack of lowering themselves into the streams, floating silently along with the current until past the sentries, then striking out for freedom.

The great popularity of escape-by-latrine led to one of the most irking harassments of prison life. After "lights out," no captives were allowed to leave their tent, barracks or hole in the ground without permission of a guard. At times when escapes were frequent, guards were detailed to escort prisoners to and from their nocturnal missions. Often there were as many as 200 prisoners to one guard. A general spread of diarrhea would run both inmates and guards frantic. The acute misery of this absurd situation was not lessened by the brutality of some guards. At Point Lookout, Virginia, survivors asserted, arrogant bluecoats repeatedly forced enfeebled Southern prisoners who wanted to go to the sinks to carry them piggy-back all the way. This might have seemed hilarious to some, but not to an ill man with a pistol at his head and a goading agony at his other extremity.

"*PRISONERS OF WAR. . . . They receive for subsistence one ration each, without regard to rank . . .*" Regulations for the Army of the Confederate States, 1862, Paragraph 724.

"*THE RATION. . . . The ration is three-fourths of a pound of pork or bacon, or one and a fourth pounds of fresh or salt beef; eighteen ounces of bread or flour, or twelve ounces of hard bread, or one and a fourth pounds of corn meal. . . .*" Regulations for the Army of the Confederate States, 1862, Paragraph 1107.

By 1864, when Andersonville was established, a Confederate soldier often was lucky if he drew as his entire daily ration half a pound of corn meal. Many fared far better at times, of course, but some were even worse off. Maj. Gen. B. F. Butler, USA, when he examined haversacks of some captured Southern soldiers, found in them only a handful or two of parched corn, not even ground into meal.

Whatever the Confederate ration was, it usually was what the Union prisoner of war received. If it was scanty and unappetizing for the captives in blue, it was equally so for the soldiers in gray. The Georgia militia who guarded Andersonville fared little if at all better than their wards.

With granary regions of the South, such as the bounteous Shenandoah Valley, methodically ravaged by the Union, and connecting railroads ripped up, there was food only in local areas untouched by the blue armies. In Georgia, General O. O. Howard's corps is said to have intercepted two Central Railroad of Georgia trains loaded with corn meal, flour and pork at Oconee, Georgia. According to the report, the Federal raiders burned both, despite assurances that the food was intended for Andersonville.

In the North, on the other hand, there were no such explanations or excuses for shortage of food in prison camps filled with Confederates. At no time did the Southern forces raid or ravage in such a way as to cut down seriously on Northern foodstuffs and their transportation.

Yet Confederate prisoners were often on short rations or next to no rations, while their Federal guards ate well. This

was especially true in 1864 when Secretary of War Edwin
Stanton deliberately cut the rations of Southern prisoners in
retaliation for Andersonville.

Stanton's ruthlessness in reducing the Confederate prisoners' rations naturally raises a question: How well were Southerners faring at the time? Official reports tell of Confederates
seizing champagne, oysters, canned meats, and other deli-
cacies in capturing the headquarters of Federal generals. But
what was on General Robert E. Lee's menu during those
days? Let fiery Lt. Gen. Jubal A. Early report:[10]

"While we were at Spottsylvania Court-House in May,
1864, battling with such immense odds, I was in command of
a corps and I received a message to come to General Lee's
headquarters at night on one occasion for the purpose of receiving some instructions from him. General Lee was then
himself suffering with a dysentery which had reduced him
very much, and rendered all of us who were aware of his
condition exceedingly uneasy, for we knew that if he failed
all was gone.

"When I arrived his dinner and supper, both in one, were
just ready and I was invited in to partake of the meal. I
found it to consist of, what to me was most acceptable, a
scant supply of hard crackers, fried fat bacon, and a beverage
made as a substitute for coffee out of parched wheat, without sugar—and this was all. *This was what the foremost commander of his age was reduced to in the then critical condition of his health.* [Italics added.]

"Such fare, if furnished to a sick or wounded Federal soldier, would have been regarded as evidence of a barbarous
purpose to cause his death. To inflame the minds of the
Northern people and prejudice the civilized world against us,
an investigation was had before a committee of the Federal
Congress who made a report on 'rebel atrocities' founded on
the testimony of men who swore to some things they had
seen, many that they had heard, and a great many more that
they had neither heard nor seen.

"The press was flooded with stories of cruel treatment, illustrated by pictures, and during the war every device was resorted to, to fix upon us the stigma of barbarous treatment
of prisoners in our hands."

[10] Jubal A. Early, *Autobiographical Sketch and Narrative of the
War Between the States*, Lippincott Co., Philadelphia, 1912.

General Early relates how "thousands of our men lay down to rest without having had a mouthful to eat all day" after the second victory at Manassas and how he as a brigadier after the battle of Ox Hill or Chantilly was "very well content to make my supper on 2 very small ears of green corn which I roasted in the ashes." Later as a division and corps commander, he added, "I have been often thankful on the road to a soldier for a biscuit from his haversack which he himself had baked. . . . I have seen . . . gentlemen of refinement, whose means before the war had enabled them to live with every desirable comfort . . . submit cheerfully . . . to actual hunger and . . . go into battle with the proud tread of heroes. . . .

"What these men were content with, the prisoners taken by their valor and who had been so well pampered in their own country, thought proper to regard . . . as evidence of a disposition to starve them."

After the climactic Battle of Gettysburg, Confederate wounded by the thousands crowded the hospitals. They had civilian friends in Pennsylvania, as indicated by Paragraph 3 of General Order No. 2, U.S. Army Department of the Susquehanna, dated at Gettysburg July 30, 1863:

"3. Any luxuries sent to the hospitals for the wounded Confederates by sympathizing friends must be handed over to the Surgeon in Charge and under his direction will be distributed equally among the Union and Confederate wounded."

One of the survivors of the ordeal of Camp Chase, at Columbus, Ohio, a teen-ager in Company H, 40th Georgia Infantry, related his experiences in a slim book 40 years after his capture.[11] By then, John H. King was qualified to speak with medical authority on the ravages and after-effects of wartime hospitalization and imprisonment. He was an M.D. and surgeon of the Confederate Soldiers' Home in Atlanta.

At Sevierville, Tennessee, young King received a bullet wound in the head which knocked him from his horse to the

---

[11] *Three Hundred Days in a Yankee Prison*, by John H. King, M.D., Atlanta, Georgia, 1904, reprinted 1959 by the Continental Book Company, Kennesaw, Georgia.

ground and left him partly paralyzed. The bullet shattered his lower jawbone and went through his neck, barely missing his spine. Captured and hospitalized for a time, he then spent nearly a year in Camp Chase with his wound unhealed, unattended and infected. Of Camp Chase he wrote:

"No bucket or pitcher was furnished to keep water in, our only vessel being an ordinary sized cup. An order had been issued that no water should be thrown about the pump by those who went there to quench their thirst. One of the unfortunates, not aware of the order, washed out his tin cup at the pump and threw out the water on the ground before filling the cup with water to drink. A guard seeing him throw the water on the ground, at once fired at him and missing his aim severely wounded an unlucky prisoner standing some distance beyond him, breaking his leg, rendering it necessary in the judgement of the Yankee surgeon to amputate the poor fellow's fractured limb. At another time I witnessed the maiming of a prisoner by a guard for the most trivial violation of an order. A ditch had been dug through the center of the enclosure for the purpose of conveying the refuse and detritus of the camp. This ditch was flushed from a large tank at the upper end, which we were required to fill every day by pumping the water, in details. An order was issued requiring all the prisoners to assemble on the south side of the ditch and bring their blankets with them. The superintendent, or prison keeper, took a stand at the end of the line near the prison wall, and the men were ordered to recross the ditch near them bringing their blankets. The effect of this, as we ascertained afterwards, was to find out who had more than one blanket. If a prisoner had more than one, he was required to drop the surplus and allowed to retain only a single blanket. One of the prisoners, not understanding the movement, stepped across the ditch before the order to do so was given, and was immediately shot down by the guard. The poor fellow's leg was so badly shattered that amputation was rendered necessary, another one made cripple for life. Of course nothing was done to these cowardly guards. Doubtless they were complimented for gallantry and are now drawing pensions from the United States Treasury, on certificates of meritorious service.

"At a certain hour at night, the guards would cry out, 'Lights out,' and if the lights were not immediately extinguished, the guard would fire into the room regardless of whom he might kill or maim. No friend of a suffering comrade dare make a light, however extreme the illness, or imminent the peril of the sufferer, or to speak above a whisper during the night watches. If so, the bullet from the rifle of a guard would come whistling into the barracks to kill or to wound some luckless sleeper.

"Attempts at escape were frequent, and met with the severest punishment. . . . A failure to escape meant a suspension by the thumbs until the anguish of pain would drive some into insanity, or ordered to hard labor on the grounds with a ball and chain fastened to one's feet and legs, or to be 'bucked and gagged' daily, for hours at a time and left to lie in this wretched condition on the frozen ground;[12] or to be maimed for life by being shot in the legs; yet, with all these tortures witnessed by us daily, in the desperation of suffering and starvation, men would often run the risk of escape. How shall we manage to make our escape from this infernal place, from the nauseating filth and stench of our prison, from the certainty of a lingering death, and the cruelty of our inhuman keepers, formed the burden of our thoughts by day and gave fantasms of vision to our dreams by night. . . .

"The walls surrounding the prison grounds were very high, twenty feet at least, and well lighted at night. On a platform, near the top, sentinels were pacing to and fro and never out of sight of each other or of the prisoners. Nevertheless, now and then on some dark or stormy night desperate prisoners would make the effort to scale these walls. In a very few instances the attempt was successful, but the majority were either shot or doomed to the torture of thumb cords.

"The entrance to the prison was secured by a large and strongly constructed double gate, always guarded by a detachment of twelve men. A number of our comrades determined to charge the guard and force their way out or die

---

[12] Punishments such as stringing men up by the thumbs and leaving them "bucked and gagged" in heat or cold were recognized disciplinary measures in both Federal and Confederate armies, although they may have been practiced with greater severity in prison camps. Army penalties were in many ways a carry-over from medieval tortures. The U.S. Army did not abolish flogging as a punishment until 1861, two years after the Navy did so. The Confederate forces never accepted flogging as a punishment. Nor did many Southerners in gray and Midwesterners in blue submit to such penalties as being strung up or bucked and gagged—they rose up in resentment.

in the attempt, reasoning that it was better to die a death from the rifle ball of a guard than to linger in misery and finally die of starvation. These desperate prisoners getting close to the gate, watched for the coming of the superintendent's bread wagon. As soon as the gates were opened, for the wagons to pass in, the gallant prisoners raised the old Rebel yell and rushed out and by the astonished guard. A fusillade of shots immediately announced these escapes, not one of which took effect upon the fleeing prisoners. A detachment of cavalry followed them however, and soon brought back the unfortunate fellows, the worse by far for their gallant charge on the guard of the gate. Poor men! As they came in, it was indeed a sickening sight to see how brutally these poor emaciated creatures had been treated. Their heads and faces bloody with the cuts of sabres and bruises of the brutes who had beaten them with clubs after their capture, until some could scarcely walk."

"You get used to them after a while, son. Rats don't taste all THAT bad."
Remark of Thomas Pinckney, of Charleston, Captain 4th South Carolina Cavalry and a descendant of two signers of the Constitution of the United States, who was penned in a prison stockade on Morris Island, South Carolina, almost in sight of the spires of his native city.[13]

In July of 1864, 40 Federal generals, colonels and lieutenant colonels were held prisoners of war in Charleston, South Carolina, much of which was then under daily bombardment from Federal long-range guns. The prisoners were confined in two permanent structures, the Roper Hospital and the O'Connor house, the latter a palatial private home. Both buildings were standing intact at the end of the war, unscarred by shells. That alone might be taken to attest that the prisoners in them were not held dangerously in the shelled area.

The Federal Government, however, protested at the time that the imprisoned 40 were being deliberately and barbar-

---

[13] As quoted by his grandnephew, J. Bryan, III, well-known author, in *The Sword Over the Mantel*, 1960, McGraw-Hill, New York.

Pinckney was among those packed into the hellship whose cruise is described here.

ously kept under the fire of their own guns. Subsequently they were exchanged for 40 officers of comparable rank from among the Confederates held in Fort Delaware, below Wilmington.

Soon afterward, 600 Federal officers ranging in rank from colonels down to lieutenants were confined at Charleston. There is sharp disagreement over whether this was a "Confederate trick" to force a further exchange or simply a routine transfer of prisoners.

At any rate, retaliation was quick in coming. On August 20, 1864, 600 Confederate officers were jammed into the hold of the small steamship *Crescent* at Fort Delaware. Among them were 12 colonels or lieutenant colonels, 16 majors, 176 captains. The rest were lieutenants. They represented 14 Southern and border states. According to one survivor's story, the 600 were selected mostly because of physical disabilities; nearly 100 had lost arms or legs, or suffered multiple wounds. Even if exchanged, many were hardly fit to battle once more for the Confederacy.

The little *Crescent*, under orders to steam to Charleston, proved to be a hellship of unsurpassed horror. A notable account of the *Crescent's* leisurely 18-day cruise was published by one of the survivors, Captain J. J. Dunkle, Company K, 25th Virginia Infantry. Even after making allowances for Captain Dunkle's vehemence, his story smacks of the worst excesses of prisoner-of-war abuse in World War II by the Axis.[14]

"Imagine our condition," he wrote. "Huddled together as close as we could stand; some having room to lie down while

---

[14] See *Prison Life During the Rebellion, Being a Brief Narrative of the Miseries and Sufferings of Six Hundred Confederate Prisoners Sent from Fort Delaware to Morris Island to be Punished, written by Fritz Fuzzlebug*, one of their number, published at Singer's Glen, Virginia, 1869, Joseph Funk's Sons, printers. Dunkle, who chose the pseudonym Fuzzlebug in a typical Victorian literary affectation, lived out his life at Franklin, now in West Virginia. Much of his account is borne out by the *Official Records of the War of the Rebellion*. *Miller's Photographic History of the Civil War* contains a photograph of the prisoner stockade or pen on Morris Island in which Dunkle and his comrades were confined. Thus, incredibly inhuman though their treatment may seem, there is little reason to doubt the substance of Dunkle's story. In fact, it was not out of keeping with the treatment of many Confederate prisoners elsewhere.

three-fourths had scarcely space upon which to stand. The heat being up to 95 degrees without steam, and of course greatly increasing when the boiler was heated for sailing; great numbers became seasick, and then the stench, filth and dirt in this crowd was almost intolerable . . . about three-fourths of us became seasick. . . . And as closely confined as we were, the spectacle was horrid—the entire floor covered with sick men—horribly sick, vomited to a fearful extent. . . ."

With the hatches battened down and a steam boiler going full blast below decks, the *Crescent* proceeded south in the summer heat and anchored off Hilton Head, South Carolina, with even the portholes closed to shut out light and air. Water was doled out, at first by the barrel and then in smaller quantities, but never enough and never pure.

Food, what there was of it, consisted of damaged pickled pork, and, according to Dunkle, of "army crackers which looked as though they had been manufactured for use in the War of 1776 . . . and would not have been eaten by the dogs of a farmer . . . completely filled with worms, bugs and other living creepers. . . .

"We suffered very much from the scarcity of water. . . . At one time we had no water for 40 hours. O, the intense suffering of those 40 hours is beyond description! No pen could convey to the mind the cruel agony of suffering without water, shut out from light and fresh air in the heat of summer, and confined with a heated steam boiler. . . .

"The scene would not have been so terrific had we not been refused light and fresh air, and had not been burnt and parched by the excessive heat of the boiler. Men sank, shrank, begged, wept, mourned, lamented, swore, raved, fainted and sickened under the dreadful blow. . . .

"Men of the strongest minds of the greatest firmness wept like babes for the precious earthly gift, water. Many bowed on their knees before their cruel tormenters, and begged like children for a single draught of water. . . .

"After this horrible agony of 40 hours, we were gratified with the return of water. The condensing vessels were put to work, and we were supplied with boiling water—*the external heat not being sufficient, we were given boiling water to augment its strength* [Italics added]. During the remainder of our stay in the boat we had no other but boiling water as it ran from the condenser. . . ."

When the *Crescent* dropped anchor off Morris Island, an approach to Charleston then held by the Federal Army, Dunkle records that "about 50 had to be carried away, being unable to walk."

The fate in store for the hapless disabled and sweated-to-the-bones Southerners soon became shockingly evident. As hostages for the Federal officers held in Charleston, they were to be penned on the sandspit of Morris Island between Federal guns at Batteries Wagner and Gregg, then shelling Fort Sumter, and the Confederate artillery firing back from Sumter and Fort Moultrie.

"Whenever a shell fell short of Wagner, it would undoubtedly fall among us," Dunkle observed.

He described their three-acre prison pen with its pine sapling stockade as enclosing "only an immense plain of white sand, which, being heated by the rays of a Southern sun, makes sufficient heat to cook an egg." The 600 Confederates were allowed 150 two-man pup tents, thus impossibly crowding four to a tent. Two regiments of Negro troops, totaling about 1,600 men under white officers, were assigned to guard the hostages. Dunkle says, "The abusive phrase, 'Look out dare, white man! I'se gwine to shoot! My bullet's burnin' to go into you!' was heard almost continually" along with "liars, thieves, rogues, and other cowardly epithets."

By now, sickness and death had cut the number of prisoners to fewer than 550. But with huge shells whizzing overhead constantly from both sides, the Federals emplaced two batteries of field artillery and 60 smaller cannon to cover the pen in case of a break. A refusal to disperse by any group larger than three officers "was followed by the discharge of a musket and the groans of a wounded prisoner—perhaps one who was lying wrapped in slumber in his tent—the ball missing the offender and finding an allodgment elsewhere. Firing upon the prisoners was of frequent occurrence.

". . . Our food consisted of three small crackers three inches square and one-quarter inch thick, two ounces of mule or horse meat, and half a pint of warm-water imitation soup. Thus we starved. . . . The rations were nearly enough for one meal . . ." Charlestonians sent boxes of food to the unfortunate, who included some fellow townsmen, but, Dunkle says, these were held up by the guards until the food spoiled.

So the survivors endured. Ailing or disabled at the start, debilitated by a hellship voyage with extreme heat and scanty water, shelled overhead by heavy batteries, shot at close range with muskets on the least pretext, fed starvation rations of the sorriest sort in the midst of ample Federal supplies, they could thank their stars for only one remarkable thing. Not a single Confederate shell burst inside their pen, although numbers of guards just outside it were seriously wounded by fragments.

"The gunners at Fort Moultrie were so expert that they could kill Yankees on every side of us, and we be almost secure from danger," Dunkle relates. But, "The Federals had a gun mounted at Wagner which invariably bursted the shell immediately after leaving the gun. They sometimes used this gun to fire directly over our pen, pretending to be firing upon Sumter, supposing that the fragments would kill some of the prisoners. . . . In this they failed. . . ."

As Maj. Gen. Sam Jones, CSA, commanding at Charleston, refused to exchange Federal for Confederate officers unless, as Dunkle tells it, privates also were released, the hapless hostages were crammed back aboard ship after 45 days in the torrid heat and constant bombardment on Morris Island. By now, their number was down nearly to 400. Half were held in Fort Pulaski, at Savannah, Georgia, and the other half imprisoned at Hilton Head. They were fed only uncooked sour corn meal, supposedly a half-ration of ten ounces but more often only four ounces a day, according to Dunkle. This they supplemented with rats, cats, and dogs when available. Several who escaped were run down with bloodhounds and thrown into a dungeon. Acute diarrhea and scurvy racked all of them. Some drank greasy dishwater at the guards' kitchen. After 60 days of this, most were loaded onto the steamship *Illinois*, amid rumors of exchange. Instead, the survivors, now down from 600 to about 200, were dumped back at Fort Delaware.

There, Dunkle says, "Our comrades scarcely knew us, so changed were our features and so haggard were our countenances. Many of us had diseases from which we never recovered. . . ."

Meanwhile, what of the Federal officers held at Charleston? They remained in the two relatively commodious three-story buildings, untouched by shells, fed the same rations given to Confederate sick and wounded. That they endured some hardships cannot be questioned. But there is little or no evidence that these were vindictively inflicted.

Does it occur to anyone that they were treated somewhat

differently than the Confederate hostages penned up in the heat and horror of Morris Island?

After reading the postwar accounts of imprisoned Confederates, it becomes difficult for fair-minded persons to shut their eyes to some statements. Summed up, these are:

> 1. While much suffering among Northern prisoners was due to scarcities and deficiencies widespread in the South, thousands of Southern prisoners were either deliberately or neglectfully starved, inadequately housed and pitifully clothed in the midst of Yankee plenty. Short rations were usually unheard of in the North except among imprisoned Confederates. Food supply in the lush farming areas around Elmira, Rock Island, Fort Johnson, Fort Delaware, Camp Chase and Point Lookout was never any great problem.[15]

> 2. While the South's far-inferior railroads were disrupted by Federal attacks in supplying Southern prison camps, Northern transportation sustained no such disruption—the widespread starving of captured Confederates could not be excused by twisted tracks and burned bridges.

> 3. While neither side expected nor prepared for the grand total of a half million or more prisoners taken during the war, the North, with vastly superior means, produced a prison system scarcely if any better than that of the impoverished and ravaged South.

> 4. While prisons on both sides were mostly miserably organized and incompetently managed, management in the South generally was no worse than in the North—and certainly no deadlier in its consequences.

> 5. While Captain Henry Wirz, a Swiss lawyer-soldier in almost daily agonies from a severely wounded right arm which never healed, proved sadly inadequate to the overwhelming task of running Andersonville, any number of similarly placed Federal officers were equally culpable of

---

[15] By contrast with the acute food shortages in most Southern cities and ravaged rural areas, which led, for example, to a women's bread riot in Richmond, the only general hardship in the North fell on the families of Union privates who were caught in the wartime inflation. A private's pay, meager at best, then proved pitiably inadequate.

prison mismanagement and presumably deserved to be hanged as high as Wirz.[16]

And what of specific brutalities?

A bibliography of those alleged by Federal veterans, all too frequently with some basis, would fill pages. Detailed accounts appear in the reports of wartime Congressional investigation committees which were bent on getting the grim facts and certainly got the grimness. Inhumanities on end are alleged until it would seem that there was scarcely a kindly soul in the entire South.

That there were some unkindly souls in the North has hardly been touched upon. The defunct Confederacy of course held no inquests of war crimes. The fallen South had virtually no presses, no paper, no voice, no audience. Not until many years later did its stories filter through.

One came from an undersized, underage Alabama cavalryman. A runt not yet 18 when captured, he was sent to Camp Morton, Indianapolis, a former fair grounds where Confederates were herded into ramshackle cattle sheds and stables whose flimsy sides and roofs admitted snow copiously in 20-below-zero weather.

"Of the cruel indignities to which the prisoners were subjected I witnessed only a small proportion," the captive wrote in later years.

"I saw Corporal Augustus Baker, a man whose heartless conduct toward us entitles him to painful notoriety, shoot a prisoner for leaving the ranks after rollcall was ended but before 'Break ranks!' was commanded. The man was too eager to warm himself at a fire only a few feet distant from the line. It was a bitter cold morning, the poor fellow had no overcoat or blanket with which to cover himself, and he ventured to the fire. Baker drew his pistol, saying with an oath 'I'll show you how to leave ranks before you are dismissed!' and deliberately shot him down. The wound was not fatal, but the intent was murderous. . . .

"On April 16, 1864, one guard at a single shot . . . killed

[16] Sometimes Confederate prisoners, happily, got the food intended for them. Often they did not. A $30,000 hospital was built at Rock Island from their ration fund, naturally without their consent. Elsewhere, penny-pinching prison commanders at times deprived scurvy-ridden prisoners of fresh vegetables simply to make their ledger balances look good.

James Beattie and Michael Healy, who were walking in front of him on garbage detail outside the prison quarters. The Minie ball passed through the bodies of both. I was with one of these men as he was dying, and heard him solemnly assert in the presence of death that they had made no attempt to escape, had disobeyed no order, and that he and his comrade had been deliberately murdered.

"On various occasions I saw prisoners beaten with sticks for no other provocation than that they would not move quickly to get out of the way or cease talking when the patrol was passing. At one time I saw an officer with a stick of firewood knock two men down, leaving them unconscious.

"To discourage all efforts at escape an order was enforced that a prisoner when obliged to go to the sink [toilet] at night should not wear his coat. Two men from my barracks one intensely cold night infringed upon this rule, were detected, and compelled to mark time in the deep snow for so long that one of them was frost-bitten and lost parts of both feet from gangrene. He died from exhaustion on the train on which we were being carried to Baltimore in February, 1865."

Does all this sound like the testimony of a man who might exaggerate or sensationalize? It comes from Dr. John Allen Wyeth, M.D., LL.D., at one time president of the American Medical Association, the New York Academy of Medicine, the New York State Medical Association and the New York Polyclinic Medical School and Hospital, pioneer institute in post-graduate medical instruction in the United States.

In his memoirs, *With Sabre and Scalpel* (Harper & Bros., 1914), Dr. Wyeth concludes his story of Corporal Baker, who pistoled the freezing prisoner, with the words: ". . . the commandant of this prison . . . testified that he had never heard of Corporal Baker shooting a prisoner. I stood within a few yards of Baker and witnessed the whole cruel proceeding. There were other witnesses. Yet the man who should have been held responsible and whose duty it was to protect prisoners never knew of it until he read my article 27 years after it occurred."[17]

[17] Young Wyeth was among 500 invalided prisoners exchanged early in 1865. He states that he never lost a day from duty in the Confederate cavalry because of sickness. After his capture, he came down with pneumonia, measles and dysentery in little more than a year. The article that he mentions appeared in *Century Magazine* in 1891.

The prisoner shot down by Corporal Baker was an enlisted man, but Confederate officers of high rank were not immune to murderous assaults while prisoners of war.

At Fort Delaware on July 10, 1864, Col. E. P. Jones, a captured Virginia militia officer, was ordered by a private of the 157th Ohio to "walk faster" on his way to the latrine. Because of a wounded foot, Colonel Jones could not comply. The private shot and killed him on the spot for "disobedience to orders."[18]

At Point Lookout prison on March 20, 1864, a newly-arrived red-haired Confederate got in an argument with a Negro guard. The prisoner was Lieutenant L. R. Peyton, 2nd Kentucky Cavalry, CSA, one of Morgan's command captured in Ohio the previous June. A white sergeant of the guard stepped up and ended the argument by shooting Lieutenant Peyton fatally. It undoubtedly taught the rest of the newly arrived rebels who was boss. The slain officer's personnel record, now preserved in the National Archives, Washington, D.C., reveals an erasure. Under "remarks," it says that he was "Shot by sergeant in the . . ." Elsewhere the missing words are supplied: ". . . execution of his duty." Possibly someone felt that the sergeant was a bit over-zealous and tried to fix the record. The same document shows that Peyton was buried in an unnumbered grave and listed as a private at the time of his slaying.

[18] *The Civil War Times*, November, 1960, page 15, article by W. Emerson Wilson.

11

The Deadly Medical Practices

"Sometimes the surgeons and the assistants washed their hands . . ."
"We used undisinfected instruments from
undisinfected plush cases . . ."
The wonder is not that so many patients
in Civil War hospitals died, but that so
many survived.

Among the most prized finds of souvenir hunters now comb-
ing Civil War battlefields are leaden bullets bearing irregular
indentations. These are unearthed most often near the sites of
old stables and barns. They, and their location, tell more of
medical practice in that war than volumes of printed words.

The indentations in the bullets are tooth marks. They mean
that some hapless soldier of a century ago clenched the bullet
between his teeth to keep from literally biting off his tongue in
the acute agony of an amputation without anesthetic.

Chewed bullets turn up frequently around stables and barns
because those unlikely places, despite their reeking dung heaps
and seething flies, served as emergency operating rooms more
often than most other types of buildings. They usually afforded
the nearest handy shelter.

Where battle lines are known or can be traced, more of the
deeply-bitten lead relics may be found around Confederate
sites than at Federal ones. Due to the blockade, the shortage
of anesthetics and all drugs became intense in the South after
1862. Even so, amputation without anesthetics was un-
common.

Fortunately for the victims on both sides, chloroform, ether
and nitrous oxide all were known and usually were available.
While no valid figures exist, amputations without anesthesia
probably occurred in not more than 5 per cent of all cases.
Usually they were due to a field hospital's running out of
anesthetics temporarily rather than to basic shortages. As in all
wars, nobody knew in advance where battles might be fought

The standup-and-fire tactics that cost so many lives in the War illustrated by this sketch from "Battle and Leaders" showing eatty's Brigade in action at the Battle of Stone's River. Later in the ar, formations became looser and intrenching became standard rocedure.

or how high casualties might run. Thus the field hospitals of hard-hit brigades might exhaust their supplies before more arrived from the rear.

Amputation was perhaps the outstanding surgical activity of the war. Not for nothing were military surgeons in that and earlier conflicts nicknamed "Sawbones." Though a jest, the nickname was grimly appropriate.

Some 70 per cent of the wounded who reached hospitals alive were hit in the arms or legs. While some were struck by artillery missiles, the great majority sustained bullet wounds from small arms. Unlike modern gunshot wounds, which are neat, precise holes if made by metal-jacketed bullets that do not expand,[1] the soft lead Civil War bullets spread on hitting a person and inflicted yawning holes. These bullets ranged from more than half-an-inch to nearly three-quarters-of-an-inch in diameter to begin with. On mushrooming into bodies, they tore holes sometimes the size of a silver dollar. Such a gaping wound in an arm or leg almost invariably wrecked bone, muscle, tissue and arteries beyond repair. Amputation was regarded as inescapable in all cases of badly shattered limbs.

Usually the patient was prepared for the ordeal by being given a stiff shot of brandy. Then he was "put under" completely by cone inhalation of chloroform or ether. Sometimes morphine was administered. An expert surgeon with a keen medical saw could then remove the wounded arm or leg in as little as half a minute. With such a master at work, a heap of limbs like a woodpile soon arose nearby. In one of its few moves toward delicacy or subtlety, wartime medical practice improved the situation by having a pit dug at the foot of the emergency operating table. The severed limbs were dropped into this. It was better psychology for the living and also handier for the cleanup or burial squad later.

More than a third of the men whose arms or legs were sawed off died. Among the better-known fatalities was General T. J.

[1] One constructive result of the Hague Conference, an international convention in 1899, was the outlawing of soft lead or expansive military bullets along with poison gas and "balloon" bombing attacks. Although the Germans used gas in World War I and the status of the bombing ban needs no comment in this atomic age, the agreement banning expansive bullets has been observed by all so-called civilized nations to date. One reason may be that soft lead bullets foul the rifling of high-velocity military weapons. In short, the continued observance may be practical rather than humane.

(Stonewall) Jackson, dead a week after the amputation of his left arm just below the shoulder. The large bone of the upper arm was splintered by a .69 calibre bullet mistakenly fired by a North Carolina soldier. The amputation appeared successful and the stump began to heal. However, pneumonia developed, due possibly to his having broken ribs in a fall from his litter. It proved fatal on the eighth day after the operation.

Some patients survived the initial shock of wounding and amputation only to fall prey to the almost inevitable infections that followed. Infection was expected as a matter of routine; the medical vocabulary of the day contained a term, "laudable pus." Yet many amputees on both sides recovered sufficiently to return to the wars, bravely going into battle with a stump limb. Factories making artificial limbs, North and South, fell far behind the demand.

By 1864, the Confederate Army carried in its "present for duty" ranks at least 10,000 amputees.[2] Generals of both armies lost limbs, recuperated, and rode back to battle. In one such instance, a runaway horse unseated an amputee of high rank before he could kick his wooden leg out of the stirrup. The unruly mount disappeared, leaving the officer not only horseless but legless.

Among the "peg-leg" generals were Lt. Gens. Richard Ewell and John Bell Hood, of the Confederacy, and Maj. Gen. Daniel Sickles, of the Union. Hood fought his greatest and most disastrous battles in 1864 after losing not only one leg but part of an arm. Sickles' brash stand in front of the Union main body at Gettysburg cost him a leg by amputation. The loss did not deter him, in postwar life, from carrying on an affair with a European queen while he was U.S. Ambassador to her court.

After the war, General Hood fathered eleven children in ten years, among them being three sets of twins. When yellow fever killed him, his wife and his oldest daughter in 1879, Gen. P. G. T. Beauregard arranged for the printing of Hood's memoirs and realized a substantial sum from them for Hood's orphaned brood.

Amputation on a wholesale scale was only one fearsome aspect of medical practice in our deadliest struggle. The practice of medicine was just emerging from the hocus-pocus of me-

[2] Dr. Richard Boies Stark, M.D., F.A.C.S., of New York, in the Virginia Medical Monthly, Richmond, May, 1960.

dieval secrecy which, in actual fact, disguised abysmal ignorance. Carry-overs from primitive procedures killed many ill
and wounded soldiers who might otherwise have recovered.

Three of the worst practices that persisted during the war
were "therapeutic" bleeding, the reckless administering of
purgatives, and a total, ignorant disregard of the dangers of
infection.

Wounded men who had lain for hours with open unattended wounds, bleeding steadily in the absence of first-aid
kits (unknown in that war) and hospital men, were carried
into field hospitals and sometimes bled anew in accordance
with the old custom of blood-letting to "purify" the blood.
Today many would be given massive transfusions instead.

The treatment of dysentery, diarrhea and allied sicknesses
was equally obsolete and backward in many cases. Soldiers
racked and reduced to skin-and-bone by "running bowels" were
administered enormous doses of laxatives at times when their
systems cried out for exactly the opposite. Not all surgeons
committed this blunder; some realized in time. But untold
thousands of dysentery and diarrhea sufferers undoubtedly
were put to death in hospitals medicinally through sheer
ignorance.

Bowel disorders were listed as the most common cause of
death among hospitalized Federal sick, with malaria second.
Typhoid, smallpox, and pneumonia also ranked high among
the killer diseases on both sides.

Bad diet and an almost total lack of sanitary precautions
aggravated the least presence of disease to epidemic proportions. Most of the food of both armies was coarse, heavy, and
devoid of proteins. In the absence of special cooking arrangements, it nearly always was fried. Often it defied digestion.
Often, too, even pork and cornmeal had to be gobbled raw for
lack of time to cook them.

In the absence of any knowledge of germs and precaution-
ary measures, the streams and ponds in areas occupied by
large armies almost always were polluted. Soldiers upstream relieved themselves into what, just around the bend, became a
water supply for empty canteens. Even in permanent winter
encampments, unsanitary practices persisted. The camp regulations of both armies prescribed that the "sinks" or toilet
facilities should be located 150 paces from the tents of the enlisted men and 100 paces from "officer's row." But the difficulty of teaching farm boys accustomed to casually "going be-

hind the barn" to walk any distance away from their blankets on a freezing night was never approached, much less surmounted. Every camp area soon became saturated with assorted germs. The first warm spell served as a signal for disease to break out. One Union general who regularly moved the site of his winter camp every few weeks was well rewarded by a lower sickness rate among his men.

Once a disease spread, medical practitioners could take some steps to curb or minimize it—there was, for example, a crude form of smallpox vaccination—but often there was little to halt an epidemic except the mercy of God. One grim irony of the war was that medical science failed to realize the causes of disease and infection. Not until 1865 did Sir Joseph Lister, the great English physician and founder of aseptic surgery, announce his discovery of disinfecting wounds, instruments and bandages by killing germs. The news came too late for thousands of Civil War victims.

The shortages of medical supplies inadvertently led the South to take two steps against infection. These, to the woe of Northern patients, did not become necessary in the North. The South, lacking sea sponges for surgical use, was compelled to cleanse wounds with rags used over and again. After each case, these were scrubbed and *boiled*. Imported silk for sutures being unavailable, the South substituted horsehair. Again, it was *boiled*. This was done to make it pliable, but also made it sterile. Such measures kept down post-operative infection.

By contrast, Dr. Robert Weir, an eminent Northern surgeon who commanded a hospital for four years, could recall only one instance among 700 amputations in which the operation was not followed by infection. In later years, Dr. Weir and medical science became more informed as to what had happened.

The operating-room sponges were kept in water buckets, like sponges used to rub down horses, and were tossed back uncleansed after each operation. As Dr. Weir described it:

"Sometimes the surgeon and the assistants washed their hands. . . . [Then to scrub the limb before amputation they used] the nice-looking sponges, filled with disease germs from previous operations which had been multiplying while resting in their pail full of water.

"Fingers laden with germs in large quantities, on them or under the nails, were stuck into the wounds and often fatal germs were inserted by the brilliant and apparently clean instruments . . . [which were wiped off but not medically sterilized]."

Dr. W. W. Keen, a Federal surgeon with much battlefield experience, added to the professional testimony:

". . . We operated with clean hands in the social sense, but they were undisinfected hands. . . . We used undisinfected instruments from undisinfected plush cases, and still worse, used marine sponges which had been used in prior pus cases and had been washed only in tap water. If a sponge or an instrument fell on the floor it was washed or squeezed in a basin of tap water and used as though it were clean."

Although the standard medical field kit of the day included fairly efficient probes and forceps, it was recognized practice for surgeons to feel for bullets inside wounds with their fingers. Some Southern doctors hit upon the trick of probing deep wounds with small wands of freshly-whittled soft pine wood; when the wood touched a bullet, the lead would leave a gray mark as evidence.[3]

More than 20 per cent of the wounds occurred in the torso. Unless the bullet went fairly straight into a man's body, without being deflected by ribs or cartilage, there was little chance of recovering it. The surgeons dressed the wound and the victim either died or recovered. If he lived, he carried the bullet inside him to the end of his days. Wounds that perforated organs were nearly always fatal. Little could be done to repair the damaged organs. From a Federal surgeon's paper published in New York, Confederate surgeons developed one helpful technique. They learned to collapse a lung to save wounded shot through the lung.[4]

Hemorrhages killed thousands of soldiers after wounds or operations. These spells of intense bleeding occurred anywhere from a few hours to two weeks after battle. Sometimes they could be checked by tourniquets, hand pressure, cold compresses or styptics. Little could be done, however, for internal hemorrhages. Often the ambulance movement of gravely wounded men over rough country roads jolted the patients until arterial bleeding began. The two-wheeled and four-

[3] *University of Pennsylvania Medical Alumni in the Civil War*, a special 100-page edition of *Medical Affairs*, Spring, 1961, published by the University of Pennsylvania and edited by Alan C. Wood and Joan Woollcott.

[4] Dr. Stark in the *Virginia Medical Monthly*, December, 1960.

wheeled ambulances, horse-drawn, proved a frightful ordeal in themselves.

Tetanus added to the post-operative perils of the wounded, especially in areas where the soil was contaminated. Barnyard emergency hospitals usually were rife with the germs. Where many wounded were sheltered in them, as at Antietam and Fredericksburg, the tetanus mortality rate ran to 89 per cent.[5] An attack of "lockjaw," as it was called, usually proved fatal. The Confederate medical manual summed it up with epitaph brevity. It said that while the list of ineffective tetanus treatments would fill a volume, "to record those entitled to confidence does not require a line."

While the North had the medicinal resources of the world to draw upon, the blockaded South turned for substitute drugs to its native fields. A text by Dr. Francis P. Porcher, professor of medicine at the Medical College of South Carolina, suggested some of the substitutions: for calomel, dandelion, butterfly weed and pleurisy root; for belladonna, Jamestown weed; for laudanum, hops and motherwort, and so on down a long list. Poppies were cultivated in the Carolinas and Florida to produce opium or morphine, with American hemlock as an alternative. Genuine drugs from Europe were run through the blockade with a priority ranking them with war munitions. Others were smuggled from the North into the South under ladies' hoopskirts and even inside children's dolls. One large china-headed doll named Nina became famous for making numerous trips with "a lot on her mind." Her china head was, of course, hollow except when packed with drugs.

On the march, the ministration of medicine was simple to an elementary degree. Dr. W. H. Taylor, a Confederate army surgeon, related that his field pharmacopia consisted of two balls of drugs carried in his trouser pockets. One was "blue mass," a laxative of calomel velocity. The other was opium. At sick call, he said, "All complaintants were asked the same question, How are your bowels? If they were open, I administered a plug of opium. If they were shut, I gave a plug of blue mass."

The diseases and risks of field duty were not the only ones that beset the health of the soldier. As in every war, the wartime "profiteers" included camp followers of the oldest pro-

[5] Philip Van Doren Stern in *Today's Health*, published by the American Medical Association, December, 1959.

fession. The venereal disease rate for the Union Army is given officially as one case to every 12 men enlisted. Spirited Elizabeth Custer, 22-year-old bride of the general, wrote to her father from Washington in disgust that 10,000 prostitutes paraded the streets of the capital in a war effort of their own. Venereal disease appears to have marched with the Southern armies, also. Some Confederate hospitals established separate VD wards. One Southern army surgeon, Dr. S. H. Stout, went farther. He was instrumental in founding an entire hospital at Kingston, Georgia, exclusively for treating venereal disease. Pills compounded of pine resin and blue vitriol, washed down with whiskey, became one form of treatment.

At the start of the war, there was only one military hospital in the entire United States and it had 40 beds. All other medical and health preparations were at about the same pathetically inadequate level. No one was prepared for a national vogue in mayhem and murder.

The Federal army in 1861 included a medical corps of 114 surgeons and assistant surgeons headed by a scantily-trained physician aged 80. Of this corps, 24 Southerners soon went over to the Confederacy. With graduates of Virginia, South Carolina and other medical colleges, they formed the nucleus of the Confederate medical corps.

The Southern military doctors were headed throughout the war by two former U.S. Army surgeons, first Dr. David C. DeLeon, a native of Columbia, South Carolina, and then by Dr. Samuel Preston Moore, of Charleston, South Carolina. Another South Carolinian serving in the Confederate medical corps was Dr. Simon Baruch, father of the nation's "Elder Statesman" of the twentieth century, Bernard Baruch.

Dr. Clement A. Finley and Dr. Joseph K. Barnes, both University of Pennsylvania medical school graduates, served consecutively as Surgeon General of the Federal army. Finley, a conservative practitioner, once countermanded orders for the construction of a hospital at occupied Beaufort, South Carolina, on grounds that the mild climate there did not require it.

Some of the medical preparation for war was prompt and efficient indeed, but the means never caught up with the soaring demand. Before the conflict surged to an end, the Federal medical corps numbered 11,700 doctors and its Southern counterpart totaled 6,000. Among the Confederates were nearly all of the 119 prewar Southern medical students at the noted Jefferson Medical College in Philadelphia. Assailed by growing hostility from abolitionists and anti-Southerners in general, the students went south to Richmond in a body under the leadership of Dr. Hunter H. McGuire, later a Confederate surgeon of note. Dr. McGuire, a member of the Jefferson faculty, arranged for all of them to enroll in the Medical College of Virginia.

Altogether, on both sides, some 17,700 doctors faced the enormous task of attending more than 3,000,000 combatants ridden by wounds and disease. The wonder is not that so many of the patients died, but that so many survived. It is a tribute both to superlative physicians and superb constitutions of patients. The burden on the medical corps is best indicated by figures that every Federal soldier fell sick or wounded *at least twice*, while every Confederate came down on the average *six times*.[6]

Soon every city of any size, in both sections of the country, supported a series of military hospitals. They were especially numerous around Washington, Philadelphia and Richmond. Forty-two, including the world's largest, girdled Richmond with bedded sick and wounded. Chimborazo Hospital, named after a peak in the Andes because it was built on the highest spot above Richmond, handled 76,000 patients in three years in its 8,400 beds. Its director, Dr. J. B. McCaw, an able young physician recalled from cavalry duty, established sewage disposal, a brewery, a bakery, special farms, herds and an icehouse. The largest Federal institution, Lincoln Hospital, at Washington, cared for 46,000 patients in the course of the war.

Hospitals themselves were often most unhealthy. The overall death rate of Federal soldiers in them is given as 14.2 per

---

[6] The Confederate figure is not exaggerated. Many fell sick time and again. One of the author's great-uncles was hospitalized in October–December, 1863, again in January–February, 1864, and on returning to duty though enfeebled, was again hospitalized within four months at Williamsburg, Virginia, where his grandfather, a captain in the Continental Line from Rhode Island, had recovered from bayonet wounds suffered at Yorktown. The third-generation rebel, Sgt. Alfred Olney, 25th South Carolina Volunteers, was less fortunate. He died of acute dysentery 17 days after admission to Jackson Hospital, Richmond. His case history is given here because it is representative rather than unusual.

cent.[7] While no comparable over-all Confederate rate is available, the rate at the largest Southern hospital, Chimborazo, ran only 9 per cent.

Part of the high fatality rate no doubt was due to the employment of inferior personnel as hospital attendants. At the outset of the war, hospitals were regarded as "no place for ladies." All attendants were men. Frequently they were irresponsible and alcoholic. Some lapped up the "medicinal" liquor they were supposed to administer to their patients. Some surgeons also were not above doing the same thing.

Within two weeks after the guns first roared at Sumter, however, women organized to render aid.[8] In this they showed far greater foresight than many of the male leaders who planned optimistically and inadequately for a short, almost bloodless war. Dr. Elizabeth Blackwell, who had become the nation's first woman physician 14 years earlier on receiving a medical diploma at Geneva, New York, took the initiative with some of her associates. Through them, 3,000 women formed the Woman's Central Association of Relief at Cooper Institute in New York on April 25, 1861. An "advance guard" of 100 women nurses were trained for three months under auspices of the association. Others soon followed. Nursing became stylish instead of reprehensible. Six society women of one prominent family enrolled and served. They fed and nursed the sick, washed and dressed rooms, ventilated and supervised hospital wards.

One unpleasant bit of technical information in the nurses' manual of the day had to do with turning on and off the flow of blood in cases of induced or "therapeutic" bleeding. It explained the application of leeches or blood-sucking insects as follows:

"The part to which the leeches are to be applied should be carefully cleansed with soap and water, and dried. Leeches will be made more active by putting them in fresh water just before applying them.

"The bleeding of leech bites may be encouraged by warm fomentations of sponging with warm water. Should there be

[7] Miller's *Photographic History of the Civil War*, Vol. VII, page 301, and other sources.

[8] See "Lincoln's Ladies in White," by Sylvia G. L. Dannett, in the *New York State Journal of Medicine*, Vol. 61, No. 11, June 1, 1961, and other sources.

difficulty in checking the bleeding, use a pledget of scraped lint with pressure. If this fails, call the medical attendant."

Dorothea Dix, a 60-year-old spinster social reformer, received an appointment from the Secretary of War to act as superintendent of nurses in all Federal hospitals. Much against male-dominated medical and public sentiment, it was decided that female nurses be admitted to all hospitals. Miss Dix made all sorts of rules to safeguard this invasion by females into male sanctums. Nurses were to be older women, plain-looking and plainly dressed. Hoopskirts, in particular, were banned.

The female invasion found itself facing repulsive situations as well as antagonistic men. A soldier suffering from a gaping, maggot-infested shell wound appealed to young Sophronia Bucklin to dress his wound. She began—and encountered nearly a pint-full of crawling, black-headed maggots. These she chloroformed with the aid of a passing surgeon and coolly removed.[9] Mrs. Anne Wittemyer, an Iowa widow, reformed hospital diet. While she was in a Mississippi Valley hospital, she heard a soldier reject food and be told, "That's all you'll get." She looked. The soldier was her brother. The food was fat pork floating in grease—hardly fit for a well man, much less an ill one. She devised a special soft diet that all hospitals soon adopted for patients in need of it.[10]

Most famous of the angels of mercy on the Northern side were Clara Barton, of Red Cross fame, and "Mother" Mary Bickerdyke. Mrs. Bickerdyke regularly overruled surgeons and once awed General Sherman into admitting that as a matter of fact "she ranks me." She fought tenaciously for the welfare of "her boys" against all manner of red tape and military procrastination.

Mother Bickerdyke and Clara Barton had their energetic counterparts in the South. One of them managed her own hospital. Sally Louise Tompkins, a Richmond belle, established a hospital in a private home at Third and Main Streets. She conducted it so well that only 5 per cent of her 1,333 patients died —nearly a record of good management for the time. When all private hospitals were placed under Government control, President Jefferson Davis commissioned Miss Tompkins a

[9] Sophronia E. Bucklin, *In Hospital and Camp*, Philadelphia, 1869.

[10] A. Wittemyer, *Under the Guns, A Woman's Reminiscences of the Civil War*, Boston, 1895.

captain in the Confederate Army so that she could continue in charge of her hospital. She accepted the commission, but refused the pay.

Another Confederate heroine actually suffered a crippling wound on the battlefield while aiding fallen soldiers. She was Mrs. Juliet Ann Opie Hopkins, of an Alabama plantation family. In 1861, Mrs. Hopkins went to Richmond and established a private hospital. On it she lavished most of her fortune, estimated at $500,000 or more. She was active under fire from the opening battle, Bull Run, or First Manassas. Gen. Joseph E. Johnston praised her work as being worth more to morale "than a brigade," and wounded soldiers regarded it as a privilege to be taken to her hospital. Although 44 years of age, she unhesitatingly shared hardships and dangers at the front. A chance bullet wounded her so severely at Seven Pines, however, that she remained lamed for the rest of her life. The state of Alabama in appreciation of her services put her portrait on its $50 currency of the 1860s. Upon her death in 1890, she was buried in the National Cemetery at Arlington with military honors.

It was just as well that women came into their own as aides to the hospitalized, for more than a few men rejected their civilian roles as physicians in favor of fighting. Some went about battling part time, others full time. Dr. M. P. Waller, M.D., a Confederate surgeon known as "the best shot in Virginia," served as a sharpshooter when not in demand in the operating room. Dr. Thomas H. Carter, M.D., another Virginia physician, fought throughout the war as a Confederate artilleryman and rose to the rank of brigadier general. In the Federal ranks, there were men like Dr. G. A. Fairlamb, a University of Pennsylvania medical graduate, who preferred the sword to the scalpel. Fairlamb commanded the 148th Pennsylvania and enjoyed twitting physicians wearing the green sash of the medical corps. One morning in 1864 he approached several of them and remarked:

"Fine morning, gentlemen. Clear sky and balmy weather. Everything getting ready for a fight. The turkey buzzards and surgeons are gathering around, ready for business."

12

How Wives Influenced Generals

"My darling husband, why are you not with us? . . . Jeff Davis has a post ready for you . . ."
Where the choice lay between a wife on one side and the rest of a general's relatives on the other, the little woman usually won. Some notable military careers were made by men allied by birth, blood, and upbringing to the side they fought against.

Nowhere among the many heroic names of the Civil War will you find those of a certain Martha, nicknamed Patty, nor of other young matrons including Frances Lucretia, Rachel and Catherine Amelia. Except for "angels of mercy" like Clara Barton, who later founded the American Red Cross, and daring female spies such as the blond rebel Belle Boyd, most of the ladies stayed discreetly away from the front lines. On the home front the propaganda force exerted by Julia Ward Howe, with her words converting an old Southern camp-meeting song to *The Battle Hymn of the Republic*, and Harriet Beecher Stowe, through her anti-slavery novel *Uncle Tom's Cabin* was of course enormous. But feminine propaganda and persuasion also took far subtler forms.

The few wives mentioned by name, and others like them, swayed the course of the war as strongly as if each were a manly battalion. They served effectively right in their own homes. For each was wed to a military leader who by birth and by rights belonged on the opposite side to the one which he served. It was the wives who helped to determine their husbands' seemingly contradictory allegiances.

The shaping of history in this instance reads like the marriage announcements of a current society page. To mention two:

In 1848 Philadelphia-born John C. Pemberton, a West Pointer and Army career officer, married demure little Martha Thompson of Norfolk, Virginia, "Patty" to her intimates.

On November 17, 1852, another West Point career soldier, stalwart George H. Thomas, son of a Virginia planter, wed Frances Lucretia Kellogg in her home town, Troy, New York.

It is not far fetched to say that these intersectional marriages, and others like them, exerted a distinct influence on the course of the Civil War.

Pemberton, a Northerner wed to a Southern woman, quit the United States Army and became a top-ranking Confederate general.

Thomas, on the other hand, led Union troops against his native South so resolutely that he went down in history as "the Rock of Chickamauga" for almost magically saving the Union Army from destruction there. He inflicted serious defeats on the Confederacy later at Franklin and Nashville, Tennessee.

Forty Confederate generals, or about 6.5 per cent of the total, were Northern-born. Fifty-two Federal generals were Southerners by birth. The majority of the "galvanized" Confederates with Yankee accents contracted their strongest ties with the South by marrying Southern belles. On the other side of the fence, intersectionally and in battle, were not only Virginian George Thomas with his New York spouse but many other Southern career officers wed to Northern women.

Where the choice lay between a wife on one side and the rest of a general's relatives on the other, the little woman usually won. Some fantastic family feuds resulted.

The home-front plight of George Thomas was painfully typical. Thomas grew up on a tidewater Virginia plantation. He accepted slavery as a fact of life. As a teen-ager, he taught his family's Negroes to read and write and spent much time in the slave quarters. Ironically he and his widowed mother and sisters were almost killed in one of the worst slave rebellions. In 1831 Nat Turner incited sixty drunken Negroes to slaughter fifty-five white men, women and children. Their path led to the Thomas plantation. If the Widow Thomas had not been warned in time to flee with her brood, the Union Army which "fought to free the slaves" might have lost a good general.

Captain Thomas was stationed at West Point in the 1850s

as an artillery instructor when he met his Northern bride-to-be. It began by borrowing books—Hawthorne, James Fenimore Cooper, and the romance of Josephine and Napoleon. Frances Kellogg, like the man she married, stood nearly six feet tall. By the standards of those prebasketball days, she was almost a giantess. Fellow officers of Thomas described her as a "noble" woman, a term which men use for a remote form of admiration.

For seven years after the wedding the couple lived at lonely posts as Army man and Army wife. Thomas fought Indians, heat, dust and contentious superior officers. Usually he won. A lone Comanche defiantly shot an arrow into his chest. He plucked it out himself.

Then came the crisis of secession. An Army wife does not give orders—at least, not openly—to her husband. Mrs. Thomas was to assert later that she never once said a word to George "upon the subject of his remaining loyal to the United States Government." She subsequently added, "No one could persuade him to do what he felt was not right. . . . From the time the actual fact of war was upon us, General Thomas's course was clear. . . ."

Regardless of how much Mrs. Thomas influenced her husband, there is no doubt that she was admirably situated to do so. When Thomas came East on leave late in 1860 and joined her in New York City, he had not seen her in more than a year. Fed up with the rawness of frontier life, she had gone home to the comforts of civilization. Thomas missed her sorely. Later, during the war, a private once applied directly to the general for a furlough. "I ain't seen my old woman, gin'ral, for four months," the private explained forthrightly. Thomas replied that he had not, at that time, seen his own wife in two years. "If your general can endure such privation," he said, "certainly a private can." The private's last words stressed the strategic position of the female in war or peace. "Don't know about that, gin'ral," he replied. "You see, me and my wife ain't made that way."

Thomas was one of the many who fought the war to save the Union, not to abolish slavery. In fact, he blamed the whole conflict on Northern abolitionists. During the war, he continued to own Negroes as personal servants. There is little to indicate that he ever "emancipated" his Negroes. After the war he simply sent them to a brother in the Deep South.

With the war ended, Thomas became even more of a Unionist. Except for kindly gestures to a few former Confederates within the close-knit fraternity of West Point graduates, he behaved like a bitter "rebel hater." He commanded the Federal army of occupation in conquered Tennessee, Kentucky, Georgia, Alabama and Mississippi and ruled more harshly, if anything, than Sherman did elsewhere in the South. One example will suffice: When Episcopal Bishop Richard H. Wilmer of Alabama instructed his clergymen not to say prayers in behalf of a Federal Government which regulated the state with bayonets, General Thomas, himself at least nominally an Episcopalian, suspended the bishop and closed his churches.

After Thomas died in 1870, a broken man not yet fifty-five years of age, he received an Episcopal funeral with highest national honors at his wife's home town, Troy, New York. Not one of his Thomas relatives attended. In the family home in Virginia, a large portrait of Thomas hung face to the wall. It had been that way since the day his two sisters, Judith and Fanny, received word that he sided with the Union. It was then that they wrote him their last letter. It was a terse request that he change his name. After the funeral, one of the sisters explained their absence, "To us, our brother died in 1861."

Could any human influence except a strong-minded wife's have counterbalanced sisters like those?

Pemberton, the Philadelphian with the Southern wife, meanwhile lived through the same kind of agonizing family predicament from the other side of the skirmish lines. Except for his Norfolk-born Patty, he had no real link with the South. His family roots went deep into Northern soil. A Quaker ancestor accompanied William Penn from England and settled on a farm in Bucks County, Pennsylvania. The farm remained in family hands for 250 years, finally being engulfed and urbanized by Levittown, Pennsylvania.

As a unit, the Pemberton family, members of Philadelphia society, opposed John's "madness" in abandoning the Union. His favorite brother pleaded with him not to take the "fatal step." On the very day that he decided to join the Confederate ranks, two of his younger brothers enlisted in the elite First Troop, Philadelphia City Cavalry, to fight for the Union. With her sons thus divided, his mother wept. His wife remained resolute.

Unlike the reserved, stately Mrs. Thomas, pert five-foot-two Patty Pemberton gave written evidence of her stand. Through it ran a refrain like martial music—"To live and die in Dixie." While John debated with relatives in Philadelphia, Patty remained South. John's mother wrote disconsolately to another relative, ". . . a letter came to John from Patty, in which she says, 'My darling husband, why are you not with us? Why do you stay? Jeff Davis has a post ready for you. . . .'"

John, who held strong state's-rights and secession convictions of his own, soon heeded his wife. Commissioned a Confederate officer, he organized cavalry for Stuart, then succeeded Robert E. Lee as commander of the South Carolina-Georgia-Florida department. He strengthened the Charleston fortifications, although he upset Charlestonians by suggesting that Fort Sumter be abandoned as of little or no military value.

As a lieutenant general, Pemberton assumed command at Vicksburg, Mississippi, control point of the great waterway. Improving its defenses, he vainly requested heavier guns to keep Federal river flotillas from prowling up and down the Mississippi.

Pemberton's crowning misfortune occurred when he was besieged by a smarter Yankee, Maj. Gen. Ulysses S. Grant. Pemberton fought stoutly during a long siege, but relief failed to come, and he was compelled to surrender July 4, 1863. He later served as an artillery officer in the defense of Richmond and remained a Confederate in spirit to his dying day.

John Pemberton and his Patty lie side by side in Philadelphia's Laurel Hill cemetery on a shady hillside overlooking the Schuylkill valley. Only a small, severely plain, marble headstone marked their resting place until the fall of 1961, although the cemetery around them is filled with ornate military tombstones surmounted with sabers, cannon and even boots. Amid this panoply was no indication that the ranking officer interred there was a lieutenant general, CSA, until the Philadelphia Chapter, United Daughters of the Confederacy, emplaced a bronze tablet with name and rank that the U.S. Government makes available to all American veterans of all wars. Pemberton's family was represented by a great-grandson, John C. Pemberton, IV, a Philadelphia banker. The author made a brief dedicatory speech, mentioning that the same cemetery is the final resting place of Pemberton, the Philadelphian who served the Confederacy, and

Captain Drayton, USN, the Charlestonian who served the Union even to shelling his own brother (see Chapter 13).

Pemberton was only one among many high-ranking Confederates of Northern birth whose hearts belonged to ladies of the South. Samuel Cooper, a native of Hackensack, New Jersey, wed the sister of a senator and darling of one of Virginia's first families, the Masons, back in 1827. In 1861 Cooper resigned as adjutant general of the United States Army and became adjutant general of the Confederate forces. In that capacity he was the senior general and military right-hand man of his old friend and fellow West Pointer, President Jefferson Davis.

The Confederacy also obtained its chief of ordnance, an exceedingly competent one, direct from the Northern ranks by way of marriage. Josiah Gorgas, a Pennsylvanian and West Pointer, wed Amelia, daughter of Governor Gayle of Alabama, in 1853 while stationed in that state. The war found him in command of the Frankford Arsenal at Philadelphia. Leaving, he headed the entire Southern ordnance effort and achieved remarkable results in producing arms in a beleaguered land with scanty mechanical resources.

In addition to losing Gorgas, one of his bright young men, aging Brig. Gen. James W. Ripley, chief of United States Army ordnance in 1861–63, also lost his favorite nephew. Roswell Ripley, a West Pointer from Ohio, married Miss Alicia Middleton, of a prominent Charleston family, in 1852 while stationed in the South, and resigned from the Regular Army three months later. When Fort Sumter was shelled, Ripley was back in uniform—as a Confederate. An expert artilleryist, he soon commanded the 146 guns defending Charleston harbor. Later he became a brigadier general and was severely wounded at Sharpsburg, no doubt by a piece of his uncle's ordnance.

The elder Ripley was not alone in his personal embarrassment and distress. Down the hall in another Washington office clerked the venerable Charles K. Gardner, Adjutant General in the War of 1812. Gardner now did his bit with a quill pen and he did it under a secret strain. His son and pride, Franklin Gardner, a New Yorker by birth, had married a Miss Mouton, of an old Louisiana family. Unlike some other West Pointers who turned civilian and settled in Dixie with

Southern brides, Gardner continued as an infantry captain until "dropped from the service" May 7, 1861, for accepting a Confederate commission. Again a wife won against her in-laws. Gardner became a major general, CSA.

The Confederacy gained by the marriage of Northern soldiers to Southerners at least three other major generals, all seasoned West Pointers. These were: Martin Luther Smith, of Danby, New York, who wed an Athens, Georgia, beauty; Samuel G. French, born in Gloucester, New Jersey, who, says Ezra J. Warner in his book, *Generals in Gray*, "acquired by his marriage a plantation in Mississippi and resigned from the Army in 1856 to supervise it"; and Archibald Gracie, Jr., a New Yorker whose family residence has become the New York mayor's mansion. Gracie, wed to a Richmond belle, served with distinction as a Confederate major general until killed by a shell at Petersburg in 1864. Throughout the war he had written faithfully to relatives in New York, the letters going through the lines in mail pouches under truce flags.

Two of Lee's principal military engineers, both brilliant young West Pointers, were Northerners wedded to Southerners. Walter Husted Stevens, of Penn Yan, New York, who married a Louisiana beauty of the noted Hebert family, ably directed the building of fortifications around Richmond. Lee later made him chief engineer with the rank of brigadier general. Charles R. Collins, a Pennsylvanian, served the Confederacy so well that Gen. Braxton Bragg requested his transfer to Bragg's army in Tennessee. Lee replied "Collins cannot be spared." Death cut down Collins, then a colonel, at Spottsylvania in 1864. Ellsworth Eliot, Jr., in his book, *West Point in the Confederacy*, comments: "At the beginning of the war he joined the Confederacy only after the greatest hesitation. His wife was a Virginian, and that proved the final test."

The war efforts of the Northerners in gray were offset in some measure by those of Southerners—loyal husbands of Northern wives—in blue.

Philip St. George Cooke, as proper a general as ever returned a private's salute, found himself caught up to his shoulderstraps in a particularly complicated family clash. Cooke, son of a Virginia plantation owner and his English wife—hence the St. George—was graduated from West Point in 1827. While a cavalry lieutenant a few years later, he married Rachel Hertzog of Philadelphia. With the war, he remained steadfastly in the Union army and rose to the rank of brevet or temporary major general. In the gray army opposing him were his son-in-law, son and nephew.

As a Union cavalry commander in the Peninsula campaign, Cooke experienced perhaps the utmost humiliation which can befall a father-in-law. His son-in-law publicly outwitted him in spectacular style. The son-in-law, wed to Cooke's daughter Flora, was none other than J. E. B. Stuart, cavalry chieftain of the Army of Northern Virginia. When Cooke sided with the Union, Stuart remarked tartly, "He will regret it but once, and that will be continuously." Later, with 1,200 troopers and a section of field guns, Stuart rode entirely around the Union army of nearly 100,000, whose flanks Cooke guarded. Cooke's cavalry pursued in vain. Stuart completed his startlingly brash four-day reconnaissance with scarcely a loss.

The Union general's nephew, John Esten Cooke, later a writer and historian, served on Stuart's staff. The general's son, John R. Cooke, resigned from the United States Army in 1861. Wounded seven times in sixteen months, he eventually became an outstanding Confederate brigadier. Father and son were not reconciled until many years after the war.

Another Southerner with a Yankee wife developed into one of the most rip-snorting combat generals in the Union Army. This was John Newton, son of an old Norfolk shipping family. Newton was graduated from West Point in 1842, became an Army engineer and, in 1848, married Anna M. Starr, daughter of a leading banker of New London, Connecticut. They had five sons and a daughter, and there never was much question of where Newton's affection and allegiance lay. In the war, he led Union infantry at Fredericksburg, Chancellorsville and Gettysburg, and specialized in bayonet charges. In one of these he lost 1,000 of 3,500 men in three minutes, but carried his objective overwhelmingly.

There were, of course, Southerners with Southern wives who remained unswerving in their allegiance to the Union. While Northern-born Sam Cooper served as the ranking Confederate general, the senior United States general at the start of the conflict was massive old Winfield Scott, a Virginian with a Virginia wife. It was Scott who said sadly of the seceding states, "Wayward sisters, depart in peace," and who, when the war became inevitable, offered command of the Union field forces to a fellow Virginian whom he thought would make a good general, a Col. Robert E. Lee.

Dark, taciturn David G. Farragut, born in Tennessee of a North Carolina mother, reared largely in New Orleans, and wed to a lady from Norfolk, dispelled all doubts as to his loyalty and emerged as ranking admiral of the Navy.

The aristocratic Rhetts of Charleston, meanwhile, were put to some patriotic embarrassment by another Naval person, a relative of theirs born in Wilmington, North Carolina. This was John Ancrum Winslow. He was related to the Rhetts on his mother's side, but the Winslow went all the way back to the *Mayflower*. Moreover, in 1837, while a young Naval officer, he married a Yankee cousin, Catherine Amelia Winslow of Boston. Catherine was strongly against slavery, and her John soon became known as a "rabid abolitionist." The Rhetts had ceased to mention his name long before he became world-famous, but they were not really surprised at his conduct. What he did, as captain of the USS *Kearsarge*, was to sink the famous Confederate raider *Alabama*. It made Catherine very happy.

General John Pemberton
Confederate Museum, Richmond, Va.

Martha Thompson Pemberton

GENERALS AND WIVES

General John Newton

Anne Starr Newton

BROTHER AGAINST BROTHER

William Culp (bottom left) fought for the Union; his brother Wesley (bottom right) was a Confederate. Both escaped injury when their units clashed in June, 1863. But Wesley was killed at Gettysburg in July. He fell on Culp's Hill, part of the family farm. The only trace found of him was his name on this musket stock (above).

13

Brother Against Brother

Although the phrase "brother against brother" became routine rhetoric for postwar orators, here is the first detailed account of the Draytons, who battled each other with cannon; the Gibbons, who led opposing infantry; the Culps, one of whom, in the Stonewall brigade, came home to die in the Battle of Gettysburg while storming Culp's Hill. How did they feel about fighting kinsmen?

How does it feel to risk killing your own brother?

Once you were boys together in a golden world that scarcely knew gloom. You ate, played, fished, swam, argued, wrestled and grew up as one flesh-and-blood. Gradually you formed opinions that divided you, or else you moved apart in the great American restlessness. War ripped the nation. You enlisted. So did your brother. You realized, "My brother is on the other side." On a sudden day, you faced the other side gun in hand. Someone, distant and impersonal, began shooting at you. The order came, Fire back. Across the top of your gunsight there flashed a memory picture of your brother's face. You wondered where on the other side he was . . . and fired.

Time and again in the intense physical and emotional agony of the Civil War, fighting men met the cruel question of whether they would shoot down their brothers in combat. Literally thousands of kinsmen, separated by convictions or circumstances, fought on opposite sides. Usually a kindly fate kept warring brothers apart. But not always. Some faced directly the stain of Cain-and-Abel sin. Their reaction often could be summed up in one scathing sentence: "He was so dead wrong that he might as well be dead." Yet beneath the bitter surface there ran a tender mourning and a remembrance of being little children together.

190

Perhaps the most dramatic personal conflict befell the brothers Drayton, one Federal and one Confederate. They fought it out almost in their own back yard with cannon.

The split in the Drayton family, South Carolina planters whose descendants still own world-famous Magnolia Gardens near Charleston, South Carolina, went back to the nullification issue of the 1830s. At that time, South Carolina threatened to secede over a states'-rights controversy that had little or nothing to do directly with slavery. Nullification, as advocated by John C. Calhoun and others, meant that a state could nullify or ignore Federal measures which it found objectionable—in this case, a high tax on imports.

William Drayton, who favored a strong Federal Government, felt compelled by the controversy to move from Charleston to Philadelphia. There he ultimately became a successor to Nicholas Biddle as president of the Bank of the United States. His sons Thomas and Percival, born in Charleston, went separate ways. Thomas, a classmate of Jefferson Davis at West Point, later left the United States Army and became a planter with a palatial home on Hilton Head Island, South Carolina. Percival, four years younger, entered the Navy at fifteen as a midshipman and pursued a naval career. Ashore he usually lived in Philadelphia or New York.

With war imminent, the two brothers went to St. Michael's Church in Charleston, according to a family legend, and beneath its classic white spire prayed for divine guidance. They walked out, shook hands and went to serve as their consciences dictated—Thomas, the older, as a brigadier general, CSA, Percival as a Union Naval commander.

General Drayton did not have far to go. He took command of a part of the "soft underbelly" of the Confederacy —the coast, with its broad, inviting bays and inlets between Charleston and Savannah. His heavily gunned twin forts, Walker on Hilton Head and Beauregard on Bay Point, commanded the entrance to Port Royal Sound. The nearby Drayton plantation mansion, Fish Hall, served as headquarters.

Against the forts on November 7, 1861, the Union launched a major Naval attack. Sixteen warships under grizzled Samuel F. DuPont made the strike. Fifteen circled between the forts, shelling both in a cannonade which could be heard seventy miles away. The Confederates hit back. Soon there were eight killed and twenty-one wounded aboardship and the sand-covered decks ran blood.

The sixteenth ship, the gunboat *Pocahontas*, hung back out of range. The gunboat's captain began to be darkly suspected. Then, with a mighty belch of smoke, the *Pocahontas* darted close to the flank of Fort Walker with all guns blazing. In short order, the Confederates abandoned the fort and Hilton Head fell. General Drayton reported that the flanking attack by the *Pocahontas* and other gunboats "annoyed and damaged us excessively. . . ."

Any who doubted the loyalty of the gunboat's captain had a conclusive answer. Only engine trouble had held him back. Lean, black-bearded Percival Drayton was Unionist enough to bombard his own kin and put shells through his brother's roof. As chance had it, no Draytons were killed. There were enough of them around. Thomas had as his aides sons Carlos and John, while a sixteen-year-old son, William, ran messages. Percival opposed not only his brother and nephews, but a distinguished naval cousin, Commodore Josiah Tatnall, who commanded the tiny Confederate "mosquito fleet" at Port Royal.

"To think of my pitching here right into such a nest of my relations, my brothers, nephews, Tatnall and others," Percival confided soon afterward to a New York friend. "It is very hard, but I cannot exactly see the difference between their fighting against me and I against them except that their cause is as unholy a one as the world has ever seen and mine just the reverse."

Percival Drayton, whose peculiar position gave him an unusual insight into slavery, detested the practice and condemned it publicly. "My brother," he wrote in 1862, "thinks I am not quite sound on the Constitutional rights of slave owners and thinks that they [slaves] cannot be looked upon as persons. My answer to him was that when a poor [fugitive slave] woman comes crying to me for the loss of her children whom she could rejoin [only] by returning to a state of slavery, she has at least two of the distinctive attributes of the rest of the human race, love of liberty and offspring. . . ."

Drayton rose high in the naval service. In 1863, he commanded the new USS *Passaic*, one of the seven Ericsson-built monitors which bombarded Fort Sumter with two other ironclads in a vain attack on his native Charleston. Ericsson and the Northern public appeared to expect miracles, he commented later, "but I for one have serious doubts that the few ironclads at our disposal can do much toward the reduction of my native city." Angered that a native South Carolinian would assail his own home, the South Carolina Legislature discussed proscribing or outlawing him along with other "traitors" serving the Union.

Drayton meanwhile harried the Southern coast and became fleet captain under Admiral D. G. Farragut. In the daring Federal attack at Mobile through floating mines, then called torpedoes, it was Drayton to whom Farragut is said to have issued his famous order: "Damn the torpedoes! Full speed ahead."

The first communication that Drayton received from his Southern relatives after the war came from nephew William, then in Texas, in the form of a boyish letter: "Dear Uncle Percy. If I recall correctly my first fight was against you when you gave us such a thrashing at Port Royal. . . ." Before the year 1865 was out, Percy Drayton died, exhausted by his war service. They buried him in Philadelphia.

Drayton was by no means the only naval officer whose sense of brotherhood suffered a bitter test under fire. One of the most famous naval engagements of the Civil War opened with two brothers each shelling the other's ship. This was the battle in which the ironclad CSS *Virginia*, ex-USS *Merrimack*, destroyed the wooden frigates *Congress* and *Cumberland* in Hampton Roads before the epochal clash with the *Monitor*.

The captain of the *Virginia* was white-haired, eagle-faced Commodore Franklin Buchanan. From an early start as a midshipman at fourteen, he had served as a U.S. Navy Officer for forty-six of his sixty years. He fought heroically in the Mexican War, founded the Naval Academy at Annapolis, and finally became a ranking Confederate naval officer by a freak of fate. Peppery "Old Buck," as he was called, resigned as a high U. S. Navy officer because he expected his native Maryland to secede. When it did not, he humbly sought to withdraw his resignation. Coldly, the Washington bureaucrats refused. Feeling cast out, Buchanan joined the Confederate service but deplored the conflict as "the most unnatural, useless, fratricidal war ever known." He prophesied almost better than he realized.

As the awesome *Merrimack* steamed toward the outclassed USS *Congress*, the sixty-two-year-old purser or paymaster of the Union ship, who ranked as a commander, requested the captain to assign him to battle duty. In reply to a question from the captain, Purser McKean Buchanan replied evenly, yes, he knew who commanded the rebel ram—his younger brother. Apparently Commodore Buchanan knew that his older brother was on the *Congress*, also. It did not deter him.

Ordering his Confederates to battle stations, Old Buck exhorted: "Do more than your duty! Those ships must be taken!"

At point-blank range of 300 yards, the *Merrimack* fired a broadside which tore through the wooden *Congress* and sent her reeling. Then the ironclad sank the *Cumberland* in quick order, and opened fire again on the hapless *Congress*.

McKean Buchanan, given command on the berth deck, saw shell after shell rip completely through his ship and strew dead and wounded like jackstraws. The *Congress* became ablaze almost from stem to stern. One hundred and thirty-six of her crew of 434 were killed, wounded or drowned. Up went the white flag.

Instantly—could he have been thinking of his brother?— Old Buck ordered small craft to rescue the survivors. From the nearby shore, Union troops opened a hail of musket and cannon fire on the rescuers. The loaded broadside guns of the *Congress*, set off by the heat of flames, apparently joined in. A number of Confederate rescuers fell dead or wounded.

Hot-tempered Old Buck roared "Vile treachery!" to his second-in-command, Lieutenant Catesby ap Roger Jones, and ordered: "Burn that damned ship, Mr. Jones, she is firing upon our boats under her flag of surrender!" **Then** he seized **a** carbine and began shooting from an exposed position on the bridge. A Minié bullet from the shore soon tore through his thigh. He fell, so seriously wounded that he had to yield command of the *Merrimack* in her historic fight with the *Monitor* next day to Jones.

Brother McKean emerged from the slaughter alive, although he had a close call. He abandoned ship with the others, and was struggling in the chilly water when a small boat picked him up. Old Buck, on recuperating from his gunshot wound, proved himself as fiery a Confederate as ever. At Mobile Bay, in command of the lone Confederate ironclad *Tennessee*, he tackled an entire Union fleet, including three monitors, and wreaked widespread damage before being forced to surrender. He and his brother McKean both lived past the age of seventy, friends to the end. Theirs was a brother-hood that not even the stress of war could break.

Not all of the brotherly strife took place between high commanders. We know more about wartime clashes of the ranking officers simply because privates, as a rule, leave fewer memoirs. The story of two rank-and-file soldiers named Culp survives, however, because of the strange circumstances under which one of them died.

Wesley and William Culp, of Pennsylvania-German stock, grew up on the edge of a sleepy small town in south-central Pennsylvania, on the family farm with its rich bottom land and sprawling central hill. The swell of land known as Culp's Hill is one of the ageless hills. Leafy paths wind amid the dogwood and underbrush. Tall trees shade the inviting greenery. Gray stones, verdant with moss, outcrop in many places. A boy can race along the paths, hide under stone shelves or stretch out on top of a slab of rock and dream.

Wesley Culp was not the type to dream. He raced the paths, climbed rocks and trees, captured and held his own little world. The hill in his youth was, to him, *Wesley* Culp's hill. In time, while brother William remained at home, Wes moved away. The blue distance of other hills beckoned. Wes headed southwest along the valleys to Shepherdstown, in what was then Virginia and is now West Virginia. It was a fatal move.

Wes worked uneventfully in a carriage factory until war broke out. Then he enlisted in Company B, 2nd Virginia Infantry, in a brigade headed by a strange sort of professor general named T. J. Jackson. After First Manassas, the general became better known as the leader of Stonewall's Brigade. Wes marched, camped and fought and received mighty few letters from home. At mail call he was one of the forlorn.

Brother William, meanwhile, joined the 87th Pennsylvania Volunteers. The 87th headed south over almost the route that Wes had traveled in peacetime. In June of 1863 it held the valley town of Winchester, Virginia. Up the valley surged a wave of gray, Stonewall's Brigade to the fore. Enveloped by Ewell's Confederate corps, a third of the Union garrison of Winchester surrendered, and the rest departed in haste. Brother Wes didn't see brother Bill, but he met a boyhood chum from the same company, Cpl. Johnston, or Jack, Skelly, Company F of the 87th. Skelly lay critically wounded. Wes bent over him. Skelly whispered a message to be delivered to his sweetheart back home if and when the circumstances of war permitted. Wes listened faithfully, but he didn't have much time to think about it.

A few days later Wes and his comrades waded across the shallow Potomac at Shepherdstown in a great invasion of the North. Late in June he found himself in increasingly familiar country, around Greencastle, Chambersburg, Carlisle. Then the Confederate march swung to the right, and the country-side grew even more familiar.

On July 1, 1863, Wes experienced a strange home-coming to his native Gettysburg. He fought his way straight down the main street as an "invader." With his fellow Confederates he drove a disorderly rout of bluecoats through the rows of tidy red-brick homes and neat stores. In a final burst of fury the Confederates forced the Federal troops out of town.

Before nightfall the Federal forces rallied to the south and southeast of Gettysburg on two hilltops. One was Cemetery Hill, with its sign, ironical at the moment, prohibiting the discharge of firearms among the graves. The other slope needed no introduction to Private Culp of the Second Virginia. It was Culp's Hill—Wes Culp's Hill.

Then darkness enforced a lull. Wes obtained permission from his captain to slip back into Gettysburg under cover of night and visit a sister, Anna Culp, living on West Middle Street. She greeted him warmly, but warned that some relatives had threatened to "shoot the rebel on the spot" if they saw him. Wes smiled, ate his dinner and told her of Jack Skelly's message for his sweetheart, a girl named Jennie Wade. Anna offered to deliver it. Wes said no, he had promised to do so himself and would get around to it after the fighting ended. He ducked out and rejoined his command before daybreak.

The next day, July second, the Confederates made a determined drive to capture Culp's Hill. Unknown to them, however, Federal reinforcements had arrived. Wes charged up the familiar slope. An enemy gun crashed almost in his face. The shot proved fatal. A comrade paused long enough to pull his body under a tree broken over by shell fire. The gray charge spent itself in vain against the hillside.

Fate next day relieved Wes Culp of his unfulfilled promise to give his wounded friend's message to Jennie Wade. Near the close of the battle, Confederates volleyed at Union snipers sheltered behind Jennie's home. Five bullets tore through the door. One killed Jennie as she stood kneading dough in the midst of battle. She was Gettysburg's only civilian fatality.

After the battle, captured Confederates sent word of Wes Culp's death to his relatives. Uncles and cousins searched Culp's Hill in vain for his body. There were 7,000 dead strewn around Gettysburg. As one cousin later explained, "We found dozens of broken-over trees and dozens of bodies under them—but we never found Wes."

The onetime captain of Wesley Culp's company left behind a clear little word picture of him. Henry Kyd Douglas, later of General Jackson's staff, wrote in his memoirs, *I Rode With Stonewall* (Univ. of N.C. Press, 1940; Fawcett Publications, 1961): "There also fell in that assault Wesley Culp, private, Company B, Second Virginia Regiment, Stonewall Brigade. The hill was named after his family and he was from Gettysburg. He was 24 years old and very little, if any, over five feet, and when captain of the company I procured a special gun for him." The special gun no doubt was a short one.

William E. Culp, Wesley's brother in blue, meanwhile, was reported "missing in action" following the engagement at Winchester, Virginia. Four days after the Battle of Gettysburg, however, William rejoined the Federal Army at Frederick, Maryland, and served out the war.

While Wes and William Culp were spared the ordeal of shooting directly at each other in battle, a distinguished Union general and the youngest of his three Confederate brothers many times commanded their men to fire into each other's ranks.

Maj. Gen. John Gibbon, a Philadelphian by birth, grew up in Charlotte, North Carolina, after his physician father moved South. Entering West Point from North Carolina in 1842, he became a professional soldier. As such, he put his war views in a sentence: "Secession is rebellion and must be put down as such." His three Southern-bred brothers, Robert, Lardner and Nicholas, disagreed. All three became Confederate officers.

In a succession of major battles—Fredericksburg, Gettysburg, Spottsylvania—John Gibbon's divisions tangled directly with Lane's North Carolina brigade, in which young Nick Gibbon led a hard-fighting company. On the foggy morning of December 13, 1862, at Fredericksburg, Gibbon's bluecoats looked up the fatal heights to see the hill crest held by Lane's brigade. Their lines veered, but exchanged fire. At Gettysburg,

July 3, 1863, Nick's unit swept forward with Pickett's great, forlorn charge which smashed in vain at an adamant Union line commanded by brother John. At Spottsylvania, turning the tables, Nick's gray brigade blazed away at the flank of John's attacking troops so furiously that it broke their nearly triumphant charge at the Bloody Angle "with severe loss."

During the long siege of Petersburg, John Gibbon yielded to an impulsive wish to see his younger brother once more. A flag-of-truce steamship ran regularly up the James from City Point, Grant's headquarters, to Richmond. John wrote to "my dear brother" Nick, suggesting an unusual wartime meeting aboard the steamer and adding that he had Grant's permission. Nick's reply to "brother John"—no "dear" about it—is a penned study in scorn. He said that while General Lee no doubt would consent to the meeting, "it is not agreeable that I meet you under the circumstances. . . ." John responded in older-brother fashion: "Under no circumstances could a meeting with one of my brothers prove disagreeable to me. Should we ever meet hereafter, you will find me, as ever, Your affectionate brother. . . ." Nick, after encountering John's unaffectionate troops in battle, apparently did not care to sample John's fondness for him. Although the brothers survived the war, family tradition has it that Nick never again spoke to John.

A curious form of conflict occurred between John and another brother, Dr. Robert Gibbon. Robert, a medical-corps officer, served as brigade surgeon of the same North Carolina unit in which Nick fought. Many of the Confederate casualties treated by Robert were inflicted by John's bluecoats. At Gettysburg 348 wounded trickled back to the brigade surgeon's field hospital. There were times when John, too, could have used a doctor like Robert. John was hit by a bullet at Fredericksburg and was badly wounded at Gettysburg. He survived both wounds and became a· famous Indian fighter after the Civil War.

Another bitter split occurred between the brothers James M. and John B. McIntosh, who eventually became cavalry generals on opposing sides. Both were born at Tampa, Florida, sons of a Regular Army colonel who fell in battle in the Mexican War. James, the older, was graduated from West Point and served on the frontier. John, after graduation from Annapolis, fought in the Mexican War as a midshipman. He left the Navy in 1850 to marry and go into business in New Brunswick, New Jersey.

James jarred John in 1861 by resigning from the United States Army and becoming a Confederate officer. John, denouncing the act as "a blot on the family honor," took a Union commission and reputedly swore never to speak to his rebel brother again. He never had the opportunity. James, rising rapidly to brigadier general, was fatally shot through the heart while leading Southern cavalry at the Battle of Pea Ridge, Arkansas, March 7, 1862. John meanwhile served in the East. He lost his right leg in Virginia at the Battle of Winchester, in 1864, and later became a major general.

No state was more painfully divided by the war than borderline Kentucky. Out of its boiling controversy there emerged two notable sets of Union-versus-Confederate brothers, the Crittendens and the Breckinridges.

United States Senator John J. Crittenden of Kentucky opposed secession and used all his influence to keep his state in the Union—but could not keep his son George out of the Confederate army. George, a West Pointer, became a Confederate major general. He resigned his commission, however, after losing the battle of Logan's Crossroads in his home state early in 1862. His lawyer-businessman brother, Thomas L. Crittenden, succeeded better as an amateur soldier than George had done as a professional. Thomas commanded Union divisions at Shiloh, Stone's River and Chickamauga, ended up a major general and made the United States Army his postwar career.

Most of the Breckinridges of Kentucky were strongly pro-Southern. John C. Breckinridge, Vice President of the United States when the South seceded and an unsuccessful Presidential candidate against Lincoln, became a major general and later Secretary of War of the Confederacy. But his cousin, the Rev. Dr. Robert J. Breckinridge, a noted Presbyterian clergyman, ardently supported the Union. The clergyman's own family, however, was badly split. Four of his sons served as officers—two on each side. Robert, Jr., and W. C. P.— "Willie" to friends—wore gray, while Joseph and Charles, a young West Pointer, served the Union.

Willie, colonel of the hard-riding 9th Kentucky Cavalry of John Morgan's command, and Joseph, a young artillery lieutenant, narrowly missed meeting in battle in the bitter fighting around Atlanta. When a Southern onslaught captured

Joseph and his battery, Willie was only a few miles away. Joseph protested loudly that nobody could send him to prison camp—his second cousin was a Confederate general and his brother a Confederate colonel. His captors released him in Willie's custody, and the brothers spent the night in a friendly reunion. Willie tried unsuccessfully to have Joseph exchanged for a captured Confederate officer. That failing, Joseph was politely led off to imprisonment, first at Macon and later at Charleston.

The four border states—Maryland, Kentucky, Missouri and Delaware—contributed to both armies in ratio of about three Union to two Confederate. Eastern Tennessee, largely hills and backwoods, gave a majority of its men to the Federal service or to irregular bushwhacking against the Confederacy. Throughout these divided areas, brothers and other relatives often disagreed and took opposite sides in battle.

There is a pathetically touching, oft-told story of warfare in divided Kentucky or Tennessee which, although not verifiable at this late date, goes like this:

Union and Confederate militia or home guardsmen face each other in a fire fight at 200 yards or so. Both lines hold fast. In a sudden surge, the Union soldiers capture one young Confederate. As he is led away to the rear, he recognizes one of the Union riflemen as his brother. Greeting the brother briefly, he calls back over his shoulder:

"Don't you go a-shootin' under that chestnut tree. Thet's Pappy a-lying onder there."

At the outbreak of the war, the Widow Hickman's family split sharply. Originally the widow and her five sons by two marriages, John and Joel Van Hook and William, Zachariah and Snowden Hickman, lived on Barton's Creek, Wilson County, in middle Tennessee. But William and Zachariah, when they grew up, moved away. William settled in southwest Missouri, in a Unionist part of the state. Zachariah, after medical studies at Nashville, became a physician at Benton, Illinois. When hostilities began, William enlisted as a private in Company M, 8th Cavalry Regiment of Missouri State Volunteers, a Union unit. Zachariah became assistant surgeon of another Union regiment, the 110th Illinois Volunteer

Infantry. Their half-brothers, the Van Hooks, and their younger brother Snowden, who had remained at home with their mother, joined the Confederate forces in Tennessee.

Dr. Hickman's regiment soon invaded Tennessee and marched into the vicinity of his family home. The doctor at that point went back to Illinois on furlough. In his absence, his regiment captured his seventeen-year-old brother. The Adjutant General's *Book of the State of Illinois*, Volume VI, Page 111, recounts how the 110th Illinois surprised a Confederate outpost of 30 mounted men in an attack at daybreak. "One of the rebels captured was a brother of one of the assistant surgeons of the regiment. He was a mere boy, seventeen years old, who after being properly advised was sent back to his aged mother, who lived in the immediate neighborhood."

If the story had ended as the report says, its conclusion might have been a happy one. Unfortunately, young Snowden was *not* returned to his mother. The colonel of the 110th notified his older brother Zachariah of his capture, apparently with that in mind. But by the time word reached Zachariah, Snowden had been shipped off with the others to a crowded Federal prison near Washington, D.C. The boy was later exchanged, but arrived at Petersburg, Virginia, so weak and enfeebled that he contracted measles and died there. His nephew, Robert E. Hickman, attorney, of Benton, Illinois, in recent years searched in vain for his grave.

The nine Bodenhamer brothers, of Webster County, Missouri, fought in and around nearby Springfield with the family odds eight-to-one against the lone Confederate brother. While Lieutenant Christian Bodenhamer, CSA, served in the 3rd Missouri Cavalry of the Confederate Army, five other Bodenhamers rode with the rival 8th Missouri Cavalry, USA. William captained Company E, and Andrew Benjamin, Martin and Thomas served with him. Three more Bodenhamers wore the blue in the Union militia or homeguard. After the war, most of them moved south to Arkansas. But the Confederate brother, unreconciled, kept going all the way to Texas.

A tragic difference of opinion divided the distinguished Lieber family, German-Americans who ranked high as scientists, educators, writers and soldiers. The oldest brother died for the Confederacy, while his father and two other brothers supported the Union.

The father, Dr. Francis Lieber, a Prussian veteran of Waterloo, fled Europe to escape persecution for his liberalism. He settled in Boston. Oscar M. Lieber was born there and became a noted geologist before he was thirty. A second son, Hamilton, was born five years later in Philadelphia while Lieber was teaching at Girard College there. A third, Guido Norman, came into the world at Columbia, South Carolina, later burned in the war, where his father filled the chair of history and philosophy at South Carolina College from 1835 to 1856.

Dr. Lieber warned against secession as early as 1851, after the South Carolina Legislature discussed the move and set the privately-owned Palmetto Armory to manufacturing 11,000 guns, swords and pistols in the first and almost only prewar preparedness move. Lieber at the time kept a few slaves, apparently as household servants, but reputedly favored abolition. His attitude did not help him in his aspiration to become President of what is now the University of South Carolina. Failing to win appointment as President, he moved north out of the secessionist atmosphere and became head of the department of history and philosophy at Columbia University. During the Civil War, Dr. Lieber wrote a basic manual for the Federal Army, "Instructions for the Government of the Armies of the United States in the Field." It was so highly regarded by President Lincoln and the military that it was promulgated as General Order No. 101 to all Federal forces. Lieber also wrote an authoritative, internationally accepted pamphlet on guerrilla warfare.

Boston-born Oscar meanwhile joined the Confederate Army. Hamilton, and Norman, the native of Columbia, accepted Union commissions. Hamilton, as a lieutenant in the 9th Illinois Infantry, had his war career cut short by the loss of an arm at Fort Donelson. Norman, who hated the South, fought so well that he was promoted and ultimately became Judge Advocate General of the United States Army. On the same day, June 27, 1862, that Norman was advanced to captain for gallantry, his Confederate brother Oscar died of wounds suffered in the Battle of Williamsburg.

In the same Virginia theater of war, two other brothers clashed directly and fatally. Both were Marylanders. One served in a Maryland regiment in gray, the other led a Maryland regiment in blue.

Clifton K. Prentiss became captain of Company F, 6th

Regiment of Maryland Volunteers, USA, in 1862. Through much bitter fighting, he rose to be major in 1864 and acting regimental commander. His brother, William S. Prentiss, meanwhile enlisted as a private in Company A, 2nd Maryland Infantry, CSA, and saw much combat.

At Petersburg on April 2, 1865—just seven days before hostilities ceased—the Prentiss in blue led his regiment in a furious attack on one of the earthwork forts guarding Petersburg. Blazing away from inside the fort was his brother William, with the 2nd Maryland, CSA.

As Clifton led the storming column over the parapet, a bullet struck at his heart. It tore away the flesh and part of the breast bone, baring his palpitating heart to view. He fell forward into the fort, beside a Confederate defender who lay desperately wounded with a mangled leg. It was William. As their blood flowed together on the battlefield, the brothers in their agony recognized each other.

After the battle, the story goes, they were taken to the same hospital in Washington and attended by the same surgeons, nurses and chaplain. Neither survived. William died in June after the amputation of his leg. Clifton, promoted to full colonel for capturing William's fort, lingered on only until August 20th.

The fate of the heroic Terrill brothers, Virginians who served as generals on opposite sides, proved equally sad. They first parted ways in college. William R. Terrill went to West Point, graduated in 1853, and made the army his career. James B. Terrill, almost four years younger, graduated from the Virginia Military Institute in 1858, then studied and practiced law.

From 1861 on, both Terrills excelled as battlefield leaders. William rose to brigadier general by 1862. He was killed while rallying a wavering brigade of Union troops at the Battle of Perrysville, Kentucky, and lies interred at West Point. James, the V.M.I. graduate, commanded the crack 13th Virginia Infantry in many battles, though he was so near-sighted that the enemy often had to be pointed out to him. In a desperate charge at Bethesda Church, Virginia, in 1864, he stumbled with an awful bullet wound. Informed that his brigade commander was killed, he staggered ahead, waved his sword, and commanded, "Forward!" A second bullet tore through his brain. He died almost at the moment that the Confederate Congress confirmed his appointment as brigadier general.

Sorrowfully, old Colonel W. H. Terrill took home the body
of his second heroic son. The grave, in a small country
cemetery, has long been lost. So has a monument, if it ever
existed, which the grieving father is said to have erected to
both his sons—Brig. Gen. W. R. Terrill, USA, and Brig.
Gen. J. B. Terrill, CSA,—with the inscription:

"God alone knows which one was right."

THE BURNING OF THE "CONGRESS"

After a painting by J. O. Davidson

14

The Infidel's Sword

*How the faith of a private soldier led his
captain, an atheist, to become not only
a devout Baptist but the "Billy Graham"
of his day.*

The Bible, in Joel 3:10, gives some edged advice: "Beat your
plowshares into swords . . . Let the weak say, I am strong."

Obeying that Biblical injunction, the proprietors of the
Nashville Plow Works manufactured sabers for the Confederacy from plow metal early in the war.

The Federal Army, perhaps swayed by Isaiah 2:4—"They
shall beat their swords into plowshares"—brought the Nashville production to an abrupt halt in 1862. The Federals
seized the militant plow works and jailed the proprietors on
charges of treason. The charges were later dropped—indeed,
no Confederates ever were convicted of treason. But no more
plowshares were beaten into swords.

On another front of the war, a saber and religion became
even more curiously involved. An almost symbolic sword, this
one in the Union ranks, led to the conversion of an outspoken
atheist. Eventually the convert became one of the most effective and celebrated Gospel preachers in the country. The
blade that wrought the spiritual transformation was a richly
decorated presentation saber, given by admirers to a brisk
young Union captain for exceptional wartime services. The
glittering weapon was gold-sheathed and bore the Latin inscription, *Vera amicitia est sempiterna*—True friendship is eternal.
The sentiment was soon put to the test.

The boyish captain of Company D, 2nd Massachusetts
Heavy Artillery, not long out of Yale University and facing
the bloodiest war in American annals, scoffed at every mention of God.

The youngest recruit of Company D, Johnnie Ring, believed in God because his dead mother had taught him to do
so.

Fate and circumstance decreed that scrawny Johnnie Ring, who already had suffered much from life, should become the atheistic captain's personal servant. During their association the captain methodically shattered every one of the boy's illusions except one. It began when Johnnie's father, a Boston customhouse employee, entrusted his son to the officer. The father explained that Johnnie was determined to go to war. Rather than have him run away to enlist, the father begged the captain, "Let him go with you."

"I asked John," the captain related later, "if he was prepared to lie on the ground all night and wake up in the morning to find his hair frozen to the ground. He said he was.

"I asked him if he was willing to have an arm or leg shot off in the service of his country. He said he was. To all the most extravagant questions that I asked him, he would answer that he was willing to suffer any privation if he could go to war.

"I asked if he was willing to do any service for me, no matter how menial. He said he would be only too glad to do so. 'Well, John,' I said, 'I will take you as my servant.'"

Johnnie shared the captain's tent, sleeping on a low couch across from his camp cot. On their first night together under canvas, the boy took a little Bible out of his pocket and sat down to read it by the pale light of an Army lantern. The captain took one look and roared, "We don't believe in the Bible around here. Neither will you after you go into war. You can't read the Bible in my tent. Everybody knows I am opposed to it, and I would not for anything have anyone see you reading it in my tent."

Johnnie, surprised and pained, gazed up at his angry captain. Gently he explained that he had promised his dead mother he would read his Testament regularly every night. The captain snapped, "If you wish to read the Testament, get out of this tent and away from me. The officers will make fun of me. I respect your love for your mother, but I don't believe in the Bible, and I don't believe it will do you any good anyhow!"

So Johnnie and his little pocket Testament went underground. He could not see to read it outside in dimming twilights and by flickering campfires. Instead, he waited until the captain was out of the tent to snatch an opportunity. One evening the captain suddenly walked in and caught him at it.

"Johnnie, didn't I tell you not to read that Bible?" the

captain said. "Now do what your superior officer commands you! Stop it now! And don't read that Bible in my tent ever again."

The boy closed his Bible and started out of the tent in tears. As he left, he said, "Captain, I love you, but you are a very wicked man."

That was the last exchange between the oddly assorted pair on the subject of the Bible. It left the captain strangely disturbed, but he had no time for soul-searching and meditation. His regiment was ordered to duty near New Berne, North Carolina, in an area occupied early in the conflict. Its job was to guard a railroad line that ran from New Berne across the Newport River to the coast.

One pitchy night while the captain checked on sentries posted at the edge of the forest, a bullet sang out of the dark. It knocked him down. Miraculously it struck and smashed the watch in his pocket and left him scarcely wounded. When he was fully recovered, he rode into New Berne on business. While there, word came that Confederates under Maj. Gen. George Pickett had captured his encampment. The gray attackers surprised the sentries, caught many of the Union soldiers swimming or playing ball and set fire to the camp. The nearby railroad bridge also began to blaze.

As the Union troops retreated across the bridge, Johnnie called out, "Where is the captain's sword?" A sergeant replied that the captain had it on, but Johnnie knew that he wore his regulation field saber. The beautiful gold-sheathed blade which Johnnie polished with such care was hanging, as usual, in the captain's tent. Johnnie, without a word, ran back across the burning bridge and snatched it from the blazing tent.

By now the opposing forces were shooting at each other across the river. The bridge was so smoky and searing that Johnnie had to lean over the side to catch his breath. The Confederate commander nearest the span saw the heroic boy and ordered his men to cease firing. Someone waved a white handkerchief. All shooting halted while all eyes were upon Johnnie, who kept on running until he reached the far shore and fell insensible, uniform afire. Comrades tumbled him in the river to put out the fire.

Days later he recovered consciousness in the United States Army hospital at Beaufort, North Carolina. "Has the captain got his sword?" he asked weakly. A nurse replied that it was right there beside him. Johnnie asked to touch it. "I am glad that I saved his sword," the boy said. Then, "Is the captain coming to see me?" The nurse said they had sent word. But as the night wore on, she called the surgeon, who took one look and called the chaplain. "You are going to see your mother," the chaplain said. "You love your mother, and you believe in your mother's God. Now don't be afraid to go." The boy replied, "I am not afraid. But can't I live to see the captain?" Then he died.

The hospital informed the captain and returned his sword with its motto, "True friendship is eternal." The captain drew the sword and read the glowing words.

"I said, 'Eternal! Will I ever see Johnnie again? Is there any eternity?' Then I went back to work with a heart positively broken. I began to think, 'Oh, if only I could see him a few minutes to ask his forgiveness for the way I treated him.'"

The captain went on to other battlefields. He rose to the rank of lieutenant colonel, always with memories of Johnnie in the back of his mind. At the Battle of Kenesaw Mountain, near Atlanta, a shell wounded him so severely that he was left on the battlefield for dead.

"In that long night of pain and agony, I thought, 'Oh! is there another life? If there is, I want to find Johnnie.' If only I could have that little boy there to pray for me! I felt an awful desire to know about eternal life—if there was such a thing."

The next day, a cleanup detail found the colonel alive. In the hospital at Marietta they debated whether to amputate his arm. Only an old nurse's objection saved it. As soon as he became convalescent, the colonel called for a chaplain. A Baptist preacher responded. The preacher said, "Colonel, you are an awful sinner; you had better make up your mind to think of eternal things."

Then, the colonel later said, the chaplain "knelt down and made one of those formal, overpious kind of prayers that didn't mean anything, and ever since that time I have had an awful hatred of all those overpious wooden professors who pretend to carry on religious work. It didn't do me any good, and then the old nurse said, 'Why don't you pray for yourself?' Then I thought of Johnnie Ring, and I prayed that the Lord would let me meet him somewhere in eternity."

Later another Baptist chaplain stopped by the colonel's bed. "He was a different type," the colonel said approvingly. "He used some good common sense. He said to me, 'You know by instinct that there is an eternal life. If you would know about its details, read the Bible.' He opened my heart to God. I said, 'If there is any service that I can give to God, I will give it—not only for myself but for Johnnie Ring too. I will try to do his work in the world, as well as my own.'"

Years later the colonel commented, "It was a brave deed for that boy to save my sword. But it was a much braver deed for him to read his Bible and stand by the religion of his mother against the powerful influence of his own commanding officer. It is far braver to do some things in private life than it is to do deeds of bravery on the battlefield."

The colonel preached those words from the pulpit in 1921, four years before his death. During his lifetime he made good his pledge for Johnnie Ring. In doing so, the former atheist became an ordained Baptist clergyman. After building up a church in Lexington, Massachusetts, he was called to the discouraging task of revivifying Grace Baptist Church in Philadelphia. His inspiration remade it into the great Baptist Temple. To help heal bodies as well as souls, he founded three hospitals. Improving minds, he established Temple University, now nineteenth-largest in the nation. From one of his famous lectures, *Acres of Diamonds*, he derived the funds to educate more than 10,000 young men.

The former atheistic young soldier was Dr. Russell H. Conwell, the Billy Graham of his day. At age eighty-two he went to rejoin Johnnie Ring.

15

Why One Hero Never Reached the Front

The true story of a sword-rattling politician who constantly maneuvered for higher militia rank, but was always "otherwise engaged" when there was a battle to be fought. From his own unpublished memoirs.

One spring day in 1861 John R. Chapin consulted his clergyman on a grave matter: Did God want him to go to war?

The question was rendered complex enough to refer to the Deity, or at least to one of His earthly representatives at Rahway, New Jersey, by a peculiar circumstance. John Chapin, who had been a militia captain, felt that he could not go to war as less than a captain. And a most curious deal had been cooked up between the embryonic volunteer battery that he headed and another one. Both units, being undermanned, would merge. Then, being overofficered, they would elect new officers in the ultrademocratic manner of the day. One unit would elect the captain, the other the two lieutenants. Obviously someone was going to have to give.

After religious consultation and meditation, John Chapin made the sacrifice. He decided to stay home. The other unit elected a captain. The two young lieutenants of Chapin's battery were duly elected as the lieutenants. Chapin went back to his wife and four children, feeling that he had served God and country to best advantage—not to mention the Chapins. A captain then drew $1,300. Chapin was making $4,000 a year as the city clerk of Rahway, second only to the mayor. He doubted, quite logically, whether his family should be required to sacrifice its living standards that much.

Although Chapin by his own account was continually panting and champing to rush into battle, he never managed to find just the right circumstances to permit him to yield

210

to his patriotic impulse. During most of the Civil War, Chapin was in uniform ready to serve, or at least had his uniform hanging handy in a clothes closet. The nearest he got to battle, by his own story, was when the great crisis at Gettysburg brought him all the way south from Rahway to Trenton, New Jersey, to guard the state capital in case the rebels broke through and crossed the Delaware. He always had his reasons for not charging into the thick of the fray. He gave them in detail years later, when there was no point in disputing them. Some sound like very good reasons, indeed. Others are at least unusual. Take the problem of kittens. Who could expect a militia officer of Chapin's experience to head a company whose lieutenants were such juveniles that they kept kittens as personal pets?

"At the first meeting of the company, I was painfully surprised to find it composed of the very flower of the youth of the place, none over twenty-two, and one under sixteen," Chapin related. "To them the war seemed a holiday excursion. To illustrate this point, let me relate an incident.

"One day while on my way to the armory, I found myself walking behind two of my boys in full uniform with knapsacks on, and, clinging frantically to the tops of those knapsacks, each had a bleary-eyed, sickly-looking kitten. Overtaking them, I found myself in the presence of my lieutenants, Bramhall and Martin, two boys whom I loved as my own sons. After receiving their salute, I quietly remarked:

" 'Boys, soldiers may be permitted to bring back from service their pets, but they seldom if ever take them with them. Were I you, I would drop those kittens before you subject yourself to ridicule!' "

The lieutenants jettisoned the pets behind a fence, but their captain remained painfully mindful of the experience. He soon let the unit merger relieve him of command. The boys went to war without kittens or Chapin. They became horse artillery, the elite of cannoneers, with every man mounted instead of seated on limbers, and made a distinguished record.

By the following February, in 1862, Chapin organized a second battery with a nucleus of twenty-seven volunteers. This time he noted with satisfaction, "They comprised many of the older men of Rahway." He began busily drilling them for war.

The first Civil War draft call, for 300,000 men for nine

months' service, soon created unprecedented furors. Rahway, a fairly populous place, was to furnish seventy-two men for the draft. "The members of the artillery company of which I had command urged me to take them in lieu of the men called from Rahway," Chapin relates. To swell out the ranks from twenty-seven to the requisite seventy-two, "many leading citizens, such as Joseph T. Crowell, president of the Senate of New Jersey, Mayor Lee of Rahway, Postmaster C. C. Hoff and others offered themselves as recruits if I would lead the battery into the field. It needed but little urging, for my heart was in the matter."

Again viewing the financial situation dispassionately, however, the bold captain spied another sound monetary argument against rushing recklessly into battle. The draft law permitted a draftee to hire a substitute for $300. If the volunteers waited until the draft took place, they could go as substitutes for the drafted men and be paid accordingly. "Dividing the pay received as such among the whole," Chapin thriftily pointed out, "each would have something to leave with his family." So they waited.

Chapin, ever eager for higher rank, meanwhile seized the opportunity to work on another personal project. He formally applied to Gov. Charles S. Olden of New Jersey for the lieutenant colonelcy of the 14th New Jersey Regiment, then being raised at Freehold. This obviously beat going to war as a mere captain. "In several interviews with the governor," Chapin said, "I urged my strong desire to serve, and his excellency promised his utmost influence to secure my election. . . ." for the lieutenant colonel, too, had to win his rank by election within the regiment.

A few weeks later the military office seeker learned that the regiment had elected someone else as its lieutenant colonel. Governor Olden, he noted sadly, was "a dear good old man, but awfully slow." Olden next informed Chapin that he doubted he had the authority to accept Chapin's patiently waiting battery as volunteers in lieu of draftees. Two regular-army recruiting officers thereupon invited Chapin to enlist his battery "for three years without the intervention of the governor."

Chapin quickly spiked that rash and dangerous suggestion. His reply emphasizes the highly democratic attitude of many toward military service. He told the Federal recruiters that "the men did not want to go for three years." They were, he added by explanation, "all men of family." Then he got down to his basic reason: "Several of them were officials, and nine months was as long as the city government of Rahway could get along without them." According to this local brand of patriotism, why save the Union at the political risk of losing Rahway?

Shortly afterward the mayor of Rahway informed Chapin that the city council had appointed a committee to call on the governor and urge him to accept the battery as volunteers for nine-month service. The governor replied that he lacked authorization to enlist the battery in the United States service for as little as nine months. He added that four steel field pieces which he was sending were for state service only and should not be taken outside of New Jersey.

With this "lame and impotent conclusion," Chapin returned to Rahway to find himself outwitted in another politico-military maneuver. A rival captain had organized a new infantry company. Included were some of Chapin's artillerymen who were willing to serve as infantry if only they could escape from the waiting list. "Most of them, however, would not enlist except under my command," Chapin records. "To overcome this difficulty, I offered to help him recruit his company if he would see that I was elected a field officer [major or up], so that my men could be with me. This he faithfully promised to do, but failed to perform, securing the lieutenant colonelcy of the new regiment for himself."

The latest disappointment was softened by a new development. Chapin received a letter from the governor, addressed to "Maj. John R. Chapin," although no mention was made anywhere of a specific promotion. In the letter, the governor introduced a committee of Princeton University students who wished to enlist in a battery for nine-month service. "If you still desire to form such a battery and will apply to the Secretary of War for the necessary authority," the governor continued in a switch of positions, "I will aid you in obtaining such authority. . . ." Chapin, with the rank of major glittering before him, rounded up the Princeton recruits and promptly found them "a fine body of boys whom anyone might be proud to command."

Governor Olden, moreover, wrote to the Secretary of War in Washington in glowing terms, endorsing a nine-month battery, "to be under command of Maj. John R. Chapin." He asserted "Major Chapin is an accomplished artillery officer

and will have no difficulty in raising a most excellent body
of men." Chapin rallied all possible support for the proposal
and, as he put it, "forwarded all to Washington and waited."

While Chapin was waiting—and he was by now a veteran
of this form of warfare—there came a landslide in his favor.
He had extensive fraternal connections. These now resulted
in an incredible development. The captain who had missed
out twice on fond hopes of becoming a lieutenant colonel and
then somehow became a major, suddenly found himself elected
a full colonel twice over. He was chosen to command two
regiments, the 26th and 27th New Jersey, then forming at
Camp Rosedale with recruits largely from the mining areas.

"I received word that, through influence among their officers, who knew me fraternally, each had elected me to the
colonelcy, one unanimously, and the other by a large majority.
I immediately repaired to their camp, where I was enthusiastically received."

The welcome was soon dampened, if not dashed. "While
awaiting my commission from the governor, appointing my
staff and equipping myself, I found that the general who was
in command, and who had a friend whom he wanted as
lieutenant colonel, had ordered the officers who held the
election not to make a report to him. This was a most unprecedented and unlawful proceeding, and I immediately
saw the governor about it. He thought he could do nothing,
inasmuch as he had no official notice of the election."

Chapin then turned to Attorney General Frelinghuysen of
New Jersey. A stormy session ensued. Chapin stated he had
been unanimously elected colonel of the 27th under a law
providing that the commanding general "shall report the result
of such election to the governor, who shall commission the
officer so elected." The wording left no option anywhere.
Yet, to Chapin's deep chagrin, a new election was ordered.

What followed would have made an amusing act for a
comic opera. "Again I was elected by a practically unanimous
vote," Chapin reports, "but again the general ordered no
report, and I was helpless. Instructing the officers in their
inalienable rights, we held a third election with the same
results. Through their ignorance of military law, they were
hoodwinked by the general yet another time. After having
twice resigned my position in private life and twice resuming
it, I finally withdrew my name, and the general had his
way."

Chapin in his memoirs apologized for discussing the remarkable episode in so much detail. "I should not have entered upon such a personal matter," he said, "were it not that it created considerable excitement in Rahway. Also, it goes to show how few men were governed by patriotic motives during the 'late unpleasantness.'"

Having recognized the sordid stuff of which other men were made, Chapin settled down philosophically to drilling his state-militia, or home-guard, battery in handling four steel rifled cannon which the governor had sent them. "We continued our drilling with the guns and in saber exercises with the thirty or forty men who stood by me," he noted, "and acquired a considerable amount of proficiency." Thus the winter of 1862-63 and spring of '63 passed uneventfully.

(That the Confederacy had non-fighting warriors comparable to Chapin is attested in pithy Lt. Gen. Daniel Harvey Hill's General Orders No. 8, as reported in the *Official Records of the War of the Rebellion*, Vol. 18, Page 1007. Hill, then directing Confederate defenses in North Carolina, became irked at the vague unavailability of local militia units. In the same tone that prompted him to disapprove an infantryman's request for band duty because "shooters are more needed than tooters," Hill wrote of the reluctant militiamen: "Others are warlike militia officers, and their regiments cannot dispense with such models of military skill and valor. And such noble regiments they have: Three field officers, four staff officers, ten captains, thirty lieutenants, and one private with a misery in his bowels. . . .")

Then the Confederate Army drove northward into Pennsylvania in the campaign which was to culminate in the Battle of Gettysburg. Chapin relates dramatically: "The governors of Pennsylvania, New Jersey and New York issued frantic appeals for every available man to rush in and throw his body in the way of the invading veterans of the Confederate Army. The battery under my command was among the first to offer and was accepted. As it was understrength, I resigned my civilian position again and, with a drummer, fifer and American flag, paraded the streets of Rahway, drumming up recruits who came in all too slowly.

"In the midst of the excitement came a countercommand from Trenton, thus placing me in the position of a mountebank or Bombastes Furiosa. Mad clear through after all the sacrifices I had made, I informed the governor that I was tired of the farce, and unless my battery was accepted, I would resign my commission and play soldier no more. Back came word to be in Trenton next day with my men and guns equipped for service in Pennsylvania.

"Now came the hour that 'tried men's souls' and showed what they were made of. No one knew where the Army of the Potomac was. We knew only that the conquering Confederates had marched unchallenged into Pennsylvania, burned Chambersburg, and were threatening Harrisburg. We were to throw ourselves into the path of this immense force of veterans who had twice defeated the Army of the Potomac and who were now marching undisturbed 'into the bowels of the land.'"

Chapin mustered his brave boys and made no bones about the crisis they faced. Perhaps he was too eloquent.

"To my pain, mortification and surprise, one third of my men declined to go. The laws of New Jersey did not permit of my compelling them, and I was forced to accept their resignations. The rest of us prepared to arrange our private affairs, load our material and take leave of our families before going to what we felt was certain disaster and death."

The shrunken little band, including the mayor of Rahway, the state-Senate president and the postmaster, arrived at Trenton. Hardly had they settled down in barracks when misleading news came—apparently based on the result of the first day's engagement at Gettysburg—that the Confederates had defeated the Army of the Potomac. Chapin rushed around to the adjutant general to obtain horses, harness and gun primers for his cannon, only to find none available. He returned to barracks "sick at heart and disgusted . . . at the inefficiency . . . after all the sacrifices we had made."

Finally, to the great joy and relief of all in Trenton, word was received that the Federals had won at Gettysburg. Chapin, however, was to continue battling against home-front odds. "The governor ordered me to fire a 100-gun salute in honor of the victory. This I failed to do, as there were no friction primers to be had. We had to use portfire, or burning rope, to ignite the powder. This soon gave out, and we fired only thirty-five times."

The stay-at-homes at Rahway, meanwhile, discharged the battery's most telling and destructive shot of the entire war. They rolled out a brass Napoleon field gun which had been left behind, and began firing salutes. While the eight-foot-long rammer was still inside the barrel the gun went off prematurely. The rammer sailed out and "struck the upper sash at the Methodist parsonage six inches above the parson's head, took out the sash, struck the far wall and dropped into the room."

Amos Clark, handling the rammer, lost two fingers and was so seriously injured about the chest that he died of lockjaw, or tetanus, a week later. He was the battery's only fatality in line of duty. Clark's fatal injury "did not deter his kinsman, Patrick Clark, from trying his hand at firing a salute with an improvised rammer without anyone 'tending vent.' His scientific knowledge led him to believe that if he forced water into the gun so that it would spurt through the vent and extinguish any lingering sparks, there would be no danger. But he learned to the contrary. A premature explosion tore his right hand terribly, and he was laid up for weeks, rejoicing that lockjaw had not set in. This ended the attempt to fire a salute at Rahway."

While his men were falling right and left at Rahway, yet another crisis beset Chapin's battery. Ferocious rioting against the draft had broken out in New York City. Officials feared it might spread to Trenton. There were rumors that 1,000 malcontents planned to seize the state arsenal and distribute its arms to rioters.

"The governor ordered me to arm my men with muskets— an arm they never had handled—against as earnest a protest as I dared make, in order to guard the arsenal. The next fifteen days found us cooped up within four walls, where rioters could have run all over us, because we could not use our guns to any effect." As usual, however, nothing happened.

After thirty days of service during the Gettysburg crisis, the battery marched back to Rahway to be mustered out. "We were handsomely received," says Chapin, "notwithstanding we had 'first marched up the hill and then marched down again.' Our guns were stored, and we resolved into private citizens once more."

The next, and last, active duty of the unit entailed a sixty-day stint of guarding railroad tracks around Perth Amboy, New Jersey, to prevent striking railroad workers from sabotaging the lines.

On the Fourth of July, 1864, there came a grand anticlimax to the war service of Chapin and his battery. They had fired the usual salutes, returned their cannon to the armory and gone home. At 9 P.M. a fire balloon sent up as part of a fireworks display came to roost on the immense shingle roof of the armory. The shingles soon blazed.

"No one thought the building would go, however, until the whole interior was a furnace. In the basement were our guns with considerable powder left in the chests from firing."

Chapin rallied his men, and they stood watching the fire and wondering what to do. "When all thought an explosion imminent, 'Little Johnny,' as we called one of our youngsters, crept through a basement window and, with sparks falling all about him, lifted the covers of the limber chests so that the firemen could play hoses through the windows and drown the powder.

"It was a plucky thing to do, and well deserves the praise I fain would give him."

It was also the battery's most heroic moment. With its equipment ruined by a friendly fire balloon, it never recovered its military composure. Needless to say, the catastrophe left the battery unequipped to go to war. Appomattox found it still waiting, with well-drilled patience, for new equipment.

Index

Adams, D. W., 110
Adams, John, 17
Adams, Brig. Gen. William W., 110
Alabama, 104-105, 189
Aldie, Battle of, 55
Alexander, Brig. Gen. E. Porter, 60
Alston, Hon. Charles, Jr., 103
American Colonization Society, 20
Anderson, Major, 21
Andersonville, 143, 145-146, 150-151, 153-156
Antietam, 146
Appomattox, 30, 83, 141
Armstrong, Sir George, 42, 44
"Artis Avis," 78

Banks, General, 46
Barnes, Dr. Joseph K., 176
Barnwell, Lieut. Edward H., 33
Barrancas, Fort, 32
Barton, Clara, 179, 181
Battle Hymn, The, of the Republic, 181
Baylor, Col. George W., 98
Beardslee, G. W., 75
Beauregard, Gen. P. G. T., 21, 31-33, 35, 40, 42, 45, 171
Belo, Major A. H., 106
Benjamin, Judah P., 21
Berdan, Col. Hiram, 112, 124-126
Bickerdyke, "Mother" Mary, 179
Big Cabin Creek, 91
"Bird of Art," 78
Blackwell, Dr. Elizabeth, 178
Blank, Professor, 78

Blue-Jacket, Chief Charles, 89-90
Blunt, Maj. Gen. James G., 133-134
Boonville, 99
Bowers, Col. T. S., 83
Boyd, Belle, 181
Bragg, Gen. Braxton, 98, 109, 187
Branch, Brig. Gen. Lawrence O., 118-119
Brantley, Brig. Gen. W. F., 110
Breckinridge, John C., 109, 199
Breckenridge, Rev. Dr. Robert J., 199
Brooks, Preston S., 93
Brown, John, 19
Buchanan, Commodore Franklin, 102, 193-194
Buchanan, James, 25, 59
Buchanan, McKean, 194
Buell, General Don Carlos, 92
Bull Run, Battle of, 30, 44, 49, 95, 180, 195
Burns, John D., 103
Butler, General B. F., 72, 76
Butler, John W., 78
Butler, General M. C., 55
Butler, Senator, 93
Byrnes, James F., 17

Calhoun, John C., 18, 100, 191
Calhoun, Col. W. Ransom, 100-103
Cameron, Archibald, 43
Cedar Creek, 69
Cevor, Captain, 79
Chancellorsville, Battle of, 97, 109, 146, 188

Chapin, John R., 210-218
Charleston Battalion, 46
Chicora, 46
Chinn, Col. George M., 71
Churchill, Winston, 17
Clanton, Brig. Gen. James H., 110
Cold Harbor, 69, 95
Colt, Col. Samuel, 62
Connally, Colonel J. K., 105-106
Conwell, Dr. Russell H., 209
Cooke, Philip St. George, 187-188
Cooper, Col. Douglas H., 85, 88-89
Cooper, Samuel, 186, 188
Crater, the, Battle of, 31, 141
Crittenden, George, 199
Crittenden, Thomas L., 199
Cross, Edward E., 94
Crowell, L. C., 77
CSS Virginia, 102, 138-139, 193
Culp, Wesley, 195-197
Culp, William, 195, 197
Curtis, Maj. Gen. Samuel Ryan, 87
Cussons, Captain, 105-106
Custer, Mrs. Elizabeth B., 56, 176
Custer, George Armstrong, 54-56, 69, 73
Custer's Massacre, 73
Cuthbert, Capt. G. B., 29-30

Dantzler, Olin M., 94-95, 101-102
Davis, Col. B. F., 58
Davis, Jefferson, 17, 20-21, 24-25, 79, 92-94, 100, 124, 150, 179, 181, 185-186, 191
Davis, Jefferson Columbus, 96-98
Day's Gap, 106
DeBray's Texas regiment, 62
De Gournay's Heavy Artillery, 61
Delaware, Fort, 143-145
DeLeon, Dr. David C., 176
D'Epineuil's Zouaves, 84

Dix, Dorothea, 179
Dixie, 85
Doles, Brig. Gen. George P., 118-119
Donehogawa, 82-84
Doubleday, Abner, 29-30, 35
Drayton, Captain, 186
Drayton, Percival, 190-192
Drayton, Thomas, 190-192
Drew, Col. John, 85-86, 88
Dunkle, Captain J. J., 161-164

Eason, James, 43
Esperanza, Fort, 47
Evans, Thomas R., 78
Ewell, Lt. Gen. Richard, 171
Ewing, Brig. Gen. Thomas, Jr., 131-132

Fair Oaks, Battle of, 70, 81
Farley, Lt. Henry S., 28, 30-35
Farragut, Admiral David G., 189, 193
Finley, Dr. Clement A., 176
Fisher, Fort, 44, 47, 76
Five Civilized Nations, 84
Five Forks, 69
Forrest, General N. B., 54, 92, 106-108, 110, 128, 136-138
Fox, Captain Gustavus V., 25
Frankford Arsenal, 74-75
Fredericksburg, 84, 188, 197-198
Fuller, Rev. Richard, 20
Furman, Dr. Irvine K., 101-103

Gaines' Mill, 81
Garfield, James A., 149-150
Garrison, William Lloyd, 18
Gatling, Dr. Richard, 72
Geer, Harold A., 56
German Volunteers, 38
Gettysburg, Battle of, 53-54, 60, 69, 94, 112, 145-146, 157, 171, 188, 190, 197-198, 217
Gibbes, Lt. Wade Hampton, 28, 30, 32, 34-35
Gibbon, John, 58, 197-198
Gibbon, Lardner, 197

Gibbon, Nicholas, 197-198
Gibbon, Robert, 197-198
Gibson, Captain, 96
Gibson, Fort, 91
Gillmore, General Quincy
  Adams, 37-40, 45-46
Gorgas, Brig. Gen. Josiah, 59-60,
  186
Gorloff, General, 73
Grant, General Ulysses S., 78,
  83, 149, 185, 198
Green, Brig. Gen. Martin E.,
  118-119
Gregg, Fort, 128, 141-142, 163
Grigsby, Col. Andrew Jackson,
  109-110
Grimes, Maj. Gen. Bryan, 110

Halsey, Lt. Michael, 102
Halsey, E. L., 36
Hampton, Wade, 54-55, 58, 104
Harris, Ray Baker, 87
Hart, Edwin, 94
"Hatchet Brigade," 63
Hay, John, 68
Hayes, Rutherford B., 63
Heintzelman, General S. P., 81
Hickok, Wild Bill, 120
Hill, Ambrose Powell, 108
Hill, D. H., 108
Hindman, Thomas C., 90, 110
Holmes, Lt. Gen. Theophilus H.,
  90, 99
Honey Springs, 90
Hood, John Bell, 106, 171
Hooker, Maj. Gen. "Fighting
  Joe," 97
Howard, Gen. Oliver O., 97, 155
Howe, Julia Ward, 181
Huger, Fort, 105
Hunter, Senator, 20

"Intolerable Acts," 23

Jackson, General T. J. "Stonewall," 60, 92, 109-110, 170-
  171, 195
James, Capt. George S., 27-28,
  '33-34

Jeff Davis Legion, 58
Jefferson Guards, 32
Johnson, General Bradley, 55
Johnson, Capt. Curtis, 58
Johnson, Fort, 27, 30, 33, 102
Johnston, General Albert Sidney,
  92
Johnston, Gen. Joseph E., 60,
  180
Jones, Catesby ap Roger, 102,
  139
Jones, Brig. Gen. W. E.
  "Grumble," 57
Jumper, Lt. Col. John, 85

Kearney, General Philip, 92
Keen, Dr. W. W., 174
Keitt, Lawrence M., 94-95
Kendall, G. W., 50
Kerr, Capt. J. F., 32
King, John H., 157
Kinsella, Arthur, 77
Kirby Smith, Gen. Edmund, 42,
  98-99

Laidley, Maj. T. T. J., 74-76
Lalane, Paul B., 31
La Mountain, John, 80
Law, Brig. Gen. Evander M.,
  105-106
Lebby, Dr. Robert, 28, 33-34
Lee, General Robert E., 18, 33,
  39, 57, 60, 83, 108, 156, 185,
  187-188, 198
Lee, Capt. Stephen D., 32-33
Liddell, Brig. Gen. St. John, 110
"Lightning Brigade," 68
Lincoln, Abraham, 17, 19-25, 68,
  71-72, 80, 93-95, 112, 124-
  125, 144, 199
Locust Grove, 89
Longstreet, James, 108
Lowe, Professor Thaddeus
  Sobieski Constantine, 80-81

MacArthur, General Douglas, 73
McClellan, General George B.,
  81

McClung, Lt. Col. A. K., 93-94
McCulloch, Ben, 119
McDowell, General, 80
McGhee, Col. James H., 58
McIntosh, Lt. Col. C., 85
McIntosh, Col. D. N., 85
McIntosh, James M., 198-199
McIntosh, John B., 198-199
McMillan, Brig. Gen. James W., 116
McParlin, Surgeon Thomas, 53
Magruder, John Bankhead, 98
Malvern Hill, Battle of, 55, 108
Marion Artillery, 30
Marmaduke, Brig. Gen. John Sappington, 99-100
Massie, Dr. Edward L., 86-87
Maynard, Dr. Edward, 49
Merrimack, 102, 138-139, 193
Metcalf, John T., III, 116-118
Michigan Brigade, 69
Minié, Captain, 49
Monitor, 102, 138, 193
Moore, Dr. Samuel Preston, 176
Morgan, Fort, 47
Morse, Samuel F. B., 66
Morton, Gov. Oliver P., 96
Mosby, Colonel John S., 57
Moultrie, Fort, 46, 100, 163-164
Mowry, Sylvester, 94

Nashville, Battle of, 142
Nelson, Thomas H., 95-98
Nelson, Maj. Gen. William "Bull," 95

Oates, Stephen B., 62
Old Fort Wayne, 90
Official Records, The, of the War of the Rebellion, 87
O'Rorke, Col. Patrick H., 114

Palmetto Guards, 28-30
Parker, Ely Samuel, 82-84
Parrott, Robert Parker, 44
Paxton, E. F., 109
Pea Ridge, Battle of, 86-87, 89, 119-120, 199

Pegram, Brig. Gen. John, 118-119
Pemberton, John C., 182, 184-185
Phillips, Col. W. A., 89
Pickens, Frances Eugenia Olga Neva, 31
Pickens, Francis W., 31
Pickett, Maj. Gen. George, 70, 207
Pike, Albert, 85-87, 90
"Pillow, Fort, massacre," 134, 137, 139-141
Pitchlynn, Col. Peter B., 91
Porcher, Dr. Francis P., 175
Porter, Brig. Gen., 38-39
Prentiss, Clifton K., 202-203
Prentiss, William S., 203
Prioleau, J. H., 42
Prioleau, Dr. W. H., 33
Pryor, Roger, 33
Pulaski, Fort, 38-41, 45, 79

Quantrill, William C., 89, 128, 130-131, 133-134

Ramsey, Brig. Gen. G. D., 74
Randolph, G. W., 103
Reynolds, Maj. Gen. John F., 115
Rhett, Alfred, 100-104
Rhett, R. Barnwell, 100
Richardson, Hon. F. D., 103
Richardson, Brig. Gen. R. V., 110
Ring, Johnnie, 205-209
Ripley, Brig. Gen. James W., 186
Ripley, Lt. Col. Roswell, 100
Ross's Texas Brigade, 62
Ruffin, Edmund, 28-30, 32-33, 35
"Rush's Lancers," 61

Scott, Dred, decision, 18
Scott, General Winfield, 23, 73, 92, 124, 188
Sedgwick, Maj. Gen. John, 120, 122

Semmes, Capt. Raphael, 104-105
Seven Days' Battles, 61, 108
Seven Pines, Battle of, 70, 81, 180
Seward, William H., 17-18, 21, 23
Shenandoah campaign, 69
Sheridan, Gen. Philip, 68-69, 83
Sherman, Gen. William Tecumseh, 46, 92, 97, 179, 184
Shields, James, 93
Shiloh, Battle of, 99, 146
Sickles, Maj. Gen. Daniel, 171
Sigel, Maj. Gen. Franz, 57, 88
Simons, Hon. James, 102
Slemmer, Lt. Adam J., 32
Smith, Senator E. D., 31
Smith, Fort, 32
Smith, Brig. Gen. Thomas Benton, 142
Spencer, Christopher, 67-68
Stanton, Secretary of War Edwin M., 82, 84, 88, 144-145, 147, 150, 156
Star of the West, 25, 32
Steigen, Capt. J. H., 38
Stevens, Commodore T. H., 46
Stoneman, General George, 81
Stone's River, Battle of, 109
Stout, Dr. S. H., 176
Stowe, Harriet Beecher, 181
Strachan, Col. W. R., 130
Stuart, J. E. B., 57, 64, 127, 185, 188
Sumner, Charles, 93
Sumter, Fort, 21, 22-25, 27-36, 40-46, 93-96, 100-102, 104, 163, 178, 185-186, 192

Taney, Chief·Justice Roger B., 18
Taylor, Dr. W. H., 175
Terrill, James B., 203-204
Terrill, William R., 203-204
Thomas, George H., 182-184
Thomas, Captain John P., 43

Tilghman, Col. Benjamin Chew, 74, 76
Todd, Mary, 93
Toombs, Robert A., 100, 108
Trimble, Brig. Gen. Isaac, 72
Tucker, Brig. Gen. W. F., 110
Tyler, Brig. Gen. Robert C., 118-119

Union League of Philadelphia, 74
U.S. Military Laws, 1776-1863, 24
USS Kearsarge, 104-105, 189

Van Dorn, General Earl, 107-108
Vicksburg, 83
Vincent, Acting Brig. Gen. Strong, 114

Walker, Captain, 62
Walker, Brig. Gen. James A., 109-110
Walker, Secretary of War L. P., 21
Walker, Brig. Gen. Lucius M., 98-100
"War Acts" of Congress, 24
Warren, Maj. Gen. Gouverneur K., 113-115
Washington, George, 18, 145
Watie, Brig. Gen. Stand, 84-86, 90-91
Westport, Battle of, 58
Wharton, Maj. Gen. John Austin, 98
White Turkey, Chief, 90
Wilder, John T., 63, 67
Wilson, Gen. James H., 69
Wirz, Captain Henry, 147, 150-152, 165
Wragg, W. T., 102
Wyeth, Dr. John Allen, 167

Yellow Tavern, 64, 69

The Author and His Book

ASHLEY HALSEY, JR., has fired more Civil War bullets than most actual combatants of the 1860's. During seven recent years of target competition in the North-South Skirmish, he became expert in using Civil War smallarms and cannon. His intimate knowledge of the conflict also stems from "growing up surrounded by war background" at Charleston, S.C. His grandfather, E. L. Halsey, commanded a battery under Wade Hampton and seven great-uncles also served the Confederacy. The author saw World War II service in the U.S. Naval Reserve. He has written extensively on military history and owns some 300 weapons of the American Revolution and subsequent wars. Some of his stories in this book were first published in The Saturday Evening Post, of which he was an associate editor for thirteen years.

WHO FIRED THE FIRST SHOT? And Other Untold Stories of the Civil War (Hawthorn, 1963) is set in Electra. It was printed by the Murray Printing Co., Massachusetts and bound by Charles H. Bohn & Co., New York.

A HAWTHORN BOOK